THE
EVERYTHING
UFO BOOK

Dear Reader,

Welcome to the world of UFO hunting. Unlike other types of paranormal hunting, UFO hunting is grounded in actual historical events, often documented by newspaper coverage, living witnesses, video and movie footage, and government documents. Whether or not people believe UFOs are real, the evidence, in the form of historical documents and news stories, is all too real. Among the different types of evidence you will encounter are records of actual military alerts, the scrambling of jet interceptors, and the tapes of radar hits on UFO targets. And the events covered in this book aren't just limited to the United States—they encompass military organizations around the world from Russia to China to nations in South America. As you embark on your hunt, you will first see the overwhelming historical evidence of UFO encounters, then you'll learn about official military and pilot UFO encounters. Finally, you will learn about the actual process of hunting itself, how to find locations and what to do when you get there.

This is an exciting undertaking and I wish you the best of luck.

Bill Birnes

UFO Magazine and *UFO Hunters*

Welcome to the EVERYTHING® Series!

These handy, accessible books give you all you need to tackle a difficult project, gain a new hobby, comprehend a fascinating topic, prepare for an exam, or even brush up on something you learned back in school but have since forgotten.

You can choose to read an Everything® book from cover to cover or just pick out the information you want from our four useful boxes: e-questions, e-facts, e-alerts, and e-ssentials.

We give you everything you need to know on the subject, but throw in a lot of fun stuff along the way, too.

We now have more than 400 Everything® books in print, spanning such wide-ranging categories as weddings, pregnancy, cooking, music instruction, foreign language, crafts, pets, New Age, and so much more. When you're done reading them all, you can finally say you know Everything®!

QUESTION

Answers to common questions

FACT

Important snippets of information

ALERT

Urgent warnings

ESSENTIAL

Quick handy tips

PUBLISHER Karen Cooper

DIRECTOR OF ACQUISITIONS AND INNOVATION Paula Munier

MANAGING EDITOR, EVERYTHING® SERIES Lisa Laing

COPY CHIEF Casey Ebert

ASSISTANT PRODUCTION EDITOR Melanie Cordova

ACQUISITIONS EDITOR Lisa Laing

ASSOCIATE DEVELOPMENT EDITOR Hillary Thompson

EDITORIAL ASSISTANT Ross Weisman

EVERYTHING® SERIES COVER DESIGNER Erin Alexander

LAYOUT DESIGNERS Erin Dawson, Michelle Roy Kelly, Elisabeth Lariviere, Ashley Vierra, Denise Wallace

Visit the entire Everything® series at *www.everything.com*

THE
EVERYTHING®
UFO BOOK

An investigation of sightings, cover-ups,
and the quest for extraterrestrial life

William J. Birnes, author of *Aliens in America*

Avon, Massachusetts

This book is dedicated to my wife, Nancy Hayfield, the editor of UFO Magazine, *whose research skills and editorial expertise makes all of my work possible. I also dedicate this book to my grandchildren, Casey, Reese, and Marcus, in the hopes that they will someday learn the hidden truth about UFOs.*

An Everything® Series Book.
Everything® and everything.com® are registered trademarks of F+W Media, Inc.

Published by Adams Media, a division of F+W Media, Inc.
57 Littlefield Street, Avon, MA 02322 U.S.A.
www.adamsmedia.com

ISBN 10: 1-4405-2513-7
ISBN 13: 978-1-4405-2513-1
eISBN 10: 1-4405-2647-8
eISBN 13: 978-1-4405-2647-3

Printed in the United States of America.

10 9 8 7 6 5 4 3 2 1

Library of Congress Cataloging-in-Publication Data
is available from the publisher.

This publication is designed to provide accurate and authoritative information with regard to the subject matter covered. It is sold with the understanding that the publisher is not engaged in rendering legal, accounting, or other professional advice. If legal advice or other expert assistance is required, the services of a competent professional person should be sought.

—From a *Declaration of Principles* jointly adopted by a Committee of the American Bar Association and a Committee of Publishers and Associations

Many of the designations used by manufacturers and sellers to distinguish their products are claimed as trademarks. Where those designations appear in this book and Adams Media was aware of a trademark claim, the designations have been printed with initial capital letters.

This book is available at quantity discounts for bulk purchases.
For information, please call 1-800-289-0963.

Contents

Acknowledgments

Thanks to Lisa Laing, my editor at Adams Media, for her patience and skill in shepherding this manuscript. Thanks also to Nancy Hayfield, my wife and the editor of *UFO Magazine*. And finally, thanks to the cast and crew of History's *UFO Hunters* and to my fellow hunters Pat Uskert, Ted Acworth, Kevin Cook, and Jeff Tomlinson for their dedication over three seasons of grueling travel and filming.

The Top 10 Things You Should Know about UFOs

1. A UFO is not necessarily a flying saucer. It is a flying object you can't identify.

2. A flying saucer is not a UFO. Calling the two interchangeably is a misnomer because a flying saucer is something you can identify.

3. Ninety-five percent of all UFOs turn out to have conventional explanations. Some UFO sightings are simply optical tricks played by atmospheric conditions.

4. The government and the military have never stopped investigating UFO sightings. Even to this day, serious UFO sightings are investigated and logged.

5. UFO sightings are not just a recent phenomenon. They have been going on, and have been captured in art, for over 10,000 years.

6. UFO sightings take place around the world. From airports in China to elementary schools in Zimbabwe, witnesses have not only observed and photographed UFOs but interacted with strange otherworldly visitors.

7. UFO sightings are actually quite common. Most people either dismiss what they're seeing or don't realize that they're witnessing a UFO.

8. Most UFO sightings are simply sightings of strange lights in the sky. Even a starlike object that seems to move across your field of vision might be a UFO.

9. There are plenty of UFO hot spots. You can spot your own UFO by traveling to places like Mount Shasta, California, or the desert alongside Area 51 in Nevada.

10. UFO incidents have played a major role in American history. Indeed, part of the rationale for the 1947 National Security Act was the UFO incident at Roswell, New Mexico.

Introduction

MOST PEOPLE HAVE A strange reaction when they're told that someone is reading up on unidentified flying objects (UFOs) or even investigating the phenomenon. This is something you should know about if you announce to your friends that you're studying the subject or even taking it seriously. Laughter notwithstanding, however, what you'll find when you begin to review the evidence is astonishing. You'll find that the number of personal experiences with UFOs that people are willing to share is much higher than you'd think. Stories of contact, of being influenced by messages received from UFOs, or the level of government documentation provide evidence that something is out there—and it's not just a bunch of delusional reactions.

There are some basic assumptions you can make about UFOs even before you start to investigate your first case. You can assume that UFOs are real, that UFOs are not real, or that you simply don't know but want to see which way the evidence leads you. This third assumption is what 95 percent of what real UFO investigators make. They simply don't know the absolute truth, but are willing to go where the evidence leads them. This is very different either from true believers, who think that every light in the sky is a message from ET, or from debunkers, who argue that unless they see an ET firsthand there are no such things as UFOs. UFO hunters are natural skeptics who look for the evidence. And if you want to start down this path, it's all about the evidence, some of which is very startling, indeed.

Are UFO investigators and researchers an odd bunch wearing tin hats and waiting for aliens to land? Maybe they're government investigators, like the "men in black" from the motion picture. Or maybe they're scientists locked in a high-tech laboratory full of bubbling test tubes and electronic equipment that can track incoming signals from space. In fact, even though all three of these are marginally correct, most UFO researchers are just like your neighbors and possibly your family members: everyday people who get up, go to work, come home to watch their kids' baseball games, and hang out on weekends. Most UFO investigators have regular jobs, but do their homework on the Internet or follow news of UFO sightings in the newspapers. They contact witnesses, fill out sighting reports, compare those sighting reports with other reports from different areas, and catalog them for future reference.

There certainly are government types who investigate UFO sightings officially, scientists who search for radio signals from distant parts of the galaxy, and people who might come off as strange because they believe that either extraterrestrials or government units are following their every move. UFO research is a big tent, and there are many different types of people in it. For most of us, however, life goes on as usual, except that we keep our eyes and ears open.

The field of UFO research comprises not only the hard physical sciences like chemistry, physics, astronomy, biology, and electronics, but the social sciences as well. Researchers search the heavens, work out formulas to account for a multidimensional universe or advanced antimatter propulsion, or look for exotic forms of life in remote places on Earth or in meteorites that fell to Earth millions of years ago. Equally important is research in psychology as it pertains to memory loss, the impact of seeing strange craft or beings, the medical issues associated with sleep paralysis or hallucinatory experiences, and the sociology of mass reactions to UFO sightings such as the ones over Phoenix in 1997.

Then there is the important and highly technical field of photo analysis, including analog and digital, still and video. Since the 1950s, so many possible UFOs have been caught on film. Photo analysts have had sixty years of work dissecting the various components of images to determine whether a photo is a hoax; is something as conventional as a cloud, a seagull, or a plane; or is something completely without explanation.

The UFO field is also the study of history, government documents, and the science of journalism as it pertains to the ongoing reporting of events the government or military would probably like to keep secret. History is an important area of UFO research because so much of the history of the United States, especially since 1945, has to do with how government policy tried to amalgamate the possibility of our being visited by life forms from another world.

All of these fields, including spiritualism and mediumship as well, comprise the UFO field of research and represent a rich tapestry of interdisciplinary investigation into an aspect of human experience that can be rewarding and fulfilling—even if people give you odd looks when you try to explain what you're doing.

Ask yourself: Have you ever seen lights in the sky that you couldn't explain? Have you ever heard stories from friends or family members about seeing craft in the sky, either in daylight or at night, that they simply couldn't identify? Not planes, not helicopters, not birds, not falling stars, not anything that made sense? These are not tales of strange creatures turning up in bedrooms or crawling through the windows in the middle of the night, just stories of craft of all different shapes that appear out of nowhere. They hover, flash different-colored lights, and then disappear over the horizon. These, at least to the people observing them in wonderment, are UFOs.

Let this book be your guide for UFO history and your own research. Happy hunting.

CHAPTER 1

Flying Saucers and UFOs

What is a flying saucer? Simply stated, a flying saucer was the name a newspaper editor gave to the way a strange crescent-shaped craft, sighted by test pilot Kenneth Arnold on June 24, 1947, skipped through the air—just like a saucer skipping over the water. "Flying saucer" didn't mean spacecraft or hostile extraterrestrial craft, but the media liked the concept and ran (or flew) with it. However, there are legitimate distinctions between UFOs—an object one can't identify—and a flying saucer, just as there are distinctions between kinds of unidentified craft and even craft you might call flying saucers. For the beginner in UFO hunting, knowing these differences and what different witnesses have described is an important first step.

Historical Definitions

The concept of flying craft with otherworldly origins goes back millennia. In the Bible, for example, the prophet Ezekiel saw a wheel, turning, with flames coming out of it. To him it was not a UFO but a flying wheel.

The Indian Vedic text talks about vertical cylindrical craft flown by the Vimana, ancient aliens who fought with each other from their flying craft. The descriptions of these craft were so precise and the descriptions of the propulsion systems so meticulous that the Nazis sought to reinvent them as weapons.

Native Americans talk of flying shields navigated by the Star People, who came to Earth and established human civilization. In times of trouble, the Star People moved entire tribes to new lands so they would survive.

During the Middle Ages, narratives of strange flying craft described them sometimes as flaming shields, spears, or moons that created fear and havoc among townspeople.

FACT

According to the Mutual UFO Network, over 95 percent of all UFO sightings turn out to be conventional craft, optical illusions, or down-right hoaxes. It's the remaining 5 percent that they investigate.

In modern times, there is much talk about flying giant triangles, flying cylinders, flying crescents, flying orbs, and flying rods, all of which fit into the category of UFOs because most people can't identify the craft—they can only describe the shape.

Why Most People See UFOs and Not Flying Saucers

The majority of sightings are simply lights in the sky. Rarely do people see structured objects clearly. There are those fortunate enough to catch the structure of an object because of the angle of light or as a result of their location—as many people did in a major sighting in 1997 called the

Phoenix Lights incident—but usually it's just a light that seems unconventional in the way it moves or in the way it is self-illuminating. As a result, most witnesses can't make a specific judgment about the object they've seen. They usually say it was something that didn't look conventional and, therefore, was unidentifiable. This, then, became the origin of the term *UFO*. It is an object that is flying that witnesses cannot positively identify as something they recognize.

It's important to stress the unidentifiable nature of the object, because when people say to a friend that they've seen a UFO, the almost immediate thought is that they've seen a spacecraft. This is not necessarily true. How can you tell a spacecraft from an interdimensional craft, or even a time ship? How do you know what a time ship looks like? Does it have a big rear spinning wheel like the time machine from the 1962 George Pal film *The Time Machine*? The truth is that no one probably can identify a time ship, an interdimensional craft, or even a craft from another planet. Therefore, what most people see are UFOs, structured or unstructured, lights or dots in the sky, because these are objects that are unconventional and there is no criteria with which to categorize them other than to say they're unidentified.

ESSENTIAL

Semantic creep occurs when a term or a word expands its meaning to something else. UFO, which was originally a neutral term denoting a flying object that could not be identified, has come to mean an extraterrestrial craft. The term has crept semantically from neutral to colorful.

However, once you say "UFO," a whole boxcar of meaning slides along the track because over the course of sixty years of sightings, flaps, and incidents, UFO has come to mean extraterrestrial craft. That being the case, the careful scientific community, not wanting to be thought of as spaceman crazy, came up with a new term, "UAP," which stands for Unidentified Aerial Phenomena. Does that sound like six of one, half-dozen of another? Of course it does, on the surface. However, there is a major difference. Because the connotation of UFO means "flying saucer" and the connotation of UAP is probably unknown, the scientific community can use UAP and escape the true believer label while sounding more nuts-and-bolts within a scientific context. It's all a matter of how one wants to be perceived.

Why It's Called a Flying Saucer

On June 24, 1947, a pilot named Kenneth Arnold was searching for a missing plane over Mount Rainier in Washington State. While searching for the plane, Arnold saw nine silvery objects flying in formation through his cockpit window. At first he thought they were birds, but they seemed metallic and didn't fly like birds. The more he observed them, the more he saw they were unconventional, wingless craft. They were shaped like crescents or soft-edged triangles. To his eyes, they seemed to skip through the air, appearing in one spot, then winking out and appearing in another spot as if they were bobbing in and out of reality. Arnold thought they were experimental aircraft from the U.S. Army Air Force.

He called in his sighting to the local airfield. When he arrived, people were already there to question him about what he saw. In describing the motion of the strange craft to a local reporter, Arnold said that they moved through the air just like a saucer that was skipping across the surface of water. And the newspaper reporter coined the phrase, "flying saucers." The name stuck, and soon every sighting of a strange craft was called a flying saucer.

Sizes and Shapes of UFOs

UFOs appear to witnesses in all sizes and shapes, which makes the term *flying saucer*, referring to any type of extraterrestrial ship, a misnomer. For example, the craft that Kenneth Arnold referred to in 1947 as "skipping through the air like a saucer skips over water" weren't saucer-shaped at all. They were soft crescents. Witnesses said this was the same type of craft that crashed at Roswell in July 1947.

Disks

The traditional shape associated with flying saucers, especially in the 1950s, are just that—disks. Captured in photographs by Paul Trent of McMinnville, Oregon, and Rex Heflin of Santa Ana, California, these craft look like flying hubcaps or wheels and are depicted in classic motion pictures, including *The Day the Earth Stood Still* and *This Island Earth*.

The Wedding Cake

Photos taken by Ed Walters in Gulf Breeze, Florida, show a multilayered circular craft, similar to the huge mother ship depicted in the movie *Close Encounters of the Third Kind* or somewhat resembling a wedding cake.

Walters became famous in the late 1980s for his stories of having seen, and photographed, a flying saucer. While debunkers and experts argued back and forth, Walters eventually sold his house, at that point a mecca for UFO enthusiasts, and moved away. Shortly after the new owners moved in, a repairman showed up saying he was sent to check one of the vents or ducts under the roof. Soon after he left, a reporter showed up, saying he had come to check on a story that Ed Walters, the prior owner, had a model of a UFO in the house. The new owners let him in, and, lo and behold, he went right to the spot where the repairman had been and found a model of a UFO that supposedly matched the photos Walters had taken. One theory about this amazing discovery was that some group—a government agency, perhaps—had sent the fake repairman to plant the model, only to be discovered by a fake reporter. By planting the model and then "discovering" the model, whoever this group was created a hoax to discredit Walters. This is an object lesson in how debunkers can create the illusion of hoaxes by planting evidence.

Giant Triangles

Marked by lights at each of the points and a camouflaged rigid structure holding the lights in place, these craft have been seen all over the world. They are able to hover, float slowly through the air at low altitudes, and fly off at incredible speeds. In Phoenix, Arizona, in March 1997, even the then-governor Fife Symington reported having seen one at close range from his own backyard. Thousands of other Phoenix residents saw it as well, describing it as the size of three football fields, moving slowly through Paradise Valley, and having a shimmering, almost satin-like surface as it wafted by. Some who saw it said that it was completely silent. Others said they heard a soft hum as it flew overhead.

ALERT

The same triangle-shaped craft seen in Phoenix has been seen over England, Belgium, and California, and it was a prominent sight over the Hudson Valley area of New York in the early 1980s, starting in 1981.

Flying Cylinders or Cigar-Shaped UFOs

Craft that resemble cigars or long cylinders are referred to as cigar-shaped craft. They are rounded at both ends and are sometimes called transport vessels because flying orbs can detach and reattach to them. They have been sighted over Santa Monica Bay in California and as far away as Kyrgyzstan along the ancient silk-trading route between Russia and China. There, a cigar-shaped craft was said to have crashed in a desolate mountain valley. A research group that reached the crash site reported that all of their electrical equipment had failed and their watches stopped. It was as if time was standing still in that area. They were forced to leave as they became sick. Shortly thereafter, a Soviet retrieval team reached the spot and lifted the craft with a huge sky crane. When another research team returned years later, the site had been scrubbed.

Arrowheads or Flying Boomerangs

The UFOs over Phoenix in 1997 were also described as giant boomerangs or arrowheads. The artist conceptions of the boomerang shape may have originated because of the cloaking-type device some observers saw on the Phoenix flying triangle. One witness, for example, said that she and her friends were observing the triangle floating over their veranda and could see hazy starlight through the structured surface. The satin-like finish didn't obscure the night, but it made the starlight seem wavy. This prompted some experts to suggest that perhaps the triangles were using a kind of camouflaging mechanism to project light onto the ground so witnesses would not be able to see the object if the orbs attached to its tips weren't illuminated. Thus, some witnesses saw a boomerang and others saw either a triangle or an arrowhead, and it all might have been the same object.

Orbs

Perhaps one of the most common close encounter sightings is the glowing orb, a round self-illuminating object that seems to float, hover, flit away, and even interact with human observers. There is debate over whether the orb, also called an "orange ball of light" or "obol," is either a life form itself or a vehicle of sorts. If it is a life form, then the orb would constitute a type of otherworldly creature or even an energy projection of an entity. If it is a craft, then some experts suggest that it is a form of a probe guided by an intelligent operator who can see and interact via the orb.

In parts of the United States, orbs have been reportedly interacting with human beings, following them and even hanging directly in front of people, instilling both awe and fear. In Utah at the Skinwalker Ranch, orbs are said to appear from within invisible portals to scout the area and then disappear.

Orbs have been spotted all over the world as far back as the mid-1940s during World War II when they were referred to by Allied pilots as "foo fighters." "Foo" was an English attempt to translate *feu*, French for "fire." The pilots believed these were fireballs that were secret German weapons. The Germans believed these were secret British weapons. However, foo fighter orbs appeared over the South Pacific as well. One of them was hit with machine gun fire by a B-29 bomber and split into different pieces. Skeptics believed that the foo fighters weren't unconventional or otherworldly after all but simply ball lightning. The problem with this explanation, though, is that the foo fighter orbs seemed to be moving intelligently, tracking the aircraft from both sides during Allied bombing runs over Germany. Ball lightning doesn't hover, doesn't move as if guided by something, and doesn't tend to linger in the air. These foo fighters actively maneuvered around Allied and German aircraft, according to the American pilots who reported on their presence.

Pinpoints of Light

Another common sighting that witnesses suggest are UFOs are bright lights in the heavens that may have no definable shape because they're so high. These lights, which could be mistaken for the North Star, the planet Mercury, or falling meteors (shooting stars), can dart around the heavens, make sharp turns in ways that conventional aircraft can't, stop and hover, and shoot off again in a different direction. Perhaps the most vivid description of these points of light come from constables in the United Kingdom who witnessed them at Stonehenge during a neo-Druidic celebration at the summer solstice.

While celebrants were dancing around the structure, police protecting the monument from any damage noticed a light in the heavens that seemed to be hanging in one place. Then, as they watched it, it began making sharp turns and traversed the entire Salisbury Plain area in straight lines and ninety-degree angles as if it were making a grid search. The police said it was one of the most astounding sights they had ever seen.

USOs

USOs are unidentified submerged objects, essentially underwater UFOs. They have been spotted as far back as Christopher Columbus's voyage to the New World in 1492. A watch officer on the deck of the *Santa Maria*, the flagship of Columbus's tiny fleet, reported to Columbus that he saw a brightly lit object underwater. Columbus was said to have observed the object himself as it traveled near the *Santa Maria* and then flew out of the water. The sighting of this craft was entered into the log of the *Santa Maria* and has become the first sighting of a submerged UFO in the history of the Western world.

USOs have been spotted by fishermen and sailors in the Gulf of Mexico, off Japan's Dragon Sea, in Santa Monica Bay near Redondo Beach, off Santa Catalina Island, and in the North Sea by crew members on the aircraft carrier USS *Franklin D. Roosevelt* during NATO's Operation Mainbrace in 1952.

ESSENTIAL

It has been suggested by experts that the different shapes and sizes of UFOs represent different extraterrestrial species. Or the same species of extraterrestrials may be using different craft for different purposes.

Sizes of UFOs

UFOs range in size from small four- or five-foot orbs to giant mother ship–type craft, whether triangular or circular, hundreds of yards across. Sizes of the flying disk shapes have ranged from twenty feet to fifty feet or more, depending on how the film still or video footage is analyzed. The Phoenix triangles were considered to be so large that for those who could only see the shimmering surface and no starlight coming through, the objects stretched over both hillsides in Paradise Valley. Other flying triangles sighted near Parrump, Nevada, were so large they simply blotted out the sky.

UFOs as Shape Shifters

Perhaps as part of a defense mechanism or the ability to generate imagery to confuse witnesses, some UFOs have been reported to have changed shape. Orbs, for example, can detach themselves from larger craft, disks, or triangles and fly independently. One triangular craft that was reported to have landed in Rendlesham Forest, Suffolk, England, in December 1980, outside of RAF Bentwaters, led a U.S. Air Force security detail through the forest and into a clearing near a farmhouse where the object split into five separate lights and took off.

Official Documentary Proof of Both UFOs and Flying Saucers

To explain the complete documentary evidence substantiating government awareness of the existence of UFOs would take at least two to three large volumes of text. Suffice to say that from the first documented crash of a UFO at Roswell, New Mexico, in 1947, later called a weather balloon and even later a Project Mogul balloon by the army air force and the U.S. Air Force, both military and civilian investigators have officially recognized UFOs in various documents.

FACT

As recently as 2010 and early 2011, the British government has released thousands of official documents on UFOs that have been investigated in the United Kingdom, documents that are all available on the Internet. You can see these files in pdf format here: *http://ufos.nationalarchives.gov.uk*. There are no real smoking guns—most of the files deal with people who report seeing lights in the sky or hearing strange noises that spooked a dog or a cat.

Sightings at Home

While the United States has been less than forthcoming about its own release of official documentary information, in 1947, General Nathan Twining of the Air Materiel Command at Wright Field (later Wright-Patterson Air Force Base) wrote memos about the importance of investigating the nature of the crash at Roswell. In 1952, briefing documents for the incoming president Dwight D. Eisenhower made official reference to the crash at Roswell six years earlier and described the official government investigation into the nature of the object (the craft) and the craft's pilots. These are incredible documents that describe the steps the government took to evaluate the craft and the incident, and assess the potential threat to U.S. security.

In 1952, the air force and the U.S. intelligence agencies investigated not only the UFO invasion of the skies over Washington, D.C., and Chesapeake Bay but the reported loss of American pilots chasing those UFOs. Many of these official references can be found in Captain Edward Ruppelt's 1956 book, *The Report on Unidentified Flying Objects* (now being reprinted). In this guide he makes reference to memos, cables, and wire reports from military sources about the appearance of these objects and their interaction with U.S. air defenses.

A similar amount of official document traffic was generated in 1965 when UFOs approached the protected airspace around Edwards Air Force Base, an incident considered so threatening that a fighter was launched to observe and intercept while other interceptors were readied to protect the air base. Two years later, UFOs were reported to have appeared over Malmstrom Air Force Base, an ICBM facility, and shut down the missile launch capabilities. Captain Robert Salas, one of the missile launch control officers at that time at Malmstrom, was an on-the-ground witness to the missile shutdown.

Sightings Abroad

At RAF Bentwaters in 1980 and again at RAF Cosford in 1995, the appearances of UFOs in highly secure airspaces generated cable traffic between the UK Ministry of Defence and the U.S. Department of Defense, each side asking the other if the craft in question was the other's. At RAF Bentwaters, the Air Force Office of Special Investigations investigated the incident within days, and agents and interrogators from this office instructed the air force witnesses to lie about what they saw to their superiors. At least one official report on the incident, written by the deputy base commander Lieutenant Colonel Charles Halt, made it all the way up the chain of command to the general staff, where it lingers to this very day.

One of the most stunning confirmations of the interest—or urgency—that the United States government has expressed concerning UFOs and their existence occurred in 1976 when Parviz Jafari, an Iranian fighter pilot, encountered a triangular-shaped UFO over the Tehran airport on a mission to intercept it. The UFO disabled the air-to-air missile weapons system on his F-4 Phantom jet as he tried to get a radar lock to fire at it and then chased him as he tried to evade it. As he flew back to base, the UFO made almost instant jumps from side to side around his airplane, finally breaking off the encounter and landing in the desert. When Major Jafari landed, USAF intelligence officers as well as plainclothes investigators met him and interrogated him about the incident. That report of his interrogation and the UFO encounter was handed to President Gerald Ford, official documents show.

Official information about UFOs has reached all the way to the White House and at least five presidents have either seen UFOs with their own eyes or have been briefed on the existence of UFOs. Accordingly, UFOs have been the subject of much official documentation inside the United States and United Kingdom, and probably other governments as well.

Misunderstandings and Misperceptions about UFOs

If you listen the next time a skeptic or debunker characterizes a UFO sighting, you'll hear a snicker factor—a joking about where the UFO came from and what it might be. Immediately you'll hear the witnesses derided as having seen something from Mars or another planet. Of course, that's a major misconception about UFOs, because only a small segment of the UFO community either believes or is willing to state where or when these things come from. For the most part, UFO witnesses either suggest that it is only a military test aircraft or something they can't explain. But the misconception is that if anyone sees a UFO, that person is seeing a craft from another planet here to eat us or take us hostage. It's a common misconception.

A common misunderstanding is that the term *UFO* means alien spaceship. It means simply what it says—that the witness was unable to identify it.

CHAPTER 2

A Brief History of UFOs

If you think that UFOs are exclusively a twentieth-century phenomenon, think again. UFOs have been around since the beginning of human civilization, and possibly even before. Some believe that human civilization was seeded on Earth by extraterrestrials and that stories of the creation are simply retellings to keep humans in the dark as to their origins. Perhaps, these people say, the reason there is a UFO cover-up is that the truth about UFOs and the arrival of human beings on Earth would be too devastating to accept.

Ancient Aliens

In cultures as diverse as those of ancient Sumer, Native American tribes, Egypt, the Maya and the Incas, and the ancient Hindus, there are vivid stories of intervention in human affairs by superbeings. Called everything from the Annunaki, the Star People, and the Vimana, these superbeings who came from the heavens not only managed the affairs of human cultures, required them to pay homage and obedience, and had a hand in the creation of humans, but also flew through the heavens on strange craft. In the Native American legends, these craft were called shields; in the ancient Indian Vedic texts, these craft were powered by a liquid metal called red mercury.

Physical records exist of what scholars like the late Zecharia Sitchin and Erich Von Daniken have called "ancient alien intervention." They exist in the form of cuneiform symbols, hieroglyphics, pictographs carved into rocks, actual ruins of ancient municipal technologies like water supply systems, and textual descriptions of appearances of aliens. Physical records also exist in the form of monuments, in ancient stone megaliths in which the technology of the cultures and societies in question could not have transported, joined, or aligned such giant stones. Does this mean that there was some form of supernatural intervention or help?

FACT

Some of the earliest pictographs from civilizations all across the world, from Egypt to Central America, contain images of crafts that appear very much like modern conventional aircraft. These pictographs are so realistic that some people think that either someone has traveled back in time or civilization was reseeded by aliens very similar to human beings today.

Ancient astronomical records point to some form of outside knowledge as well. For example, how could the ancient Maya have known about the existence of a black hole at the center of the Milky Way galaxy when it wasn't discovered until late in the last century? Did the Maya have telescopes? Were they able to determine the position of the solar system in the Milky Way to position their calendars? Did they even have the concept of planets in relation to the sun, and, if so, how could they have plotted a course for Planet X, which they called Niburu, supposedly due to orbit past Earth in 2012, causing untold destruction?

How do you account for physical records that point to advanced knowledge and technologies far beyond the tool-making and construction capabilities of ancient cultures? These records, across many different cultures, point to some form of outside intervention and help.

UFOs in the Bible and Apocryphal Texts

According to some members of the UFO community, who have claimed to be in the loop of official government investigations into the UFO phenomenon, the Old Testament itself is a record of extraterrestrial intervention. Many ufologists have said that the very nature of otherworldly or extraworldly intervention speaks directly to an ET presence on Earth.

ALERT

It's not an either/or situation, that you either believe in the Bible or you believe in UFOs. Many of the stories that come from the Bible about human history could well have gotten entangled with very real UFO sightings and encounters. Most UFO researchers are as religious as the average person. They simply believe that there are some encounters with anomalous objects that can't be explained conventionally.

Genesis

The story of Genesis is the story of the creation of humanity by an extraterrestrial or otherworldly force. Human beings were created, manufactured out of native elements on Earth—"100 pounds of clay" for the creation of Adam.

In Genesis, human beings are created, and their first act of disobedience involves listening to the advice of a native reptilian being that walks upright and hangs out in the trees. The next act involves the mating of the children of Adam and Eve with the children of the Nephilim, translated loosely as "giants" but actually meaning "those who came down from the heavens." Were the Nephilim another extraterrestrial species who populated Earth before the Annunaki fabricated human beings? Was this interbreeding so prohibitive to the function of humans that a flood had to be generated to wipe out the Nephilim and their hybrid human offspring? If so, does the appearance of the Nephilim in later portions of the Bible, including King Og and the giant Goliath, mean that the attempt to wipe out the Nephilim and their hybrid offspring was unsuccessful? This is just one of the many mysteries and discrepancies of the Bible that points to another source of the story of creation.

QUESTION

Where does the name *Adam* come from?
The name *Adam* means "man," coming all the way from Proto-Indo-European. In Hebrew, the concept of man or "human" means "derived from dirt" or "made from dirt." This is why *humus*, meaning "soil," is from the same root as "human." Today, such names as Adams, Adamson, Andrews, and Anders all have their roots in the name *Adam*. In the movie *The Matrix*, Keanu Reeves's character, "Neo," literally means "new," representing the "new man."

Biblical historians know that the modern Bible is a redacted version of many ancient texts, a version that was assembled by ancient editors trying to reconcile the different stories of creation with one another. Books or texts that were left out of the Bible are sometimes called *apocrypha* or apocryphal texts. One of the major apocryphal books that was left out of the Bible, as it was handed down through generations, is called the book of Enoch.

The Book of Enoch

Quoted by Saint Jude in the New Testament (Jude 1:14–15), the book of Enoch is attributed to the great-grandfather of Noah and the seventh son of Adam. This book, while not appearing in the New Testament today, was considered a part of the Gospel by the early church fathers. Enoch might be called the first contactee who talks about the Nephilim, those who fell from the heavens, and the first contactee to take journeys to other worlds. Blasphemous though it may be, the book of Enoch, revered by many ancient scholars before being excised by later church councils, might well be the first first-person narrative of UFO contact ever compiled.

Joseph's Abduction

The Lost Books of the Bible is a collection of ancient works that never made it into the formal Bible because they were excised by the early Church fathers. In one of these books, there is a remarkable passage about Joseph before his wife, Mary, gave birth to Jesus. In his own words, Joseph describes what can only be termed a vision of being levitated. Joseph says he rises through the air where he sees birds frozen in midflight and looks down at people on the ground. He says he sees a table spread with food with "working people" sitting around it. But, he says that their hands are laid upon the table and they're not moving, frozen in position. Those people who were putting food in their mouths were also motionless, not chewing any food. And all the people were looking skyward. All the animals around them were standing stock-still. Joseph sees a bright, magnificent light and receives a prophecy of the salvation of Israel.

This would seem like a typical biblical prophecy foretelling the coming of grace, except for some of the details: Joseph's levitation, the frozen people, birds still in the air, and the sheep standing stock-still. All of these bespeak a version of an alien encounter with those who are not part of the encounter being frozen in position. This is also similar to what happens in many alien encounter and abduction episodes.

Ezekiel Saw the Wheel

One of the most vivid biblical stories of a UFO encounter is the story of the Old Testament prophet Ezekiel, who sees a wheel turning in the sky amidst flame and smoke. Out of the wheel emerges a strange four-sided being who instructs him, calling him the "Son of Man," to warn the king to mend his ways in order to avoid destruction. Is Ezekiel a contactee who has seen a flying saucer and the ET who emerges from it?

UFOs in Roman Times

One of the earliest sightings of UFOs came during the Second Punic Wars when Hannibal was making war on Rome in 218 B.C.E. The historian Livy, documenting the Punic Wars, wrote "a spectacle of ships was observed gleaming in the sky." Were these objects large enough to resemble ships? The following year, witnesses said they saw a group of bright orb-like lights in the sky. And two years later Livy again reported that witnesses saw a large "stone" flying in the air. Livy pointedly said the object was flying and not a stone hurled from a catapult.

During the reign of Emperor Theodosius in 393 C.E., burning "flying round shields" appeared over Rome. Other witnesses saw burning globes. Today they are called orbs.

UFOs in the Middle Ages and the Renaissance

One of the great historical documents of the early Middle Ages is the Anglo-Saxon *Chronicle*, a history of England from the conquest of Roman Britain to the arrival of William the Conqueror. Written by various scribes in different monasteries and abbeys, primarily in the time of West Saxon's King Alfred, these chronicles were organized by year. In 793, one chronicler notes that fiery dragons appeared in the sky, and the town's inhabitants who witnessed the event were so frightened they fled inside a church.

FACT

Christopher Columbus might have seen a UFO. From the captain's log on the *Santa Maria*: "Saturday, 15 September, 1492. And on this night, at the beginning of it, they saw fall from the sky a marvelous branch of fire into the sea at a distance of four to five leagues from them." It was the first recorded sighting of a UFO in the New World.

In 900, another chronicler writes that reddish flying shields appeared in the skies over Saxon England near a castle, causing residents to seek shelter inside the palace walls. The archbishop of Lyon also recorded the appearance of what he called "sailors," who emerged from a flying ship and were stoned by residents of a village. But the stones caused them no harm, and they chased the residents inside a church. One has to ask whether these chronicled sightings were fantasies, rumors, or real events expressed in the language and outlook of the day. In some respects, they differ very little from what might be called an actual historical account of Ezekiel's sighting. Similarly, in 1290, in the Yorkshire *Chronicles*, there is a description of a flying disk—a flat, round, silvery object that flew over an abbey and caused great consternation and terror among the clerics who lived there.

Although one can easily walk through history, citing reports in various chronicles of the appearances of UFOs, none is more intriguing than two sixteenth-century UFO battles in the skies over Europe, the first of which was in Nuremberg in April 1561.

ESSENTIAL

Under the rules of evidence, particularly in federal court, there is something called "judicial notice," which means that if there is an independent, usually unimpeachable, source, such as an almanac recording a sunrise or the phase of the moon, a court will admit that as evidence. If you use judicial notice as an argument, then you can say that as far back as 1561, valid evidence was presented for the existence of UFOs in the form of the Nuremberg *Gazette* broadsheet report of a battle between UFOs in the skies over Nuremberg, Germany.

According to the Nuremberg *Gazette*, a lot of men and women saw a very alarming scene where various objects were involved, including balls:

. . . approximately 3 in the length, from time to time, four in a square, much remained insulated, and between these balls, one saw a number of crosses with the color of blood. Then one saw two large pipes, in which small and large pipes, were 3 balls, also four or more. All these elements started to fight one against the other.

It was a "dreadful apparition," according to the *Gazette*, that filled the sky and was a "frightful spectacle" for all the men and women in the town who witnessed it.

What was it? Two alien cultures fighting with each other as they came into contact over medieval Europe? A religious apparition? A mass hallucination? You can easily dismiss the late Renaissance townspeople as either superstitious, technologically ignorant, or both, but that would be a mistake of prejudgment. Whatever it was, the multiple-witnessed event was described in such detail from different positions that it didn't seem to be a wild hallucination or a mass panic at a strange configuration of clouds. And five years after the event, Hans Glaser created a woodcut that illustrated the event, memorializing it to accompany the news report of the event. It is one of the most striking depictions, both in text and in art, of a violent UFO encounter.

In August 1577, over Basel, Switzerland, another apparent battle between UFOs also took place. This one, also memorialized in a newspaper report, was between fiery dark spheres, some of which turned red when they were hit and either exploded or simply vaporized.

The interesting similarity in these events, only sixteen years apart, is that they both involved what witnesses believed to be airship battles—at a time when there were no airships—using forms of explosives, and both were memorialized in print. In the late sixteenth century, with the invention of movable type in Europe, print had become the late medieval and early Renaissance version of today's Internet. It was the beginning of newsprint, modern newspapers, and events that might have been suppressed by the church or simply tucked away as strange unrealities found their way into popular circulation.

UFO Representations in Medieval and Renaissance Art

In addition to strange UFO-like images in Egyptian hieroglyphics, Sumerian pictographs, and Mayan ideographs, depictions of unidentified flying craft also appear in some prominent late medieval and Renaissance paintings. For example, in a sixteenth-century fresco from a church in Europe, one can see what can only be described as a space capsule with a needle-like nose cone and a clear windshield streaking across the sky over the heads of an assembled group of people seemingly unaware of the presence of the craft. In another painting from the fifteenth century by Ghirlandaio, you can see the Virgin Mary with a flying disk over her head. In yet another painting of the Virgin, there is a man in the foreground pointing up at an object in the sky, and his dog, standing next to him, is barking at the object.

One can argue, of course, that the UFOs in these paintings are some sort of fantasy on the part of the painters, but that is not in the province of the art of this period. It would make no sense for a flying capsule, one that looks like the old Gemini space capsules, to appear in a medieval or Renaissance painting, because these objects were intellectually beyond the ken of artists six hundred years ago. A painting of an angelic spirit would be just that, not a nuts-and-bolts spacecraft. Therefore, one has to wonder where the artist saw or heard about these objects.

UFOs in Early America

UFO sightings were not confined to Europe. In the American colonies, witnesses including fishermen in Massachusetts and one of New England's most important theologians and authors saw UFOs. Their observations were taken very seriously by historians, and as a result, UFO historians have a treasure trove of information about UFOs in early America.

The Muddy River Sighting

America's first recorded UFO sighting, and possible alien abduction, took place on the Charles River in Boston in 1639. The sighting report was considered so reliable that Massachusetts governor John Winthrop recorded it in his official history of New England. Governor Winthrop wrote:

In this year one James Everell, a sober, discreet man, and two others, saw a great light in the night at Muddy River. When it stood still, it flamed up, and was about three yards square; when it ran, it was contracted into the figure of a swine: it ran as swift as an arrow towards Charlton [Charlestown], and so up and down [for] about two or three hours. They were come down in their lighter about a mile, and, when it was over, they found themselves carried quite back against the tide to the place they came from. Divers[e] other credible persons saw the same light, after, about the same place.

Among the interesting features of this report is Winthrop's mention of the witnesses being carried back up the river to the place where they started, against the tide, without any memory of their journey. Was this also the first mention of what has come to be known as *missing time*, a period of time in which activity can't be accounted for?

Cotton Mather's UFO Sighting

As recorded in NASA's *Chronological Catalog of Reported Lunar Events*, in November 1668, the New England fire-and-brimstone preacher, the Reverend Cotton Mather—a minister who was rational enough to put the Salem Witch Trials to an end—said that when he was observing the moon through a telescope, he saw a "star-point" of light moving on the surface of the moon.

ALERT

The citations in NASA's *Chronological Catalog of Reported Lunar Events* are purely anecdotal, at least insofar as the early Colonial sightings are concerned. All you can gather from the report is that Cotton Mather "said" he saw strange lights moving above the lunar surface. What they were, no one knows.

George Washington's ET Vision at Valley Forge

Here's a story that never made it into the official history books but was told to the army newspaper *Stars and Stripes* by the self-described oldest living survivor of the Continental army encampment at Valley Forge, Pennsylvania, at the centennial celebration of American independence in Philadelphia. In a moment of utter despair at snowbound Valley Forge, his troops demoralized, hungry, ill-clad and -shod, and staggering under the deep freeze, General Washington sought refuge in a grove of trees, where he prayed for guidance. In answer to his prayers, he told his staff, he saw an angelic vision who foretold the American victory in the war and the glorious future of the new union. This vision renewed Washington's resolve, which he communicated to his troops and inspired them to weather the winter and renew the resistance to the British in the spring.

Was this vision a figment of Washington's tormented imagination, a hallucination brought on by the overwrought commander-in-chief, who could not bear the suffering of his troops? Or was it a divine message sent to the person whose courage and perseverance were central to the outcome of the war? UFO historians have said that visions such as these, described by writers as far back as biblical times and the times of the ancient Greeks and Romans, are extraterrestrial beings whose presence is understood by the contactees to be spiritual or divine. Whatever the nature of Washington's visitation, his story, told in his own words to the members of his staff, mark a recounting of remarkable contact between America's founding patriarch and a representative of the other world.

UFOs in the Nineteenth Century

The nineteenth century in America began with the report of a UFO sighting communicated by the third president, Thomas Jefferson, of an account by William Dunbar in Baton Rouge, Louisiana. Dispatched from Natchez on June 30, 1800, the communication read:

A phenomenon was seen to pass Baton Rouge on the night of the 5th April 1800, of which the following is the best description I have been able to obtain.

It was first seen in the South West, and moved so rapidly, passing over the heads of the spectators, as to disappear in the North East in about a quarter of a minute.

It appeared to be of the size of a large house, 70 or 80 feet long and of a form nearly resembling Fig. 5 in Plate IV.b

It appeared to be about 200 yards above the surface of the Earth, wholly luminous, but not emitting sparks; of a colour resembling the sun near the horizon in a cold frosty evening, which may be called a crimson red. When passing right over the heads of the spectators, the light on the surface of the Earth, was little short of the effect of sun-beams, though at the same time, looking another way, the stars were visible, which appears to be a confirmation of the opinion formed of its moderate elevation. In passing, a considerable degree of heat was felt but no electric sensation. Immediately after it disappeared in the Northeast, a violent rushing noise was heard, as if the phenomenon was bearing down the forest before it, and in a few seconds a tremendous crash was heard similar to that of the largest piece of ordnance, causing a very sensible earthquake.

Aliens Versus Cowboys

In another wild story out of the *Nebraska Nugget*, cowboys herding cattle on June 6, 1884, were startled by a loud whirring sound over their heads. They saw a dazzling white light and saw an object that crashed on the other side of an embankment. They made their way to the crash site where they saw "pieces of machinery," debris from the crash. The heat at the crash site was so intense it made them back off, but they noticed that the entire area was scorched. However, they located what seemed to be the largest part of the craft, and when one of them looked directly at it, he collapsed from the intensity of the light and, perhaps, the radiation or electric field. The newspaper described the object as a ship of about fifty feet long, twelve feet in diameter, and shaped like a cylinder, hissing and smoking in the grass. It was made of a very light metal. It had crashed in an area that was very remote and far away from any roads. The story gives no resolution to the event, only reporting what the three cowboys saw.

The Texas Airship Mystery

Once reported as the first official UFO crash in America, the Texas Airship Mystery is the story of a purported crash of an unidentified flying object into a water pump windmill tower in Aurora, Texas, in April 1897. According to the *Dallas Morning News* from April 19, 1897, "About 6 o'clock this morning the early risers of Aurora were astonished at the sudden appearance of the airship that had been sailing throughout the country. It was traveling due north, and much nearer the Earth than before." The ship, a small metal-clad dirigible-like craft powered by propellers, crashed into a windmill and exploded on Judge Proctor's property. Residents recovered a small burned-beyond-recognition body from the wreckage and buried it in a nearby cemetery. Was the craft a UFO?

UFOs on the Moon

Beginning in Elizabethan England in the sixteenth century and continuing through colonial New England with a sighting by minister Cotton Mather, strange lights and structures have been observed on the lunar surface. These sightings of lunar anomalies are all documented in a surprising historical report from NASA summarizing 500 years of lunar anomalies. The report, *NASA Technical Report R-277, Chronological Catalog of Reported Lunar Events*, published in 1968, is unclassified and freely available, and it notes the different sightings, reveals how they were reported and by whom, and describes what the observers have seen.

CHAPTER 3

The Beginnings of Modern Ufology

After World War I, through World War II, and into the 1950s, the legends surrounding UFO sightings became a hard reality. German secret aircraft provided one source of anomalous sightings. But floating, seemingly intelligently guided illuminated orbs, mistaken for plasma balls or ball lightning, were seen during this time along with structured craft in the shape of crescents or soft triangles. Thus, when researchers began to investigate the historical facts surrounding these sightings, the modern age of ufology began.

Ghost Rockets of Scandinavia

Prior to World War II, from 1932 to 1937 in Scandinavia, hundreds of witnesses reported seeing unidentifiable aircraft in the skies. Of course, this was a time when aircraft were still relatively rare in some parts of the world, and it was also a time when the Luftwaffe was expanding and preparing for its role supporting the Nazi push east and north. But when the reports were compared with each other, witnesses said that what they'd seen were not conventional airplanes. Rather, many of them said what they saw were huge aircraft, some of which were also accompanied by sets of multicolored lights in the sky, seemingly not attached to any rigid structure.

German experiments in unconventional aircraft took place in the 1930s, including the Horten brothers' flying wing, a very unconventional aircraft for its time. Other researchers in the history of Nazi weaponry have suggested that after 1936 the Germans were reverse-engineering a flying saucer that they had recovered from a crash in the Black Forest. This disk was reportedly able to take off and land vertically based on an exotic propulsion system, using what is now known as the Coanda effect, to create lift around the disk.

UFOs During WWII

In the Second World War, pilots from both the Allied and Axis powers had UFO sightings. The first of which has become known as the Los Angeles Air Raid or the Battle of Los Angeles.

Flying Saucers over Long Beach

From the night of February 24 to the early morning of February 25, 1942, the sky over Santa Monica Bay in Los Angeles County was alive with antiaircraft fire as gunners tried to shoot down a strange object that they, at first, believed to be a Japanese bomber or reconnaissance aircraft. It was only ten weeks after the attack on Pearl Harbor, and a Japanese submarine had already attacked a land installation just up the coast in Santa Barbara. All of California was in a war panic.

The 37th Coast Artillery Brigade fired thousands of antiaircraft shells at the object or objects, depending upon which witnesses saw what, but they couldn't bring the craft down. Some of the shells fell back on Los Angeles itself, exploding on the ground. Other shells exploded in midair, sending shrapnel back to the ground for beachcombers to pick up. At least six people died during the attack, some from falling debris in damaged buildings and some from heart attacks.

After the event, which was covered by the *Los Angeles Times* as well as other major newspapers that reported a possible Japanese attack on the U.S. mainland, Frank Knox, Secretary of the Navy, said that this was just a false alarm resulting from a collective case of "war nerves," jitters after the submarine attack north of Los Angeles.

In 1983, the U.S. Air Force investigated the event and said that the antiaircraft gunners mistook a flight of meteorological balloons for enemy aircraft. However, UFO investigators and historians argue that it is inconceivable that coast guard gunners could not even knock down one balloon and that the balloons themselves seemed to be flying against the prevailing upper air currents. The case still remains a mystery, but it inspired the Sony motion picture *Battle: Los Angeles*, in 2011.

FACT

After the famous air raid in 1942, beachcombers and police looked for fragments of a UFO along Long Beach, Redondo Beach, and Venice Beach. One police officer found what looked like a strange fragment and traded it to a car parts dealer for a set of spark plugs, which were rationed during World War II. Seventy years later, it turns out that the piece of the UFO was really a piece of shrapnel from an antiaircraft shell that fell to Earth and exploded.

Foo Fighters

Originally, these strange balls of light in the air were reported by the U.S. 415th Night Fighter Squadron in the skies over Europe after D-day in 1944. Observed by pilots from both sides, the Americans originally thought they were German secret weapons, while the Germans thought they were American weapons. But foo fighters were also spotted over the South Pacific, where one was even fired on and seemed to have been shot down.

Professor Michael Swords of the Center for UFO Studies said that foo fighters—the term comes from an Americanization of the French *feu* for "fire" because these orbs looked like floating balls of fire—were taken very seriously by Allied military intelligence personnel, and the mystery of their true nature or identity has never been resolved even to this day. They appeared in the skies penetrating fighter formations and simply seemed to observe without interfering in any operations. The Allies and the Germans saw them as hostile because they came close to the warplane squadrons even though they did not engage in any hostile fire.

In the South Pacific in 1945, a B-29 bomber encountered a foo fighter and fired on it from one of the gun turrets. The object seemed to split or disintegrate into other objects and then disappeared. Explanations that foo fighters were manifestations of ball lightning also fell short of the mark because pilots who observed them said they seemed intelligently guided, tracked the planes, and stayed in the sky too long. These were among the first UFO sightings of World War II.

The Horten Flying Wing and Postwar UFO Sightings

Among some of the best-kept secrets of World War II were the highly advanced weapons developed by German scientists. Most people know about the V-1 "Buzz Bomb," the first cruise missile, and the V-2, the first ballistic missile, both of which were launched against England during the latter part of the war. Some people also know about the advanced jet fighter, the Me-262, the Germans deployed toward the end of the war as well, a fighter that out-maneuvered the most advanced Allied fighters.

Few people, however, know about the Go-229, the German flying wing that was jet-powered and employed stealth technology and, if deployed, could have evaded British radar. However, the craft, even though it was being developed as early as the 1930s and relied on the technologies developed by the Horten brothers for their flying wing, was never deployed because the war ended. That technology was engineered by the Allies and today is represented by the American F-117 and the B-2 Spirit stealth bomber that is in service in the Middle East.

Other German weapons included a rocket plane and an attempt at a space capsule to give the Germans an orbital or suborbital strategy to defeat the overwhelming numbers of Allied warplanes bombing German cities at the end of the war. The German weapons, as exotic as they were, nevertheless pale in comparison with what the Nazis referred to as *Die Glocke*, one of their "Wonder Weapons," a class of weapons so powerful, so game changing, that their potential would be enough to secure a Nazi victory. Nuclear weapons were also included in this class.

Die Glocke, or the Bell, was a bell-shaped device powered by counter-rotating cylinders of a special type of mercury called "red mercury." The radioactive field generated by the counter-rotating cylinders was so intense that many German scientists and the concentration-camp slave laborers who worked on the device were burned by radiation or died of radiation poisoning.

The device was based on ancient descriptions of a flying saucer from the Hindu Vedic records, specifically the descriptions of the Vimana, craft piloted by the deities that fought battles in the air with each other. The Nazis studied these records in their attempt to prove that the Aryan race was ancient and descended from a race of extraterrestrials from the planet Alderbaeran. The Vimana were the craft that these extraterrestrials possibly flew. Therefore, the German scientists tried to reverse-engineer such a craft from the descriptions in the ancient texts.

Although there is a great deal of debate over just how successful the Germans were, interrogation records of the interrogation of SS officers who worked at the Owl Mountain complex revealed to the Soviets that the Germans had a craft so powerful and so secret that they believed it could win the war even in the last weeks. At least one former scientist said that the craft was actually a time machine that could go back where the Germans would reverse the course of history. The SS colonel who managed the project, an electrical engineer named Kurt Debus, ultimately escaped as the Soviets closed in and wound up in the United States, eventually as the launch control officer at Cape Kennedy in the 1960s. During this period, a bell-shaped object landed in Kecksburg, Pennsylvania, and was retrieved by NASA and the U.S. military shortly after it touched down.

UFOs over Hanford

Based upon the eyewitness testimony of navy Hellcat pilot Rolan Powell, pilots stationed at a naval air station near the Hanford nuclear plant at Richland in Washington State were tasked with defending the plant against a possible Japanese attack. Hanford was a very sensitive installation because plutonium was enriched there to provide the first weapons-grade nuclear material for the bombs that would be dropped on Japan.

Rolan Powell says in his book that a squadron of Hellcats were scrambled to intercept an unidentified object that was hovering over the plant and get a visual on it. When they made visual contact, they reported that the object was huge, had an oval shape, and was the size of three aircraft carriers with some sort of vapor flowing out of portholes on the edges.

The air controller ordered the Hellcats to pursue the object, pushing the propeller-driven warplanes to match the object's altitude, which was above the Hellcats' ceiling of over 37,000 feet. As some of the planes exceeded their ceiling, their engines began to stall, and they had to get back to base. When some of the pilots questioned the order, they were told to catch up to the object regardless of the consequences and if their engines failed to glide back to base. It was a do-or-die order.

The pilots did their best to catch up, but it was no use. As they approached the hovering object, it floated off and disappeared. It made no overt threats or took any aggressive action, only moving away in self-defense. The planes returned to base and reported the sighting as an object they could not identify.

This encounter over Hanford was perhaps the first time that a UFO inspected U.S. nuclear processing facilities. But it would not be the last, beginning a long history of UFO interest over our nuclear plants and weapons facilities.

UFOs over the Pacific Northwest

Just two years after the end of World War II, the northwestern United States had two reported UFO sightings. One was a questionable event over Maury Island in Washington, and the other a credible sighting over Mount Rainier in the Cascades. These two sightings and the Roswell incident the following month began the age of modern ufology in the United States.

Maury Island

Controversy still rages over this event, which ostensibly began on June 24, 1947, when Puget Sound boatman Harold Dahl said he saw a formation of flying craft shaped like doughnuts over his salvage boat. Dahl was salvaging logs that had fallen off barges and selling them back to the lumber companies. He said that one of the craft overhead seemed to be in trouble, and when the other craft formed up around it as a kind of an escort, the troubled craft ejected a substance that looked like molten metal. Dahl called the substance "slag." Some of the slag hit his boat, he said, killing his dog, injuring his son, and damaging the boat. Although Dahl did not report the incident at first, he said he received a visit from a gentleman in a black suit who invited him to breakfast where, over their meal, he described the incident that Dahl had allegedly witnessed and warned Dahl not to discuss the incident in any way if he wanted his family to remain safe. It was a threat that Dahl ignored.

Dahl told his associate Fred Crissman, a wannabe intelligence agent who was reputed to have been one of the people on the infamous grassy knoll during the JFK assassination, about the strange craft and the slag. Crissman said that he also retrieved slag from the beach, material that he sent out for testing. Meanwhile, just days later, Kenneth Arnold, a pilot, reported seeing a flight of crescent-shaped craft over Mount Rainier in Washington, craft he said skipped through the air like saucers skimming over water. The newspapers deemed the craft a flying saucer, and, within days, newspapers all across the country reported the sighting of "flying saucers."

Crissman approached Kenneth Arnold about writing a book or articles about his sighting and asked him to investigate the Dahl sighting. Although Arnold found no evidence to support what Dahl had claimed, he contacted two army air force pilots and intelligence agents who had investigated his sighting and found him to be reputable. The pilots, Captain William Davidson and Lieutenant Frank Brown, flew up to Washington from California in a B-25 Mitchell bomber and were persuaded to take a box of the slag back to California. On the flight back, however, something went horribly wrong, perhaps as a result of the heavily magnetic slag, and a fire broke out on the plane, which crashed in Kelso, Washington, killing both pilots.

Whatever Dahl said he had seen and whatever had transpired between Dahl and Crissman had suddenly become very serious. In an FBI interrogation about the incident, Dahl finally said that the entire event was a hoax, a lie that he had made up. He recanted his story. However, after his recantation, he recanted his recantation and said he had been forced to admit the story was a hoax. As a result, today UFO historians are left with either a hoax or the first UFO sighting in modern ufological history. It is a story whose veracity is still being debated.

FACT

One of the conspiracy theories concerning the mysterious Fred Crissman, a wannabe secret agent, was that he was investigated by the New Orleans District Attorney Jim Garrison as being a conspirator in the JFK assassination. The conspiracy theory states that he was one of the culprits on the infamous grassy knoll from where, allegedly, the deadly shots were fired at President Kennedy.

Kenneth Arnold at Mount Rainier

Just about a day after the Harold Dahl sighting, pilot Kenneth Arnold, flying a rescue reconnaissance mission over Mount Rainier, spotted a formation of silvery crescent-shaped objects, which he thought at first was a flock of birds, in the distance. These things reflected the sun but moved in a strange skipping motion through the air. He clocked their speed and estimated they were traveling at over 1,200 miles per hour, way beyond the speed of birds or of any other aircraft he knew about. Arnold said he believed that what he saw might have been air force test craft, but when he landed at Yakima and described what he had seen to his friend and airport manager Al Baxter, the story spread like wildfire. When he was interviewed by the *East Oregonian* newspaper on June 25, the reporters believed that Arnold had seen something conventional. The army air force also took Arnold's sighting seriously, although they suggested that he had seen guided missiles.

Even though Arnold's sighting was corroborated by Fred Johnson on Mount Adams, who said he saw six of the craft that Arnold said he saw, Arnold's life completely changed after his sighting. His story gave him unwanted celebrity as the man who saw things from Mars, but it also set off what would become the flying saucer craze, especially after the newspapers released the army-approved story of the flying saucer crash at Roswell a week later.

Roswell, New Mexico

Perhaps the most famous event in UFO history in America, if not around the world, is the July 1947 reported crash of a flying saucer—actually a crescent-shaped object—in the desert outside of Roswell, New Mexico. The incident was reported by the army air force itself before it was retracted days later by the same army air force. Roswell is also the most written-about and researched flying saucer event in the United States with scores of books, at least one *New York Times* bestseller, and hundreds of articles. Roswell witnesses continue to tell their stories, many of them corroborating facts that they not only handled strange and unearthly material but saw extraterrestrials with their own eyes.

To recount the entire case, conspiracies, and double-crosses, and the way the case unraveled over the past sixty-four years, would fill more than one book. In brief, enlisted personnel at the Roswell Army Air Field, home of the 509th Bomber Squadron, spotted strange objects flying over the runways at the beginning of July. Around July 4—different witnesses provide different dates—a rancher called Mac Brazel reported to Chaves County sheriff George Wilcox that a strange object had crashed near the Foster Ranch, where he worked, spreading debris across a wide area. Brazel brought some of the debris to Wilcox for safekeeping.

According to Inez Wilcox, the sheriff's wife, the sheriff called the army air force base, and the base intelligence officer, Major Jesse Marcel, was dispatched to the location to see what had happened. He brought with him the Army CIC commander Captain Sheridan Cavitt. Together they drove out to the ranch, saw the debris field, and brought some of the material back to the base to assemble crews to collect the debris. Along the way, Marcel stopped off at his house to show the debris, which included a thin piece of metal that could be crushed and bounced back into shape and a thin I-beam with strange lettering on it, to his wife and his son, Jesse Jr., who is today one of the last living witnesses who handled the Roswell crash debris.

Changing Official Stories

The next day the army sent out a full recovery team to gather up all the debris, along with the bodies of strange little grayish creatures and one living gray creature, to bring back to the base. That day, General Roger Ramey of the 8th Army Air Force arrived at the base and told the assembled officers that although two separate crash sites were discovered, the army would admit to the one and keep the other a secret. Lieutenant Walter Haut, the base public information officer, upon the orders of his boss Colonel William Blanchard, released a story to the press that the army had captured a flying disk in the Roswell desert.

The crash debris was flown back to 8th Army Air Force headquarters at Fort Worth, Texas, where Ramey ordered Marcel to admit that he'd only mistaken a weather balloon for a flying saucer. With that admission, the newspapers printed the story that the disk was only a weather balloon, and the fervor died down. The crash debris and the one living alien along with his dead copilots were then sent to Wright Field in Dayton, Ohio, where the army began extensive experimentation on the live alien.

FACT

The first U.S. atomic bombs were transported to the South Pacific from the Roswell Army Air Field. The nuclear warheads for those bombs were processed at Hanford in Washington. Both Hanford and Roswell were sites of UFO surveillance, Hanford in 1945 and Roswell in 1947. Since the late 1940s, UFOs have been watching nuclear sites on a continuing basis, including Malmstrom in 1965, RAF Bentwaters in 1980, and missile silos in the Soviet Union.

The story of Roswell entered the popular culture in the 1950s as a rumor, but it was marginalized by all of the flying saucer monster movies during that decade. However, in 1978, Jesse Marcel could no longer keep silent and began telling the story of what really happened at Roswell and what he'd been forced to say. Other witnesses inched forward, and soon many writers were investigating the story. The air force managed to come up with two different cover stories in the ensuing years. The first was that the object that crashed was really a Project Mogul balloon, a high-altitude contraption intended to sniff out Soviet nuclear test residue in the upper atmosphere. The second cover story was that the alien bodies were really crash dummies. But both stories fail.

In 1947, Project Mogul balloons were simply standard weather balloons tied together and made of the same material they had used during the war. Any army air force personnel would have recognized the neoprene rubber, especially because the weather balloons were manufactured right across the street from the base. And as for the crash dummy story, that fails because crash dummies were the size of real human beings, not four-and-a-half-foot, child-sized people, plus crash dummies didn't come into use until the 1950s.

The Secret of the Japanese Balloon Bombs

One of the best-kept secrets of World War II was the moderate success of the Japanese balloon bomb attacks on the U.S. mainland. Stories that were unearthed after the war revealed that the bombs launched by the Imperial military attached to balloons were carried across the Pacific on wind currents and reached U.S. destinations as far east as Mississippi River communities. One family in Oregon suffered fatal injuries as a result of a balloon bomb explosion. But that was not the only problem.

The Japanese were lacing their bomb payloads with weaponized anthrax, a biological attack with a weapon of mass destruction on the civilian population of the United States. Because of the potential of civilian panic and because the U.S. military did not want the press and broadcast media to serve as artillery spotters for the Japanese military, the government imposed a complete press blackout about the bombs. No one knew about the attacks or about the anthrax supposedly contained in the payloads.

This press blackout contributed to the government's strategy in covering up the Roswell incident, not just because they didn't understand what had crashed, but because they didn't know who launched it. Could it have been an advanced balloon bomb still floating on air currents for two years, a doomsday weapon, a secret Japanese weapon that had finally reached its destination? As the Cold War was beginning and the threat from the Soviet Union became very real, it made perfect sense for the government to try to get a grip on what had crashed at Roswell before releasing the information to the general public, especially if the government believed either it was a weapon or, worse, some species of extraterrestrials were in league with a hostile foreign power.

A Witness Speaks Up

Shortly before his death in 2005, Walter Haut, the army air force lieutenant who had released the flying saucer story to the press and who had over the years steadfastly denied knowing any of the real story behind the Roswell event, swore out an affidavit, to be released after his death, in which he finally stated that he knew the entire story. He told of having gone to the debris field and of having seen the actual spacecraft as well as the bodies of aliens covered up on stretchers. He revealed that General Ramey had double-crossed Major Jesse Marcel and made him the fall guy and of masterminding the cover-up from Fort Worth. It was a stunning document when it was released in Tom Carey and Don Schmidt's book, *Witness to Roswell*.

ESSENTIAL

> There were so many fake stories to cover up the real Roswell story that it's easy to mix them up. First there was General Roger Ramey's weather balloon story. Then the air force's Project Mogul story and later their crash dummy story. And in 2011, there was the flying wing/ Dr. Mengele deformed pilots story. The real story is what the public information officer at the Roswell Army Air Field released in July 1947—the army captured a flying disk in the Roswell desert. No cover-up there.

For many people, Haut's deathbed statement, properly notarized, witnessed, and sworn out in the presence of his attorney, closed the book on Roswell. It really was a flying saucer. And it really changed the course of history.

Wright Field and Marion Magruder

The crash debris from Roswell, along with the alien bodies and the live alien, journeyed to Fort Worth and then on to Wright Field in Ohio with the Air Materiel Command under the command of General Nathan Twining. It was at Wright Field that the initial scrutiny of the debris would take place and where some policy might be set for the disposition of the captured alien. The dead aliens, of course, would be autopsied to find out what they were made of. But the live alien provided a unique opportunity to find out what it actually was, especially if anyone could communicate with it.

In order to help in the setting of policy and to get some initial reactions to the implications of an ET presence on Earth from officers the military could trust, the army air force turned to the class of 1948 at the National Air War College in Georgia. These were seasoned flyers, officers who had made their mark in the war and who were being eyed for higher command and even general staff status in all branches of the military.

One such officer was Lieutenant Colonel Marion "Black Mac" Magruder, the hero of the battle of Okinawa who brought night-fighting techniques and tactics to the United States Marine squadrons facing off against the Japanese kamikaze pilots. Magruder had learned night-fighting and radar-vectored tactics from the British, who successfully used them in the Battle of Britain against the Luftwaffe bombings. Magruder brought them to the U.S. fleet in the South Pacific.

In July 1947, Magruder and the rest of his National Air War College class were flown to Dayton, Ohio, ostensibly to come up with policy suggestions for a way to handle something the army air force was grappling with. What the class members didn't know was that the policy involved figuring out what the crash at Roswell meant for the military. At first, the class members, according to what Magruder told his children, saw some of the debris from Roswell. Then, in a shocking moment, and Magruder remembered this moment until the day he died, they saw the live extraterrestrial.

Magruder told his children that the most frightening thing about the extraterrestrial was that it looked more humanoid than human even though he knew that it wasn't a human being. It had a large (but not overlarge) head, pinkish skin, large eyes, almost no mouth, and no ears that he could discern. The strangest thing about its appearance, Magruder said, was the way it moved its long, spaghetti-like arms as if in a wavy motion. It looked "squiggly," he said, and that's what he nicknamed it "Squiggly."

The extraterrestrial was able to communicate with him, Magruder said, not through human speech or language, but through mental impressions.

The creature communicated to Magruder that the military was subjecting it to tests, painful tests, tests that were killing it. And the sadness that the entity communicated to Magruder saddened and stayed with him until 1998, when Magruder died. He told his children, "It was a shameful thing what they did to that thing. Wherever it came from, it was one of God's creatures, and they had no business killing it."

CHAPTER 4

The 1950s: The Decade of the Saucers

It was during the 1950s when the saucer craze really took off. It was the time of great science fiction movies like *Invaders from Mars* and *This Island Earth*, with the gruesome insect monster and the white-haired humanoid aliens. It was also a time when there were dogfights between flying saucers and air force jets and eerie photographs taken by people who spotted flying saucers hovering over roads or farms. And through it all, despite the photos, the newsreel films, and the ET contactee movement itself, the government steadfastly denied anything alien was out there. The government furiously tried to explain what was outmaneuvering the fastest jets and interfering with NATO nuclear exercises. The 1950s was indeed the Decade of the Saucers.

UFOs over the Northwest

The May 11, 1950, sighting of a flying saucer in the skies over McMinnville, Oregon, by Evelyn Trent set off a controversy among experts, skeptics, debunkers, and shadowy government Men-in-Black types that has not been resolved over sixty years later. It began at 7:30 in the morning when Trent was walking back to her farmhouse (from the outside field) and spotted a disk-shaped object moving slowly overhead and reflecting the morning sun. It seemed to be made out of metal. She couldn't identify it and called to her husband, Paul, to come out to take a look. He also saw it, as did Paul's father, although very briefly. When Paul saw the object, he considered it noteworthy enough for him to run back inside the house to grab his still camera and run back outside to snap off a set of photos.

Thinking only that these were photos of something strange and never intending to find himself at the center of a windstorm of controversy, Paul showed the photos to his banker, Frank Wortmann. Wortmann soon hung them for display in his bank window in McMinnville. The photos caught the attention of reporter Bill Powell, who got Paul Trent to lend him the negatives so he could examine them. Actually, he was examining the negatives to see if the photos had been faked, because the image of the flying disk on the photo was clear enough to be unmistakable. In fact, the images were so compelling that the story of the photos was picked up by national and international media, and one of the photos landed on the cover of *Life* magazine in July 1950, just months after Paul took it.

As you can imagine, the photos touched off a whirlwind. If real, appearing on the cover of this country's most popular magazine was undeniable proof of the existence of flying saucers, a growing craze in America since Roswell in 1947. If fake, which the government and debunkers would try to show, then it was worth a good laugh even as Paul and Evelyn Trent's reputations were tarnished.

Unbeknownst to the Trents, however, the photos were taken from the *Life* magazine archives and loaned out to astronomer William Hartmann, who was working as an investigator for the Colorado Project at the University of Colorado. The Colorado Project was a committee that had been asked by the air force to assess the possibility of the reality of UFOs and their potential threat to U.S. national security. The committee was actually a setup with a predetermined outcome, which was to get the air force out of Project Blue

Book, the public cataloging of UFO sightings and encounters. It was the air force itself that asked the Colorado Project at the University of Colorado to do this because they desperately wanted to close down Project Blue Book and concentrate on investigating UFO accounts in secret. William Hartmann found the Trents to be reliable people, and ultimately the Colorado Project was unable to find a conventional explanation for the photos.

FACT

Even though the Colorado Project's outcome was rigged by the air force, the committee members were in favor of continuing research into UFOs. According to the report, the committee members found many of the cases they investigated unexplainable. However, in the executive summary, Edward Condon, the scientific director of the project, argued that UFOs were mostly not real and presented no threat to national security. The air force, using that executive summary as a pretext, closed Project Blue Book and got out of the UFO business, at least as far as the public was concerned.

Over the ensuing years, skeptics and debunkers came out of the woodwork to argue that the photos had been faked. But Dr. Bruce Maccabee, a photo analyst for the U.S. Navy and the CIA's go-to analyst on UFO cases, eventually showed that the photos could not have been doctored or faked and were more likely real than not. The photos remain as some of the best evidence for UFOs in history.

The Summer of the Saucers

It was almost a scene out of a science fiction movie. It captured the headlines on major newspapers across the country and was featured on Movietone newsreels in motion picture theaters. It spawned any number of science fiction movies, not only in the 1950s, but in this millennium as well. Yet, despite a denial and implausible explanation from Intelligence Director Major General John Samford of the U.S. Air Force and Air Force Director of Operations General Roger Ramey (of Roswell fame), it was as real as any incident could be and witnessed by thousands of people including air force pilots, officers on the ground, air traffic controllers on their radar screens, and even the national media. It was the invasion of the flying saucers over Washington, D.C., in July 1952.

On the weekend of July 19 and again on July 26, 1952, a swarm of flying saucers invaded the airspace above the District of Columbia. The director of the air force's Project Blue Book, Captain Edward Ruppelt, said that he had personally been warned of the flying saucer presence by scientists working for what he said was a three-letter agency. He was therefore on a quasi-alert. But what happened, and the aftermath of those events, surprised even him. He described it all in his book *The Report on Unidentified Flying Objects*.

Confronting the Flying Saucers

What made the flying saucer invasion of Washington, D.C., such an intense event was not just the presence of these craft in significant numbers but the aggressiveness of their appearance. These craft didn't simply fly over the White House once; they lingered in restricted airspace and hovered over military installations. Picked up on air traffic control radar at first, then on military radars across the entire area, they seemed to challenge the air force fighter jets as they scrambled to intercept them. As the jets approached the seemingly motionless flying saucers, the craft were apparently able to sense the moment the air force pilots were trying to get a radar lock on them, and at that very moment they sped off, breaking the lock.

In a dangerous air-to-air game of combat cat and mouse, the saucers waited for the air force jets to arrive on the scene, allowed them to close in, even played tag with them as they navigated back and forth across the sky, and then sped away when the pilots attempted to lock weapons on. There was no attempt on the part of the saucers to camouflage themselves or even hide. They appeared in plain sight seemingly in answer to the standard skeptic's question, "If flying saucers are real, why don't they just land at the White House?" The saucers, presence at the White House seemed to say, in response, "We are, we did, and not only at the White House but over the Pentagon, the Capitol, and the Washington Monument as well." And the photos exist today to prove it.

Throughout both the two weekends, Captain Ruppelt rushed to keep up with unfolding events. In conference calls with air traffic controllers and air force officers in Washington, while he remained at Wright-Patterson Air Force

Base in Dayton, Ohio, Ruppelt cataloged as much of the sighting reports as he could and confirmed with both personnel on the ground and indirectly with pilots in the air that what they were truly seeing on their own cockpit screens was what the control towers said were there. And photographs from the ground showing a formation of saucers over the Capitol indicated that what the radars were seeing was there as well.

Reporting the "False Images"

After two weekends of intense activity, the saucer invasion seemed to fade away as quickly as it arrived. And in its wake, on July 29, General Samford of the air force, according to retired marine Major Donald Keyhoe, agonized over what he would tell the American people at a Pentagon press conference. Just as General Roger Ramey had covered up the truth about the crash at Roswell, so General John Samford told the press that what the radar operators saw were false images on their screens that could have resulted from any number of technical issues including temperature inversions. Other radar installations were simply not functioning properly as were some of the radars in the fighter jets that scrambled to confront the saucers. With a little encouragement, the air force pilots themselves had to agree that they were in error in their sightings and that there was nothing there at all. And in the end, except for a few people who would emerge years later to tell their stories, the news of the flap faded away.

FACT

Captain Edward Ruppelt, the director of Project Blue Book, had no staff and had to fly back and forth on his own between Washington, D.C., and Dayton during the saucer invasion over the capital. He was almost regarded as AWOL because he couldn't get back to his office on schedule.

Four years after the summer of the saucers, Captain Edward Ruppelt revealed in his book *The Report on Unidentified Flying Objects* the true story of what happened in Washington, D.C., and stated that what the air force had experienced were actual UFO sightings and in-air encounters with craft that could outfly its fastest jets. In other words, if anyone wanted proof that Earth had been visited by flying saucers, he could find it fully revealed in Ruppelt's own account of what happened.

The Flatwoods Monster

Some people consider the story of the Flatwoods Monster to be the weirdest story coming out of the history of UFOs in America at this time. It was so compelling that even the celebrated paranormal researcher Ivan T. Sanderson investigated it. The event took place during the summer of the saucers in 1952 in Braxton County, West Virginia, and it was witnessed by many people, some of whom are still alive today and talking about it.

Whether it was a story of a monster, an extraterrestrial landing, or the crash of a UFO that deployed defensive measures, the Flatwoods Monster reminds those who investigated it of the premise of the robot creature, Gort, in the 1951 feature film *The Day the Earth Stood Still*. Because the flying saucers of Washington, D.C., and the crash of a UFO in Braxton took place almost a year after the movie came out, some skeptics argued that the folks in the mountains of West Virginia must have mistaken the headlights of a pickup truck in the fog for a monster because of the influence of *The Day the Earth Stood Still*.

ESSENTIAL

You can attend the yearly UFO celebration in the town of Flatwoods and meet some of the locals, who still tell the story of the Flatwoods Monster. You can find information about each year's festival at *www.flatwoodsmonster.com*.

Perhaps the two most researched titles about the 1952 flying saucer air war over Washington, D.C., and the Flatwoods Monster are *The Braxton County Monster* and *Shoot Them Down*, both self-published titles by UFO researcher Frank Feschino. In his investigation of the Flatwoods case, Feschino interviewed the eyewitnesses and pieced together a story about how three young boys walking in the woods at night came upon the sight of two large red lights gleaming at them through the fog. As the boys looked more closely, they saw what looked like a giant, a monster, gliding toward them. They fled back to the house of one of the boys where they told his mother, who then rounded up a local member of the National Guard and went back to the area with the boys. They also saw a large humanoid object, moving through the trees in a gliding motion, and they, too, fled.

The site was also explored by the local sheriff, who didn't see the creature or object, and was also visited by a local reporter. Other people in the town of Flatwoods said they saw the creature, however, and the entire event went down in history as the story of the Flatwoods Monster.

Operation Mainbrace

Operation Mainbrace (September 13–25, 1952) was the first major NATO joint air-sea exercise to block Soviet submarines from invading over the North Sea and penetrating the Atlantic sea lanes. It was conceived in 1951 by Columbia University's president, retired Supreme Allied Commander in World War II and president-to-be Dwight Eisenhower, and it turned out to be one of the most famous UFO military encounters as well. Military personnel onboard the NATO fleet and pilots witnessed not only UFOs surveilling the operation but unidentified submerged objects (USOs) surveilling the submarine activity as well.

The fascinating nature of these UFO sightings was that they were observed on multiple naval vessels by multiple witnesses, appeared on radar screens, and were picked up by aircraft radar as well. There was no doubt among the sailors on the U.S. aircraft carriers *Wasp* and *Franklin D. Roosevelt* that there was something unusual in the skies. For example, on the very first night, crew on the Danish destroyer *Willemoe* spotted a large blue triangle in the sky moving quickly over the fleet. One of the officers estimated the object's airspeed at over 900 miles per hour, faster than any jets then in service in NATO.

On September 19, ground observers at RAF Topcliff in Yorkshire, England, as well as the pilots on an RAF Meteor warplane spotted a disk-shaped craft that was following the plane and swinging back and forth in the sky as the pilots came in for a landing. The Meteor, seeing that it had a bogey on its tail, climbed sharply while the flying disk stopped dead in the sky, hovered while rotating, then sped away.

Then on September 20, from the deck of the USS *Franklin D. Roosevelt*, there was a sighting so interesting that it made its way into the air force's Project Blue Book. It was silvery and spherical and flying across the sky behind the fleet. One of the reporters covering the exercise from the deck of the *FDR* snapped off some photos of the object that made it all the way up to Air Force Intelligence and landed on the desk of Blue Book director Captain Edward Ruppelt, who said that the photos were "excellent." He also said that he could estimate that the object was flying quite rapidly because of how quickly it traversed across the sky from photo to photo. The photos were shot in sequence. Personnel investigating the intrusion of military airspace inquired whether a balloon had been launched from one of the ships. They found that there had been no balloon launches, thereby eliminating that possibility. Even today, readers of Project Blue Book can find one of the photos of the object taken from the USS *FDR*. It's of poor quality, but it definitely shows that something was there.

The very next day a squadron of RAF warplanes over the North Sea spotted a UFO following them, again in restricted military airspace. When they turned to give chase, the UFO simply flew away. As they approached land, one pilot noticed the UFO behind him and turned, but the UFO simply disappeared.

There were other sightings over Europe during that week that seemed to indicate that in 1952 the world was under active inspection by whomever was in charge of those craft. Was it a portent of a possible ET invasion, headed off by Eisenhower's reported meeting with the extraterrestrials after he took office, or was this simply active surveillance of the world's nuclear powers as Cold War tensions arose? Maybe the answer is hidden away in the records of one of the NATO powers. But it's an answer that to this day has never been made public.

Dwight D. Eisenhower

For the Supreme Allied Commander of World War II, confronting the Soviet Union and the Warsaw Bloc in the nuclear age was a daunting endeavor, especially because Eisenhower was an antiwar advocate. In fact, he was reported to have said that every single bullet fired in war deprives a child of that money for an education. And it was Eisenhower who warned America about a military-industrial complex. But Eisenhower seemed to take UFOs very seriously, especially because he was an observer on Operation Mainbrace in the North Sea in 1952. According to a member of the bridge crew on the USS *Franklin D. Roosevelt*, Eisenhower was on the bridge when a bright light in the sky overhead passed over the small armada for ten minutes. No one on the bridge spoke. When the UFO had flown off, Eisenhower advised the bridge crew witnesses not to speak about it and left.

Ike Meets the Extraterrestrials

Accordingly, by the time Eisenhower received the MJ-12 briefing documents, he had already observed a UFO firsthand and certainly had been apprised of the appearance of UFOs over Washington, D.C. Eisenhower's familiarity with the UFO issue has also sparked rumors that he was willing to meet with the aliens to negotiate an understanding. That meeting took place in 1954, according to UFO and conspiracy researcher Bill Moore, himself the subject of much controversy because of his unproven conspiracy theories. On a vacation trip to the Smoke Tree Ranch near Palm Springs, California, Ike suddenly went missing the night before he was to attend a church service. Where did he go? Allegedly, Eisenhower was driven to Edwards Air Force Base where he met a group of extraterrestrials who had landed there.

Eisenhower's disappearance was not a matter of circumstantial evidence. The press noticed he was gone and had begun to report on his disappearance when Eisenhower's press secretary shut the story down. He said that Eisenhower had broken a cap on his tooth and had to be rushed off to the dentist. But, the story goes, no dentist in the Palm Springs area ever acknowledged treating the president. Hence, the mystery remains. Also, there was a mystery about why the president had scheduled a trip to Palm Springs right on the heels of a trip he had taken to Georgia with his family. The only thing that can be proven is that Eisenhower disappeared from view the night before his attendance at a church service. Was it a trip to Edwards?

The purpose of the alleged meeting is a matter of conjecture, but some UFO historians believe that such a meeting took place either for Eisenhower to look at the debris from a crashed flying saucer or to meet with ETs who had landed. What did they talk about? One theory is that Eisenhower and the ETs negotiated what amounted to an understanding in which the United States wouldn't scramble jets to fire on them, only to observe, if they agreed not to make public displays of their appearances. This would explain the end of invasions over Washington, D.C.

President Eisenhower might also have wanted to learn what they were looking for, if anything. Could they have communicated to him their concerns over the growing nuclear arsenals among nations and the possibility that with all that dry nuclear tinder a simple spark could devastate the planet? If they were here to mine resources, those resources would be contaminated by a nuclear holocaust.

FACT

As a student as well as a maker of military history, Eisenhower was well aware of how miscalculations resulted in horrendous military and civilian casualties. Therefore, in order to avoid a nuclear miscalculation, the results of which were too disastrous to contemplate, he suggested that the Soviets have fly-over rights to inspect what the United States was doing with its nuclear facilities just as the United States would have over the Soviet Union. Khrushchev agreed. Ultimately, spy satellites in the ensuing decade would change the technology of surveillance. However, open skies with the Soviets might have been inspired by open skies with the extraterrestrials, which were far better than the 1952 flying saucer invasion fiasco.

Kingman, Arizona

The 1953 reported crash of a UFO in the Arizona desert near Kingman has been the subject of much debate over the years. Some serious UFO researchers believe the entire event was a hoax, while others have said that the event really happened and enabled the U.S. government to retrieve the bodies of ETs, which they packed in ice and shipped off to Wright-Patterson. The story of the crash and retrieval was first reported by UFO researcher and author Ray Fowler in *UFO Magazine*.

The story was told to Fowler by witness and participant Arthur Stancil, an engineer who was working for a government contractor when he was suddenly given a top secret assignment. That assignment was to travel from Nevada to Arizona where he was loaded onto a bus with other personnel and driven out to a remote desert location near the city of Kingman where the group inspected what looked to be the crash of a large disk. The disk had a hole in its side, which, Stancil speculated, might have come from an explosion inside the craft or the penetration of a rocket. In other words, the craft may have been shot down.

ALERT

The Kingman crash story is a classic example of how one person's anecdote about having seen a dead alien can turn into an entire story of a captured alien that still lives in a secret location deep inside a top-secret air force base. According to at least one self-described scientist, he has not only seen the alien from the Kingman crash but communicated with it.

The group of personnel inspected the site, inspected the craft, and then were summoned back to the bus. Before that happened, however, Stancil said that he had a chance to peer inside a tent, where he saw the apparently lifeless body of a creature that he estimated to be four feet tall, wrapped in a silvery one-piece flight suit, and wearing a kind of skull cap. Stancil's story seemed to have been corroborated by personnel at Wright-Patterson, who said they witnessed the arrival of three small body bags containing bodies that were about four feet tall.

The Contactees

By the 1950s, the flying saucer craze had become part of popular culture. Whether because the CIA, as it has admitted in its report on its history of involvement with UFOs, was deliberately marginalizing the subject by feeding popular media with UFO stories or whether UFOs were captivating enough on their own, the public was gobbling up anything to do with flying saucers. Part of the craze, fed at the beginning of the decade by the *Life* magazine cover of Paul Trent's flying saucer photo and the stories of flying saucers over Washington, D.C., also had to do with various personalities who came forward to say that they had been in actual contact with extraterrestrials. These extraterrestrials, they said, brought a message to humanity of both dire consequences resulting from environmental disasters and war and of hope if we heeded the warnings from our interplanetary friends.

Were these self-described "contactees" true messengers or wannabe cult leaders? Whatever the ultimate answer, there is no doubt that they were true personalities whose stories of meeting humanoid aliens from Venus were intriguing.

George Adamski

Science fiction author George Adamski said he had contact with Nordic-type people from Venus, took photos of what he said were their "beam ships," and said that the so-called space brothers had come in peace to make sure our planet and its inhabitants were sustainable. Adamski, although the object of much criticism, was honored by the nation of Granada in 1976 with a commemorative stamp for "The Year of the UFO."

Howard Menger

Howard Menger claimed to have had his first contact with an extraterrestrial from Venus in a wooded area near High Bridge, New Jersey. He claimed to have had another encounter when he was in the army years later. After he moved to Florida, he routinely held meetings with friends, one of whom said he corroborated Menger's story of alien contact when he actually saw the creature during a night-long vigil over his sick child.

Menger's child was so sick, in fact, that there was doubt he would make it through until morning. As Menger kept vigil, his medical doctor friend looked out the window to a distant hilltop where he saw a strange figure clad in a silver jumpsuit. The figure seemed to be looking at the Menger house as if taking note of the goings on. Sure enough, in short order, Menger's son began to recover. Menger's friend attributed the boy's miraculous recovery to the appearance of what he believed was a Venusian. Howard Menger wrote and self-published a book called *The High Bridge Incident* in 1959, in which he described his contacts and displayed photos of some of the Venusians he claimed had visited him.

George Van Tassel

Aircraft engineer, aircraft inspector, and airport owner George Van Tassel moved out to Giant Rock in Landers, California, to open his own airport on land he leased from the federal government. While living at Giant Rock, he claimed to have had a vision of being transported to a spaceship in Earth's orbit where he met a council of extraterrestrials. The following year, he said, the space aliens, human-looking creatures from Venus, came down to Earth to visit him. They instructed him to build a structure that would enhance human life and give those who visited the structure a special longevity. Building this structure according to the design of the aliens became Van Tassel's lifelong obsession, which he ultimately completed.

Called the "Integratron," this structure had a large dome and was said to have been designed according to the theories of legendary inventor and engineer Nikola Tesla to have the power to extend human life by channeling natural energies. The structure still stands today in Landers and is the site of many conferences by New Agers and those interested in the history of ufology. There are those who believe that the structure actually channels power and can both enhance and extend the lives of visitors.

ESSENTIAL

For a great experience, visit the Integratron yourself. You can also attend one of the many festivals at the Integratron and the Giant Rock. Visit *www.integratron.com* for details.

Frank Stranges

Frank Stranges, the author of *Stranger at the Pentagon*, who died in 2008, was a friend of Howard Menger and an attendee of many of his 1960s conferences. Stranges wrote about an extraterrestrial named Valiant Thor, who looked almost like a movie star and had the ability to shape shift, turn invisible, and otherwise camouflage himself so as to move in and out of secure government facilities in complete secrecy. Stranges wrote that Val Thor communicated with President Eisenhower at the White House and with Richard Nixon. Nixon walked into the meeting between the self-described alien and the president. He asked if Thor had been on the flying saucer that flew over Washington in 1952 that "had us all in a dither."

Thor explained to both the president and the vice president that the extraterrestrials had Earth under surveillance since 1945 when the military first exploded an atomic bomb. Thor was asked to follow the Secret Service to an apartment especially made for him inside the Pentagon where he would stay. However, Stranges wrote, Thor stayed in constant communication with his ship and was able to move freely in and out of the Pentagon because he could telepathically place his image on a security badge that granted him egress and ingress. Val Thor and his crew also were guests of Howard Menger's conventions, although they dressed themselves in conventional clothing of the period to observe the goings on inconspicuously.

RAF Woodbridge/Bentwaters UFO Dogfight

Numbered "Case 2" in the Colorado Project's famous *Scientific Study of Unidentified Flying Objects* (read the report yourself at *http://files.ncas.org/ condon*) is the strange case of a five-hour series of UFO sightings in 1956 over the RAF bases Woodbridge and Bentwaters, operated by the U.S. Air Force. These cases, like the Washington, D.C., flying saucer intrusion, involved sightings on ground aircraft radar, and visual sightings by pilots, as a fleet of up to fifteen unidentified craft showed up on U.S. radar. Then a single UFO, hovering in the sky, eluded a British Venom fighter jet launched from RAF Lakenheath to intercept them. As the Venom fighter passed the UFO that it had spotted visually, the unidentified craft suddenly turned and began tracking the fighter. What was most amazing about this maneuver, according to the records, was the Venom pilot's own statement that he never saw the craft change course. One minute he had it as one of the "clearest" radar targets he had ever seen. Then, almost invisibly, the craft turned up on his tail as if the two craft were in a dogfight.

Although the Colorado Project itself was a setup, a rigged study to get the air force publicly out of the UFO business by closing down Project Blue Book, the body of the report itself was far from a debunker statement. In fact, the experts involved in the report stated that some cases were unidentifiable and unsolvable and recommended they be subjected to further study. In the case of RAF Woodbridge, Bentwaters, and Lakenheath, the report said:

> [This] is the most puzzling and unusual case in the radar-visual files. The apparently rational, intelligent behavior of the UFO suggests a mechanical device of unknown origin as the most probable explanation of this sighting. However, in view of the inevitable fallibility of witnesses, more conventional explanations of this report cannot be entirely ruled out.

But the executive summary of the report, written by Dr. Edward U. Condon, ignored the expert opinions in the body of the report that favored the additional investigation of UFOs and argued that because these phenomena clearly posed no threat to national security, they should not be of interest to the air force.

CHAPTER 5

UFO Encounters Become Deadly Serious in the 1960s

With the close of the 1950s, the end of the Eisenhower years, and the ascension of John F. Kennedy to the White House, the fun of flying saucers gave way to the NASA astronaut program and serious concerns about encounters with UFOs by American spacecraft in Earth's orbit. High-flying U-2s, as well, were thought to confront high-flying UFOs. The 1960s ushered a more solemn era regarding UFOs. The 1960s also marked the beginning of the involuntary abductee event as well as direct UFO intrusion into U.S. affairs. Distinct from the 1950s contactee movement, where individuals spoke of friendly contacts with extraterrestrials, abductees like Betty and Barney Hill described hostile abductions. Air force captain Bob Salas described a hostile intrusion into a U.S.-guided missile silo, and air force bases in California went on full alert when UFOs appeared just outside restricted airspace near Edwards AFB. No matter how vigorously the military downplayed UFO reports, it was clear that somewhere, deep inside a secret government entity, UFOs were taken very seriously.

The Abductees: Betty and Barney Hill

The beginning of the 1960s was also the beginning of the involuntary abductee movement. Unlike the voyage of George Van Tassel to the alien ship in orbit around Earth, Betty and Barney Hill's story of their unwilling visit to an alien spaceship proved truly horrifying because of the impunity of their ET kidnappers. The Hills' story was a headline-making event that became a bestselling book (*Interrupted Journey,* by John Fuller) and a television movie starring James Earl Jones entitled *The UFO Incident* in 1975.

It began outside of Portsmouth, New Hampshire, in September 1961 when Betty and Barney were driving home late at night from a vacation. They spotted a strange light in the sky, traveling with them. Barney got nervous because the light seemed to be tracking them. When he stopped the car and got out to take a better look at the light, it seemed to come closer. That made Barney exceedingly nervous, and he and Betty tried to get home as quickly as they could. But before they could reach their familiar surroundings, Barney noticed the light—now it was clearly an object—in the road in front of the car. Even stranger, there was a group of what looked like "little men" standing in the road, creatures that neither Barney nor Betty could recognize. This was too much. Barney reached for his gun and got out of the car, but before he could put up any defense, the creatures surrounded him. Betty also tried to flee, but the creatures grabbed her, too, and dragged her and Barney to a nearby clearing. And that's where their memories stopped.

Missing Time

The next thing Barney and Betty remembered was that they were in their car driving up the street to their driveway. They had a very uneasy feeling about the passage of time because the distance from the point they encountered the object and the little creatures to their street should have taken less than an hour to drive. But here it was four hours later, according to the clock on their car's dashboard. What happened during the intervening time?

Inside the house, Betty and Barney had an uncomfortable feeling that something had been ripped right out of their lives. Where were they for four hours? Were the four missing hours simply an illusion, a figment of their own imaginations? There were other odd things as well. Their watches had stopped running and Barney's binocular strap was torn. Yet he had no memory of that. Betty remembered vividly, though, the light following them, the object in the road ahead of them, and being grabbed by the little creatures. Her memories stopped when she was in the clearing. She made sure that the black dress she had been wearing was put safely in the closet. She didn't know why, at first, but she felt it was important. Then, putting the nightmarish events behind them, Barney, who was very agitated, and Betty went off to bed, upset by their spotty memories of what they had encountered on the road.

Betty Investigates Her Own Experiences

The next morning, Betty called her sister about the events the night before and talked to her niece, Kathy Marden, about the entire event. Kathy remembers that her aunt was very specific about what happened to her. She remembered all the events leading up to the little creatures grabbing her and Barney and taking them to the clearing. It became a topic of conversation even though Barney himself was not that happy about talking about it. He said that he thought he had a "mental block" about remembering everything. He was troubled by it. Betty also called Pease Air Force Base to report the event and was interviewed by an officer there. The follow-up report suggested that the Hills had misidentified Jupiter for a spacecraft.

Betty also filed a sightings report with the National Investigations Committee on Aerial Phenomena (NICAP), a group started by Major Donald Keyhoe, a bestselling author years earlier who in his book *Flying Saucers Are Real* said that UFOs were a real phenomenon that the government knew about and was covering up. She was visited just about a month after her encounter by Walter Webb of NICAP, who said that not only did Betty believe what she said happened to her but that she and Barney really did have an encounter with extraterrestrials. By this point, Betty had started having vivid dreams of the event, dreams of being led up a ramp to a craft with Barney and being subjected to a variety of what seemed like tests by strange-looking, large-headed creatures.

Barney's Physical Symptoms

Soon Barney began experiencing physical symptoms that he couldn't pin down. For example, he kept on talking about raised welts and pain around his genital area for no apparent reason. The family doctor said there was nothing wrong with Barney and suggested he might be troubled by emotional issues. Barney visited a psychiatrist, who, hearing the story, suggested that Barney see Dr. Benjamin Simon.

The Regression Sessions

Dr. Simon was a psychiatrist specializing in memory recovery to help remediate the problems caused by a trauma. It wasn't called posttraumatic stress disorder in the 1960s, but during World War II, Dr. Simon helped pilots suffering from trauma confront their fears by facing the event and getting back into the cockpit. In January 1964, Dr. Simon took on Barney and Betty as patients, but he was certainly not prepared for what they would tell him during their hypnotic regression sessions. He began with Barney, who described having a cuplike device placed over his genitals through which the creatures with terrible eyes extracted a sperm sample.

ALERT

Many in the UFO field believe that memories recovered from a hypnotic regression session are automatically true. In fact, many psychologists argue that recovered memories through hypnosis are more the result of the hypnotist's suggestions than the subject's real memories. That's why memories recovered through hypnosis are generally inadmissible evidence in court cases.

When Dr. Simon first heard the Hills' respective stories about being taken aboard a spacecraft by little creatures where the two were examined invasively in some sort of medical tests, he decided not to allow the Hills to have a conscious memory of the events they had recovered through hypnosis. He tape-recorded the sessions and had the tapes transcribed, but he decided that he would work with the Hills individually to make sure for himself that what they believed had happened to them really did happen.

However, events overtook both the Hills and Dr. Simon. Although Dr. Simon eventually wrote an article for a professional journal in which he said that he didn't believe that extraterrestrials abducted Barney and Betty, he believed that they believed their own stories and were not fabricating them. In his *Psychiatric Opinion* article, Dr. Simon said that the Hills' experience was unique, a conclusion that many professional analysts and scientists have said about the Hills' case to this day. But even though Dr. Simon's sessions with Betty and Barney soon came to an end, the story did not.

Eighteen months after they began seeing Dr. Simon, reporter John Lutrell of the *Boston Traveler* obtained an audio of the Hills' hypnosis session. Intrigued, he managed to get reports of the talks the Hills gave to UFO groups and to NICAP. He published a story in the *Boston Traveler* about their chilling experience, which was picked up by UPI, and the story of the event broke into the newspapers worldwide. A year later author John Fuller worked with the Hills to write a book about their experiences called *The Interrupted Journey*. The book became a bestseller and is still in print today.

FACT

Betty and Barney Hill were a very private couple because they were partners in an interracial marriage at a time when interracial marriages were outlawed in some states. Therefore, the last thing they wanted was to become the poster couple for hostile alien abduction. Yet, through no efforts of their own, that's exactly what they became.

In 2007, Betty's niece, Kathleen Marden, with coauthor Stanton Friedman, published a fuller account of the Hills' experiences, along with new scientific information supporting their story, in their book *Captured*.

Hard Evidence in the Hill Case

Although many skeptics and debunkers have gone to great lengths to find fault with the Hills' story, they have never adequately been able to explain Betty's memories of a star map shown to her onboard the craft in which the extraterrestrial medical examiner pointed to as the home planetary system of the ETs. Some people thought Betty's drawing of this system, made while she was fully awake, was simply a confabulation. However, subsequent measurements and designs made of the planetary and star system Betty said was shown to her matched the twin star system Zeta Reticule, which was not known to astronomers in 1961. How could

Betty have conjured up something so accurately when even astronomers didn't know of its existence?

Betty's other memory was that the medical examiner onboard the craft inserted a long, thin tube into her, through which he extracted her eggs. This procedure, oocyte retrieval, was also not known in 1961, coming into use years later by obstetricians for in vitro fertilization.

Finally, Betty's dress that she had saved was later analyzed by organic chemist Dr. Phyllis Buddinger, who discovered that the strange pink stains in the very places where Betty said she was grabbed by the little creatures, stains that only appeared less than twenty-four hours after the event, were of an organic nature and had protein markers in them. In other words, they were types of fingerprints from an external source.

Betty Hill as Spokesperson for the Alien Abduction Phenomenon

Right up to her death in 2004 from cancer, Betty continued to talk about her experience to authors, researchers, and on television shows. She became a celebrated character in the UFO community. Barney Hill, who died in 1969 from a cerebral hemorrhage, was more reticent about going public, but the release of the Hills' story to the newspapers, done without their knowledge or consent, transformed him into a celebrity as well. The Hills' case is still the most and best documented story of an alien counter in U.S. UFO history with its strong witnesses, medical proof that something happened to them, scientific evidence backing up the story, and physical trace evidence of the encounter. This case introduced the alien abduction concept in America, which is now a major field in ufology.

Philip Corso and Reverse Engineering

In his 1997 book *The Day After Roswell*, retired army colonel Philip J. Corso revealed that between 1961 and 1963, during his years at the Army Office of Research and Development as a deputy to Lieutenant General Arthur Trudeau, he was tasked with filtering some of the Roswell crash debris into American engineering. This was a process called *reverse engineering*, a practice that had been carried out in the Foreign Technology Division of

Army Research and Development for years. Indeed, the United States wasn't the only country that reverse-engineered technology. The Soviets engaged in it at the end of World War II when they reverse-engineered a U.S. B-29 bomber. The Chinese reverse-engineered U.S. nuclear warheads from plans that their spies smuggled out of the U.S. nuclear defense industry.

Corso revealed that the army had been reverse-engineering Roswell technology since 1947, when the first solid-state circuits from the spacecraft were taken to Bell Lab scientists Walter Brattain, John Bardeen, and William Shockley. After trying, and repeatedly failing, to create a workable transistor for years, seeing the working piece of technology from the spacecraft enabled them to develop the first successful model in December 1947. Shockley developed an improved version in 1949, and by 1951, the transistor was a commercial success.

General Trudeau and Army Research and Development

At first, the army was upset that Bell Labs applied for and received the patent for the transistor. For that reason, the reverse-engineering projects languished for the next decade until Lieutenant General Arthur Trudeau moved over from the director of Army Intelligence (G-2) to Army Research and Development, then a backwater command inside the Pentagon. Once there, he discovered not only that there was a cache of crash debris from the Roswell crash that was a potential technological gold mine but that the government had already sent some material to Bell Labs. Trudeau convinced his friend in the Senate to authorize a budget for reverse engineering. It was agreed that whatever technology Trudeau and his team developed would be patented by an American corporation, usually one already working on that technology. Senator Strom Thurmond of the Armed Services Committee believed that seeing what amounted to a finished model, a fully complete product of that technology—albeit extraterrestrial—would enable companies to leapfrog over false starts and get to the finish sooner. Trudeau agreed. He brought Corso in from the Maryland National Guard, where he was serving out his final year as a reserve officer, and named him director of the Foreign Technology desk and then as deputy director of Army Research and Development. Trudeau set Corso to work on a plan to get the Roswell technology into American industry before foreign governments or other intelligence agencies could get their hands on it.

The Roswell Goodies

Among the pieces of technology that Corso said he discovered in the file of Roswell debris in the Pentagon were a fiber optic cable, flat round computer circuits, a fabric that was indestructible and remarkably tensile, and a cutting tool that was later reverse-engineered into one of the first laser weapons. Corso also discovered one of the original Walter Reed Army Medical Center autopsy reports on the deceased extraterrestrials, which he described in *The Day After Roswell*. According to Corso, and undisputed by the development companies he named or by the Pentagon, the reverse engineering of the cache of Roswell technology helped spawn a golden age of invention during the mid-1960s.

The Lonnie Zamora Incident

Lonnie Zamora was a police officer in Socorro, New Mexico, on August 24, 1963. Zamora was on patrol at 5:30 in the afternoon when an explosion off in the distance caused him to abandon his chase of a speeding vehicle. He set off to investigate what he thought might be a detonation in a shack of dynamite he knew was in the direction of the explosion. To his surprise, and ultimate dismay, as he drove nearer to the shack, he saw an odd metallic object ahead of him in the distance.

Although at first glance Zamora thought it might have been a car accident and thus the source of the explosion and fire, he realized that this was no car. In fact, this was an object of a type he'd never seen before—metallic, ovoid, with a red insignia on the side. The object was resting on legs or landing struts. Alongside the object were figures he thought to be children dressed in coveralls. He radioed in a report to his dispatch and then approached the object for a closer look. At that point, he heard a roar and saw a flame shoot out from the base of the object. The object took off, seemed to retract its legs, and headed off into the sky.

Just after the object took off and disappeared from view, a state police officer appeared and took a statement from him. The incident was reported to the military, which also followed up with an investigation of the object. In his statement to military officials, Zamora said:

Noise was a roar, not a blast. Not like a jet. Changed from high frequency to low frequency and then stopped. Roar lasted possibly 10 seconds was going towards it at that time on the rough gravel road . . . At same time as roar, saw flame. Flame was under the object. Object was starting to go straight up slowly up . . . Flame was light blue and at bottom was sort of orange color . . . Thought, from roar, it might blow up.

When the roar stopped, he heard a whining sound going from high tone to low tone, which lasted about a second. He then said:

Then there was complete silence . . . It appeared to go in [a] straight line and at same [constant] height, possibly 10 to 15 feet from ground, and it cleared the dynamite shack by about three feet . . . Object was traveling very fast. It seemed to rise up, and take off immediately across country.

Initially, all of this would have been one man's statement, not corroborated by any other witnesses, had it not been for the follow-up investigation that turned up real physical evidence of the presence of something exactly where Zamora said it should have been. The ground investigation team discovered that on the spot where the object landed and then took off there were landing impressions, and the desert sand had been fused into glass by extreme heat. This intrigued UFO investigator, University of Arizona atmospheric physics professor James McDonald, who had the sand sample analyzed. All the analysis turned up was fused sand, but, oddly enough, an air force investigation team contacted the materials analyst, took the samples from her, and advised her never to speak of this case again.

Other Witnesses Support Lonnie Zamora

Four years after the incident, two witnesses contacted Project Blue Book scientist Professor J. Allen Hynek to report that they, too, had seen the object when they were driving near Socorro. They had heard reports of Zamora's sighting and wanted to confirm that they had seen a disklike, egg-shaped object taking off from the desert. Specifically, one witness said, "a round, saucer or egg-shaped object ascended vertically from the black smoke . . . After climbing vertically out of the smoke, the object leveled off and moved in a southwest direction." He said he could see that silver object had what looked like portholes along the side and a red mark near what he thought might have been the stern. The red mark looked like a *Z* insignia.

ALERT

A recent disclosure by a UFO researcher has uncovered a story about students at the New Mexico Institute of Technology who were engaging in a prank caper at the time the Zamora sighting took place. The prank involved faking a landing of a space capsule, complete with crew members in jumpsuits. Was this the ultimate cause of the Zamora sighting? This is an item still up for debate.

The Zamora sighting was listed in Project Blue Book but was never officially resolved. Subsequent investigations by the military revealed that there was no military activity in the area on that day, and that the landing impressions in the sand where Zamora said he saw the object could not otherwise be explained. The case, controversial among skeptics and debunkers who called Zamora's credibility into question, remains unsolved today.

UFOs over Santa Ana, California

Rex Heflin was a highway inspector for Orange County, California. He was driving across Myford Road in Santa Ana on August 3, 1965, in his county truck when, through his windshield, he spotted a hat-shaped object in the sky. It looked like a flying disk or a hubcap, but it seemed clearly metallic, reflecting light, and it wobbled as it flew over the road. Heflin grabbed his Polaroid 101 camera lying on the seat beside him and quickly began to snap photos, pausing between them to pull the developing packet out of the back. As the object flew across his field of vision from the windshield to the passenger side of the truck, Heflin was able to get a succession of four photos, the last one of a black smoke ring hanging in the air just after the object sped away. He later said he could see that there was a band of light on the object that seemed to be sweeping around it like the sweep arm of a radar line around the screen. As he watched the object cross the highway, he tried to radio his dispatch, but the radio in his truck was completely dead while the object was in view. It later came back on its own once the object flew away.

At first, Heflin believed he had just observed one of the unconventional test aircraft from the El Toro Marine Base, which was not too far away. However, the black ring of smoke fascinated him. He drove toward the ring, which was still hanging in the air, rising in altitude but still very cohesive, and photographed it. This was his fourth photograph. Then he finished his rounds and drove back to the Orange County Highway Department headquarters, where he showed the Polaroids to his colleagues. It was only then that folks began suggesting that Heflin had seen a flying saucer and not an aircraft from El Toro.

The Story Spreads

If only the story of the photos had stayed within the small group in the Orange County Highway Department, Rex Heflin's life would have gone on as it had before. But that was not to be the case. He had no interest in UFOs and certainly didn't want to become known, either to the public or to the powers that be inside the government, as the person who had captured some of the best photos of a flying saucer since Paul Trent over a decade before. But the interest among his friends and relatives was so great that Heflin lent the first three photos to some family members who showed them to the local Orange County newspaper, the *Santa Ana Register*. A *Register* reporter made a routine inquiry to the El Toro Marine Base to ask whether any special craft had been launched or whether they had any reports of a UFO. The newspaper's chief photographer, without asking Heflin's permission, published the three photos—Heflin had not turned over the photo of the black smoke ring to anyone—in September 1965. That caught the attention of the National Investigations Committee on Aerial Phenomena (NICAP).

NICAP experts, including such celebrated UFO researchers as Ann Duffel and Dr. Robert Wood, researched the case for the next three years, visiting the Myford Road site, examining the Polaroid photographs, and even examining the truck radio to see if it had any malfunctions that would have caused it to cut out only during the appearance of the object Heflin was photographing. They could find no reason for the radio's performance other than some form of electromagnetic interference that occurred when the object was overhead. They concluded that the photos were not hoaxed photos and that the object, whatever it was, had to have been really there.

The Men in Black

In September 1965, a little over a month after Heflin's sighting, an individual who claimed that he was from NORAD, the North American Air Defense Command, arranged a meeting with Heflin to borrow the photos for analysis. Since Heflin had lent them to the marines, Naval Intelligence, and the air force, and all of them had been returned, Heflin had no misgivings. The individual claiming to be from NORAD warned Heflin in very specific terms not to discuss his sighting or the photos with anyone. When the individual appeared at Heflin's doorstep, he showed him an ID card with no photo. Heflin noticed that parked out front was a dark car with lettering on it that he could not read. He thought he could make out a second individual in the car, but, strangely, the interior of the car seemed to be emanating a purplish glow. Also, just as strangely, Heflin's hi-fi, which he had been listening to and was playing clearly, suddenly began to crackle from inside the house with an interference he had never noticed before as soon as the man claiming to be from NORAD appeared at his front door.

For some time after turning over the photos, Heflin and the investigators from NICAP tried to track down the photos, which had not been returned. NORAD personnel, when contacted, said they dispatched no agents to meet with Heflin and that they searched their offices "from top to bottom" and found no records of their ever having sought the photos. They could not find the photos, either. Heflin concluded that the photos had simply been stolen by someone posing as a government investigator.

Despite the ongoing research into the photos and the repeated meetings with scientists and investigators, including a team of British documentary filmmakers, Heflin continued to work with the Orange County Highway Department until he retired with a severe bronchial disease brought about by his exposure to smog and lead particulate matter from gasoline exhaust fumes. He moved to northern California. One day, in 1993, the Heflins received a phone call asking them whether they had looked in their mailbox that day. The caller then advised them to check the box and hung up. There, in the mailbox, with no postmark on it, was an envelope containing the three original photos that Heflin had lent to the man claiming to be from NORAD. After the return of the originals, they were subjected to enhanced computer analysis, ultimately showing that the photos were real, not hoaxed, and that the smoke ring in photo four could well have been left by the UFO when it picked up smog and particulate matter as it traveled through the atmosphere.

The Military Investigates Heflin

While NICAP was conducting its investigation, the U.S. Marines, Navy, and Air Force also conducted their own investigations. They pried into Heflin's background, contacting his acquaintances and his supervisors at Orange County, and copying his photos for their own analyses. The air force's Project Blue Book investigation was noteworthy because the investigator wrote that he could find no evidence whatsoever that Heflin was perpetrating a hoax. Nevertheless, Project Blue Book officially reported that the photos were faked. As the investigations continued, and curiosity seekers continued to contact him, Heflin did not in any way actively pursue any publicity. Like many inadvertent UFO witnesses, he simply answered questions when asked, but he did not seek any gain from the photos he took or the story he told.

Eventually, Heflin's story caught the attention of Professor James McDonald of the University of Arizona, a climate physicist and a rigorous investigator of UFO phenomena. McDonald became part of a group of scientists and aerial phenomena investigators who investigated the case and evaluated all four photos, trying to figure out the nature of the smoke ring that Heflin said the unidentified object left in the air. Although their investigation took many twists and turns, the ultimate conclusion after years of research substantiated

Heflin's sighting as real. Today, the photos are regarded as some of the most important pieces of evidence of the reality of flying saucers.

Kecksburg, Pennsylvania

On the night of December 6, 1965, all the way across the country from Santa Ana, California, a bright fireball appeared in the sky over rural western Pennsylvania near the small town of Kecksburg, an outlying suburb of Pittsburgh. Observers had sighted the fireball over Michigan and Ohio, as well as over Ontario, Canada, before it headed into Pennsylvania. Witnesses in Kecksburg said they saw the object slow down in the sky, make a long sweeping S-turn, and land, not crash, in a heavily wooded area outside of town. At least one woman said that she saw wisps of smoke from the landing site, and her son said he also saw the object come to Earth.

In a scene that resembled a real-life re-enactment from *War of the Worlds*, local residents followed the streak of light to the gully where they estimated the object had come to rest, where a member of the area's volunteer fire department said he saw the object resting in the trench it had dug as it plowed into the ground. He described what he saw as a bell-shaped or acorn-shaped metallic object with a band around its base on which he thought he could make out lettering that reminded him of Egyptian hieroglyphics. A truck driver, who also said he was one of the witnesses to the object in the trench that night, said that he got very close to it and saw it glowing a purplish blue.

As quickly as residents gathered, milling around the area to get a view of the object, they noticed that an armed military unit was right on their heels. And the Pennsylvania State Police moved in as well, moving bystanders out and clearing the way for military vehicles. The army personnel, who some say were not wearing any identifying insignia, brought in equipment to lift the object out of the gully. Other researchers say that NASA personnel were involved as well and arrived at the scene almost instantly, as if they were expecting the object to appear.

The object, whatever it was, was loaded onto a flatbed and hauled out of the area, some say toward Ohio, while the army and state police cleared the area of witnesses. Subsequent requests for information from the army turned up denials that anything had landed. Reportedly, the army said that its personnel had scoured the area for any signs of wreckage or downed objects, found nothing, and left. NASA also denied any reports of having retrieved an object from the woods. This stands in stark contrast to the eyewitnesses who say they not only saw the object moving through the sky but that they saw it land and observed it glowing and smoking in the trench that it dug.

QUESTION

Is there a link between the Nazi Bell and the Kecksburg object?
The project director of the Nazi Bell was Colonel Kurt Debus, an SS officer and electrical engineer. Twenty years later, his war crimes officially erased, Kurt Debus was the launch director at NASA's Cape Kennedy. He was in charge of NASA when NASA teams recovered the radioactive Kecksburg bell-shaped object. Did the Bell jump forward in time?

Sometimes referred to as "Pennsylvania's Roswell," the Kecksburg incident has been investigated and researched for over forty-five years and has been the object of Freedom of Information Act requests from NASA as well as other government agencies. Yet what remains today are the starkly contrasting statements between the eyewitnesses and the government. Even the claims of the government that the falling object was either a meteorite or a Soviet Cosmos satellite have been rejected by UFO researchers based on astronomical data and reports that the objects came down in different locations and that the behavior of the Kecksburg object was not that of something that was falling but something that was landing. One of the heroes of the Kecksburg incident is Leslie Kean, who led a successful Freedom of

Information Act lawsuit against NASA regarding the Kecksburg incident. The lawsuit resulted in a release of documents, indicating that courts were sympathetic to FOIA requests about UFO incidents.

Edwards AFB Incident

On the very early morning of October 7, 1965, Technical Sergeant Chuck Sorrels, an air traffic control officer at Edwards United States Air Force Base near Palmdale, California, noticed a group of strange lights, flashing red, blue, and green, coming over the field. He could not identify these lights, except to confirm for himself that these didn't look like conventional aircraft. The base was a restricted airspace and any intrusion would call for an interceptor to be scrambled to investigate. Sorrels called the Los Angeles Air Defense Command, which reported to NORAD, to report the lights and the strange maneuvers they were making. The Los Angeles Air Defense Command contacted towers at neighboring air force bases in the area including March, Norton, Hamilton, and George in Victorville, California, to confirm that they had targets on their screens as well. They did.

Sorrels kept a watch on the objects on his radar scope, noting that they were clear targets, not ground clutter, which are reflections of the ground on low-hanging clouds, or temperature inversions, which are false fuzzy targets on a radar scope caused by sharp differentials of temperature at different levels of the atmosphere. Sorrels also noted that these targets were now hovering just outside of the restricted airspace. If this was an invasion of something, they were waiting and watching.

The Incident Escalates

Major Struble of the Los Angeles Air Defense Command was now faced with the decision to order an interceptor to close in on the lights to get a visual identification. In order to do so, however, he had to get an approval for his order from a junior officer, a captain at Edwards AFB, to authorize the flight. The officer, Captain Edwards, was officially designated as the base "UFO Officer." As intriguing as that sounds, the title simply meant that he was in charge of investigating unidentified aerial phenomena over the base, not flying saucers.

During this period of the Cold War, USAF interceptors were equipped with nuclear-tipped air-to-air missiles for purposes of shooting down multiple Soviet bombers should they ever decide to attack North America. Therefore, dispatching one of the F-106 interceptors on alert status at one of the bases was not a casual command. It was serious. Nevertheless, given the multiple sightings of objects in airspace uncomfortably close to the base and the multiple radar hits from Los Angeles Air Defense Command and from civilian Los Angeles Center Ground Control Approach radars, Captain Edwards authorized the scramble of an F-106 from George Air Force Base. At the same time, Captain Daryl Clark of the 329th Fighter Interceptor Squadron stationed at Edwards was the alert pilot that night, and from the runway he also observed the lights that Chuck Sorrels saw as did the pilot of the interceptor dispatched from George Air Force Base, who tried to track the source of the lights. He reported seeing objects, but they dispersed as he approached their formation.

An Areawide Alert

An intrusion into restricted military airspace is a serious event, usually requiring reports from all the personnel involved from enlisted and specialist ranks all the way to command ranks. The Edwards AFB incident was no exception. Radar tapes were collected, as well as audio tapes of the radio transmissions among tower officers at Los Angeles Center, Los Angeles Air Defense, and the air force bases at Edwards, George, Hamilton, Norton, and March. The air force concluded that the visual observations were only mistakes and that the radar operators were only observing temperature inversions or ground clutter, conclusions hotly disputed by Chuck Sorrels in his later television interviews. Coming as it did during the Cold War and only a few years after the Cuban Missile Crisis, the Edwards AFB intrusion is one of the major events in the history of UFOs versus the military from 1944 to the present.

Malmstrom AFB Missile Silo Incident

Malmstrom Air Force Base in Montana is a Strategic Air Command Minuteman missile facility, a key part of America's nuclear strike force and a longtime nuclear deterrent. As you can imagine, the air force takes the ongoing maintenance and operations of these facilities seriously, and the crews that staff the guided missile bases are some of the best-trained technicians in the entire military. One mistake, one glitch not remedied by a crewmember, and the loss of a deterrent during time of war might be catastrophic. Equally catastrophic might be the loss of control of a nuclear-tipped guided missile; a launch by mistake, and the entire world would be at war. Therefore, any incident at the Minuteman silos is a deadly serious event.

Just such an event, according to Deputy Crew Commander (at that time air force captain) Robert Salas, a graduate of the United States Air Force Academy and now an author and UFO investigator, happened on March 16, 1967, when a reported observation of a UFO in the airspace over Malmstrom shut down the ability of launch control to communicate with its missiles, effectively cutting off control to the facility. This was not an event to be taken lightly.

A Frightening Ice-Cold Night to Remember

Bob Salas, author of *Faded Giant*, writes that on that clear, cold night in Montana's Big Sky country, one member of an air force team outside the silo noticed a light in the sky different from the surrounding canopy of stars because it was zigzagging. Then this airman noticed another light in the sky begin the same maneuvers, only this light came closer and looked larger than the pinpoints of starlight. He asked his supervisor to look at the lights. He agreed that these were not conventional aircraft but something else, and he phoned a report to Captain Salas, the launch control officer inside the silo.

Salas ordered the air security personnel to keep a watch on the lights, not knowing what they were actually seeing. But a few minutes later the supervisor called Salas back to say that there was a large red glowing light hovering outside the base gate. This time the air security officer seemed clearly frightened. One of the airmen who had gone to investigate the light was injured and had to be evacuated by helicopter.

As this conversation was unfolding and Salas called his commander to brief him on the conversation, both officers heard a klaxon horn go off inside the capsule housing the launch control center. Salas says that when he and his commander looked at their control boards, they saw that a "No Go" light was flashing, indicating that one of the missile sites was down.

Security lights were also flashing. Something had taken the missile site off-line, a very serious condition.

Salas's commander began a query operation to find out what was wrong and why the lights were flashing. Almost instantly, another klaxon alarm went off and a new series of lights indicated that six to eight missiles had been taken off-line and were "No Go."

Salas said that he left the control room to interview the security guards on the surface to find out more about the red glowing lights they had seen. The injured guard had already been evacuated, but the other guard said that there had been a red glowing disk-shaped object hovering over the gate. The timeline of this event corresponded to the missiles under Salas's control going off-line. A subsequent patrol of the area also confirmed that another red glowing unidentified object had been spotted, and this time when the patrol tried to report the sighting, they discovered that their radios were inoperable and could not communicate with the base.

Salas summed up the incident initially without attributing any direct causality, stating briefly that the missiles in the affected silos were rendered inoperable at the same time that security personnel above ground saw a disk-shaped craft hovering near the base. Subsequent maintenance checks by Boeing and by air force engineers to determine the nature of the malfunction in the launch control systems found no anomalies anywhere. The control panels, launch control systems, and communication systems were all checked and rechecked to find any problem that could have caused six to eight missiles to become inoperable. Nothing was found. The only event, the event that cut out electronic communication between a security patrol and the base, was the sighting of unexplained, unidentified lights in the sky in very near proximity to the missile silos that were shut down.

CHAPTER 6

The 1970s: Alien Abduction Becomes Up Close and Personal

By the 1970s, close encounters seemed to become more menacing and seemingly more invasive than the previous decade. The Travis Walton case, made famous by the media and the motion picture *Fire in the Sky*, served as a warning to UFO hunters to be careful what they're hunting because UFOs could be hunting them. While the two self-described Pascagoula River abductees were laughed at by the media, other witnesses corroborated the stories of abductee-claimants Hickson and Parker. Then there was the Delphos, Kansas, case, one of the most studied UFO cases because of the physical trace evidence and the very compelling photos. It seemed that as America became more UFO-savvy, those who were navigating these craft were becoming more interested in the lives of individual human beings.

Trace Evidence

A sighting in Delphos, Kansas, in 1971, is one of the great cases that combines credible multiple witnesses with physical trace evidence, government involvement, and residual physical biological effects that something anomalous took place. In fact, the case won an award in 1972 from the *National Enquirer* for being the best UFO case of the year backed up by scientific evidence.

On November 2, 1971, at approximately 6:30 P.M., sixteen-year-old Ron Johnson along with his dog, Snowball, was out tending the family's sheep when he saw a mushroom-domed, disk-shaped object descending through the trees on the family's land. The object hovered only a few feet off the ground and so amazed Johnson that he tried to get a better look. But the brightness of the object forced him to squint, so he could see no specific details on the surface except for the shape. He remembered that he did hear a machinelike sound as the object descended toward the ground. Momentarily blinded by the object, which had now begun to rise, Johnson quickly regained his sight and ran inside the house to get his parents. His parents, alerted, came outside where they saw the object as it ascended still bright and about the size of the distant moon in the sky. They were shocked.

FACT

Because trace evidence is a key element in any crime scene or accident scene investigation, its presence at a UFO encounter site is vital because it is evidence that something—probably something anomalous—took place there. Therefore, UFO investigators as crash or landing scene analysts look very hard for any piece of physical evidence they can take to a lab for analysis.

Their shock would turn to utter amazement, however, when they saw that on the ground just below where the object was hovering there was a glowing ring that looked crystalline. The same type of glow was on the leaves of the trees where the object had first descended. Johnson's mother touched the substance and remarked that it felt slick, but her fingers suddenly became numb.

The next morning, the family returned to the site where they had seen the ring and discovered that the glowing ring was still there. Remarkably, though, it had rained the night before and the ground was wet everywhere except for the surface of the ring. It looked like the soil where the ring was simply shed the water or was impervious to it. The ring remained through the winter snow, but again, unlike the surrounding soil, the soil where the ring was would not admit any water. Snow sat on the ring as if it were the surface of a car. The soil remained impervious to water.

The Story Circulates

Within days, the local newspaper picked up the story, this time calling it a UFO incident, and the news about the ring on the soil also attracted the interest of both the county sheriff and undersheriff, as well as the highway patrol. They, too, filed a report, remarking that the doughnut-shaped ring was completely dry despite the precipitation and that the discoloration of the soil matched the "slight" discoloration of limbs on the tree above the area where the witness had said the object had descended. Photographs of the ring even after almost four years still showed that the soil had a whitish color.

The entire incident was investigated by Ted Phillips, who photographed the area and turned soil samples over to chemist Phyllis Buddinger. When *UFO Hunters* investigated this case, we evaluated the soil sample and were able to report that, forty years after the incident, the soil was still impervious to water. We also uncovered two facts of interest. First, the witness Ron Johnson, although he did not report it at the time, revealed that he could not account for a period of time between his trying to get a better glimpse of the object and his realization that the object was ascending through the trees. He does not know what happened during that missing time and has been reluctant to recover those memories. Two, he later discovered that his dog, Snowball, was in discomfort around its snout. He took the dog to the vet, who was able to retrieve a long, metallic, insect-like object that looked like it had been implanted into the dog. Whatever it was, Johnson has kept this object to this very day, still reluctant to explore what that object might be.

The Importance of the Case

This was a case that combined a family of witnesses, a police report verifying the existence of physical trace evidence on the ground, independent corroboration that the imperviousness of the soil continued for over forty years, a case of missing time, and the physical trace evidence of the implant of a metallic object inside the witness's dog's snout. Certainly these facts make the Delphos case one of the better cases in American UFO history.

The Pascagoula River Incident

On October 10, 1973, witnesses in New Orleans saw a strange circular object fly very low over a housing project. The witnesses reported seeing a UFO. On October 11, 1973, at 9 P.M., two workers at the local shipyard, Calvin Parker and Charles Hickson, were fishing on the bank of the Pascagoula River in Mississippi when they heard a buzzing sound nearby. Hickson and Parker were at first puzzled by the sound until they looked around to see a glowing ovoid-shaped object, with a blue haze around it, floating right above the ground. Suddenly, as Hickson and Parker stared in disbelief, a sally port doorway opened in the object and out of it floated a trio of strange beings—not earthly, Hickson would later say—who came toward the two fishermen. The five-foot-tall beings had a humanoid shape, legs, no necks or eyes, slits for mouths, gray wrinkly skin, claws in place of hands, and heads shaped like bullets, but they did not walk. They levitated themselves, defying gravity. They floated toward Hickson and Parker, the first two creatures grabbing Hickson and the third taking hold of Parker. Then, while the men were paralyzed with fear, the creatures began floating the two men through the air and into the object, which they now realized was a craft.

Parker, overcome by terror, lost complete consciousness while Hickson, though awake and conscious, was completely numb and unable to move. The two men were separated, each in a different chamber, possibly an examination room. Hickson remembered that he was floating in midair inside the room while a large eye, floating along with him, scanned him from head to toe. Then it left him alone in the room, still floating.

After about a half-hour, Hickson and Parker—now fully conscious—were floated back out of the craft and deposited back on land. Parker was in a complete state of terror, while Hickson, although frightened by the ordeal, was glad to be back on land. The two men watched as the craft, its hatch now closed, gently rose and then ascended through the atmosphere.

Hickson and Parker, simply fishing on the bank of a river, had been floated aboard some sort of craft by unearthly creatures, scanned, and floated back through the air to the riverbank at which point they watched the craft take off. Their first act was to phone Kessler Air Force Base in Biloxi, Mississippi, where they were told to report their abduction to the local sheriff, which they did, after trying to tell it to the local newspaper. But the sheriff, as anyone could imagine, after asking whether the men had anything to drink, confined the two to a room and left them there. Convinced that the men were hoaxing the story, the sheriff had a clever plan. He bugged the room to record the men's conversation, believing that between them they would reveal the truth and the sheriff could send them home.

ESSENTIAL

Not all witnesses will be airline or military pilots or public safety officials. In fact, most witnesses are just everyday folks whose paths cross those of anomalous objects or even beings. The tip here is not to judge a book by its cover. Go with the story first to see if you can find any corroborating evidence and consistency. Then look for physical traces. Think about the backgrounds of your witnesses last, but keep in mind that debunkers will always attack the witness credibility, even resorting to personal character attacks if they want to.

The Sheriff's Gambit

Imagine the sheriff's surprise, however, when Hickson and Parker, still in a state of fright, began to go over the details of what they remembered. While Hickson tried to calm Parker down, assuring him that he wasn't crazy, the sheriff realized that whatever happened to them, they weren't making it up. They believed the incredible story they had told him. The next step was a lie detector test, which they passed. Then the story unfolded in public after the sheriff told the local newspaper, which spread the story to other papers, and Hickson's and Parker's boss at the shipyard also wanted to disseminate the story. Ultimately, the story caught the attention of such reputable UFO researchers as Dr. J. Allen Hynek, formerly of Project Blue Book, who commented that he believed the story was certainly not terrestrial.

Over the years, debunkers have attacked the story as the joint delusion of two country fellas who drank a little too much as they cast for fish. And that's how it might have remained except for another witness from the local naval base who also reported seeing the oval-shaped craft flying over the highway on the same day. The U.S. Coast Guard personnel and some fishermen also reported seeing an oval craft with a telltale amber light on it under water in the Pascagoula River. Multiple witnesses, therefore, gave the Hickson and Parker abduction story the corroboration it needed.

ESSENTIAL

When scrutinizing a UFO story, try to look behind the story to see if the storyteller witness provides any hint of trace evidence or any other evidence to back up the story. Lie detector tests, such as the one that Hickson and Parker passed, are good. Also, Hickson and Parker were tape-recorded in a sealed interrogation room by the sheriff and still stuck to their story.

Fire in the Sky

Travis Walton's personal story of his having been abducted by a UFO and returned to Earth days later, thoroughly investigated by the police and many UFO researchers, was the subject of his own bestselling book, *Fire in the Sky*, and a feature film of the same name starring D. B. Sweeney, Robert Patrick, and James Garner.

The Abduction

The incident began on November 5, 1975, when logger Travis Walton, then twenty-two years old, and his crew had quit for the evening and were heading back out of the forest in Snowflake, Arizona. It was just after 6 P.M. and already dark when, as the crew drove away, they saw a bright light from right behind the hill ahead of them. As they drove closer to the light, they came to a clearing and saw that the light emanated from a large silver disk hovering in the air right above the clearing.

The driver and crew boss, Mike Rogers, stopped the truck so the men inside could get a better view when Travis Walton jumped out to get an even better look. While his crewmembers in the truck shouted at him to get back in, Walton approached the disk until he was almost directly under it. At that point, the disk began to make a noise similar to that of a turbine. Then it began wobbling from side to side. Seeing the disk seem to react to him, Walton moved away from the spot under the disk very slowly as if not to spook it. That was when, according to the witnesses in the truck, a blue-green beam of light shot out from the disk and hit Walton directly. He rose directly into the air about a foot and then was thrown backward, Walton says, about ten feet where he sprawled flat on his back and lost consciousness. Mike Rogers and the crew, seeing him lying motionless on the ground after flying through the air, thought he was dead and drove out of there, seized by fear.

Less than a mile down the road, however, Mike Rogers and the crew decided that, whatever had happened, they had better go back and retrieve Walton. But when they reached the clearing, not only was the silvery disk gone, but Walton, or Walton's body, was nowhere to be found. They searched the area but turned up nothing. They knew that they had to report what they saw to the police. They also realized that what they saw would be a tough thing to get the police to believe.

The Crew Under Suspicion and the Police Investigation

They were right. When the crew spoke to the police, a deputy sheriff, and then Sheriff Martin Gillespie, they were met with a very skeptical response. After all, they said that a flying disk had appeared in the woods, lifted Walton up in a beam of light, then threw him backward ten or so feet, at which point they fled, and when they returned, Walton had disappeared. What was clearly a missing person case also sounded like a murder case, with the murderers having hidden the body. The whole story sounded plain strange.

After the police and some of the crew returned to the clearing, the temperature was dropping precipitously and there were fears that if Walton were somewhere in the woods, he would quickly succumb to exposure. They wrapped up the nighttime search and returned the next morning, this time with helicopters and mounted police, but still could find no trace of Travis Walton. Within days, however, the story of the UFO started to spread and that attracted UFO investigators to the area, who began interviewing the witnesses. The story evolved into a UFO abduction.

The police were not UFO believers, however, and suspected either a hoax set up by Walton himself or foul play. They administered polygraph examinations to the crewmembers and discovered that, as crazy as the story seemed, the crew members believed it. They all passed the polygraph test, which confused the police even more. As the search continued over the next few days, an even more amazing event took place.

The Phone Call and the Return

On the following Monday, Walton's brother-in-law received a phone call from Travis Walton himself, a panicked, terrified call pleading for help and saying that he was in a phone booth not far from Snowflake and needed to picked up immediately. Grant Neff, Walton's brother-in-law, phoned Duane Walton, Walton's brother, and together they drove out to the gas station phone booth where Walton placed the call, and drove him back home. He was shaking, so sick to his stomach that he couldn't keep down any food, suffered some weight loss, and was still in a state of panic. The brother and brother-in-law decided not to call the police immediately, but the phone company had traced the call from the phone booth and notified the police. The investigation moved to another stage, especially when the sheriff sent two of his men to dust the phone booth for fingerprints and found out that Walton's prints were not there.

Walton's Account of His Experiences on Board a Spacecraft

By the time Walton had undergone a medical exam, he had recovered enough to tell his story to the sheriff, and the story was even stranger than Walton's disappearance and reappearance. Walton said that he last remembered the beam hitting but had been knocked completely unconscious in the woods. When he opened his eyes, he was in a room with a bright light. He thought at first, he told me in our radio interview, that he might have been in a hospital but had no memory of being taken there. His sense of being in a hospital room, however, quickly vanished when his vision cleared and he could see that there were three small (under five feet) figures surrounding him. And they weren't human.

They wore something that looked like jumpsuits, were completely hairless, had heads much larger than normal with tiny mouths and noses, and had huge eyes that were mostly dark. The eyes, he said, just kept staring at him and were terrifying. He had the presence of mind, though, as he fought through his fear, to rise up and get off the bed. He shouted at the entities to get away and grabbed what he believed to be a cylindrical object made of glass. At least he thought it was glass, and he swung it menacingly at the creatures who backed away. They exited the room, leaving him alone. Now it was time for an escape.

ALERT

In the movie version of *Fire in the Sky*, D. B. Sweeney, portraying Travis Walton, is depicted as being covered with a slimy substance, like an insect goo, and is stuffed into a tiny cubicle onboard the spacecraft. Travis Walton explained on the radio show *Future Theater* that this was done just for dramatic effect and was not at all what really happened to him. He actually woke up on a hospital-type bed when he was onboard the spacecraft.

Walton said that he found an entrance to a corridor and made his way down it, still unsteady on his feet. The corridor led him to a room that was circular and had a chair in the middle. Lights came up in the room as he walked in and, in retrospect decades later, Walton thought it might have been a control room. He sat down in the chair and immediately he could see images of stars or star systems on the ceiling. He played with the controls a little, a lever alongside the chair, but gave it up quickly and got up off the chair. The stars disappeared from the ceiling. As he walked around the room looking for a doorway out, he turned around to see another creature in the room. This time, it seemed human.

The creature was tall and wore a blue coverall and had a clear helmet over his head. Walton tried to communicate with it, asking questions, but the creature only indicated for Walton to follow it. He did, down a hallway and a ramp and into a large open area that Walton could only describe as similar to an aircraft hangar. Inside, he saw other disks, perhaps flying saucers, but he didn't have time to linger because there were three other human creatures in the hangar, one of whom was clearly a woman. He asked them questions, but they didn't answer. They led him into another room with an examination table on it, motioned for him to lie down, and when he did, the woman put a mask over his face. Before Walton could pull it away or fight her off, he lost consciousness. And the next thing he remembered was waking up back at the gas station near the phone booth where he was picked up. He looked up at the sky and saw the silvery disk over the road. Then it shot away and he was all alone. That was when he placed the phone call to his brother-in-law.

FACT

Although a common perception among science fiction fans is that all extraterrestrials look frightening and monster-like, many people who have claimed to be visited, contacted, or abducted by extraterrestrials say that there is one group who look just like human beings. These are the "Nordic types," who appear to be benevolent, almost as if they and we share a common ancestry.

The Attack of the Debunkers

In the aftermath of the story, both supporters and debunkers in and outside of the UFO community popped up. Debunkers said that Walton was inconsistent in his story, that he failed a polygraph exam, while supporters said the polygraph exam was unprofessional at worst and completely not up to modern standards at that time at best. Hence it was inconclusive. The sheriff thought at first that Walton had been drugged and taken to a regular hospital and in a confused state imagined he was in a spacecraft. Arch debunker, the late Phil Klass, said that Walton had seen a movie about flying saucers, giving him the idea, and that the entire story was a confabulation to get out of trouble on a logging contract with the U.S. Forest Service that the crew couldn't complete on time. In fact, Klass, who, it would come out years later, was working for the CIA to embarrass UFO witnesses and debunk their stories, embarked on a personal mission to discredit Travis Walton. However, the story has stood up over time as one of the best multiple-witnessed

UFO abductions. In 1978, Walton wrote his own story called *The Walton Experience*, which screenwriter Trace Torme adapted for the motion picture *Fire in the Sky.*

QUESTION

How accurate are motion pictures about UFO events?
Most people think that if you see it in a movie based on fact, the facts are usually portrayed accurately in the movie. However, this is often not the case. For example, folks who saw the movie *Fire in the Sky* saw Travis Walton enveloped in a mucus-like substance as if he were larva while onboard the spaceship. That, according to Walton, was inaccurate. Walton said he simply woke up on a hospital-type bed in a room he thought was a hospital.

The impact of Walton's story was so great that Phil Klass set up a fake witness to lure Walton into believing him so that he could expose the entire story as a hoax. But the fake witness failed a lie detector test and was exposed as a fraud. This last event, the deliberate attempt to hoax a witness into believing a fake witness, is another example of how debunkers usually try to trick witnesses by creating their own hoaxes.

Walton has rewritten *The Walton Experience* and is currently in the process of updating his original book again. He still makes appearances at UFO conferences and was a recent guest on the radio show *Future Theater.*

The Val Johnson Incident

This incident, in which an alleged UFO collided with a deputy sheriff's patrol car, is one of the best physical trace evidence cases in ufology. Although the nature of the evidence itself is still debated among debunkers and researchers, some of it is very hard to dispute as anomalous.

The incident began on a lonely country road in Marshall County, Minnesota, at 2 A.M. on August 27, 1979, when Deputy Sheriff Val Johnson was on patrol near the town of Stephen. As he reached an intersection along the road, he saw a beam of light in the distance. Even though at first he thought it was an approaching car at high speed, what quickly captured his attention was that the light was not from a headlight but was an actual glowing ball. It wasn't a car at all, and it wasn't slowing down as it approached. Suddenly the light was all around him as if it had swallowed his car. As he lost consciousness, Johnson said that the last thing he heard was breaking glass.

The Johnson Report

Deputy Johnson remained unconscious for over half an hour. When he came to, he noticed that his dashboard clock in his police unit had stopped for fourteen minutes. He also noticed that his wristwatch, not connected to the car's electrical system at all, also lost fourteen minutes. Johnson realized this when he checked his clocks against the official time from his dispatch after the incident. Thus, whatever event shut down the car also shut down his watch. Johnson also noted the damage to the car from what he assumed to be the impact with the object. The car's windshield was shattered. His red police emergency light was broken as was a headlight. Interestingly, the car's radio antenna was bent back at a ninety-degree angle but not broken. This is similar to the shafts of grain in a crop circle that are bent and flattened by some force but not actually broken. In addition, inasmuch as this was still summer and the car had been driving along country roads, the radio antenna had gathered material from squashed insects. Where the antenna was bent, the insect material was missing, but it was present on the rest of the antenna.

FACT

Typical of attacks on witnesses, debunkers said that Johnson was either drunk or had fallen asleep and crashed his car, using a collision with an orb or UFO as an excuse to explain his actions. They disregarded the physical trace evidence, such as the nature of the skid marks on the road and the car's radio antenna, and attacked the witness.

Trace Evidence

As for the car itself, when deputies arrived on scene in response to Johnson's call for backup after the incident, they found that his car had been pushed off the road and turned sideways, halfway into a ditch. They also found that the skid marks showed that even after Johnson had applied the brakes and the engine was apparently off, something had moved the car along the road and spun it sideways. How could this have happened with the engine off and acting as a brake on the car? The skid marks backed up Johnson's story that something had impacted and probably moved the car, and that it was not the police officer who had caused the accident. Again, physical trace evidence, extrinsic to the actual damage to the car, verified that something had happened to Johnson that was not a result of his driving.

Johnson himself was injured physically as a result of the incident. He was rendered unconscious, lost time, and suffered a bruise and an injury to his eye that a doctor characterized as a "welder's burn." Johnson was also shaken badly by the entire incident and eventually left the police force as a result of the national publicity that resulted from the story.

The Physical Evidence Lingers

Two other elements in the aftermath of the incident also served to corroborate that something anomalous happened. First, the police car itself could no longer maintain a battery charge. Whatever hit the engine caused the engine to drain the car's battery. Even today, that car, stored in Minnesota, will not hold a battery charge. When a new battery is installed, the battery will drain almost immediately and the car will not start. Moreover, the new battery will not take a charge and must be replaced. Nor will the car start.

Second, after the incident, UFO investigators flew over the area to see if they could make out a pattern for the beam of light, also referred to as an orb. In scanning the area with infrared equipment, they discovered that there was a swath of discoloration along the road where the orb traveled up to the spot where it hit the police car. They discovered that along the orb's route was a farmhouse. Curious about whether anything might have happened at the farmhouse, they asked the folks who lived there if they had experienced any strange effects in the house or knew about the incident.

A strange thing did happen, the family told investigators. They were away on the night of the incident on a trip. But when they returned home, not knowing what happened just down the road, they noticed that the clocks in their house had stopped for fourteen minutes. This turned out to be another piece of extrinsic evidence corroborating that something anomalous happened in that area, an event that coincided with the swath of darkness picked up by the infrared camera tracking the path of the orb.

The Johnson case, although heavily debunked by folks like Phil Klass, who claimed that Johnson hoaxed the entire event because he was a drunk driver, still hasn't been explained away logically or scientifically.

Debunker arguments are sometimes more implausible than a UFO explanation. For example, when the late Phil Klass suggested that Deputy Johnson was drunk and fabricated the story, he never bothered to explain the existence of the physical evidence on Johnson's police unit. Also, no one in the sheriff's office believed Johnson was under the influence. A subsequent physical exam would have more than likely turned up evidence of elevated blood alcohol, indicating inebriation. No such evidence was ever put forth.

CHAPTER 7

UFO Incidents in England in 1980

In 1980, events involving UFO encounters in the United Kingdom became more bizarre than at any other time in the modern history of British ufology. In separate cases, the level of intensity of UFO encounters shook the timbers of British police and military institutions. Personnel at the very top of those institutions became involved in trying to control the information about what the experiencers encountered. A constable was ultimately forced to sign a national security letter effectively muzzling him and preventing him from conducting his own investigation into his experience. A UFO encounter at a very sensitive nuclear weapons base in the United Kingdom wound up involving Prime Minister Margaret Thatcher and the head of the British Admiralty, as well as investigators from the U.S. Air Force, the U.S. National Security Agency, and British Intelligence. The incidents in the United Kingdom were also remarkable because of the degree of cover-up, both in the United Kingdom and in the United States. The year 1980 was important for UFO researchers, especially in England.

The Alan Godfrey Abduction

This case is one of the stranger UFO incidents because not only did it occur during a UFO flap over England in the latter part of 1980, but it linked a number of otherwise disparate events. There was the discovery of a corpse on top of a coal heap, with a UFO sighting nearby. A herd of cattle disappeared and strangely—unexplainably—reappeared later. The officer who investigated the cause of death of the body found on the coal heap was abducted, and upon his release he found that he had miraculously recovered from an injury he suffered while making an arrest over a year earlier. These events ultimately forced the officer and abductee—Constable Alan Godfrey—to sign a national security nondisclosure letter linking the disparate incidents. Something about these seemingly unrelated incidents had touched a raw nerve among the police and national security powers that resulted in their wanting Godfrey silenced about the entire event.

The Body

The incident began with a police report that a body had been discovered on top of a twelve-foot-high coal tip in the town of Todmorden. Godfrey was one of the responding officers who reached the body discovery scene at 4:10 P.M. on June 11, 1980.

As Godfrey related the story, upon inspecting the body lying on its back on top of the heap, he noticed that it was completely clean and free of coal dust, as if the deceased had just taken a shower. He wondered how a person could have climbed up this coal mound and not gotten any coal dust on him. Then he noticed the deceased's expression. It was one of pure fright, just like something out of a horror movie. What could have scared this person so that his face was frozen in terror while he was on top of this coal heap?

The more Godfrey inspected the body, the deeper the mystery became. As if the lack of any coal dust even under the victim's fingernails, the body on its back, and the terrified look on the corpse's face weren't enough, Godfrey noticed that the body looked like it had been undressed and redressed, but redressed by someone who did not know how to put on clothing. For example, the corpse's shirt was missing but his jacket was buttoned as if the person doing the buttons didn't know how buttons were supposed to match up with buttonholes. It wasn't just the case of a hurried missing of a button—the entire jacket was put on incorrectly and buttoned in such a way that, to Godfrey's eyes, the dresser didn't know what a jacket or a button was. It was uncanny.

FACT

Crime scene investigators will look carefully under a victim's fingernails or in other spots for residue from the crime scene. According to Locard's theory of transference, whenever an object or body, human or otherwise, comes in contact with something else, material is transferred between the contacting entities. This theory is one of the most important aspects of crime scene investigation.

The deceased's wallet was missing, and his pants were also put on incorrectly. Godfrey also noticed that the man's head had been partially shaved at the base of his skull and that in the shaven areas were burn marks. But the burn marks looked as though they were impressed into his skin, as if he had been wearing some type of headband that burned him in spots. In the areas where there were burn marks, Godfrey could make out the presence of an ointment of some sort, as if it had been applied to make an electrical connection.

In spite of the apparent mystery, Godfrey and his partner tried to be as logical as they could. The cleanliness of the body might have been due to the incessant rain that had been coming down, washing away the coal dust and stains—unlikely, of course, because anyone who has handled coal knows that coal dust has an oiliness to it that needs a solvent, like soap, and a brush to scrub it off. But perhaps the rain might have cleansed the corpse. The rain had not removed any of the ointment, however, and it did not explain the odd way the man was redressed.

The Investigation

Upon examination, the police determined that the deceased was a Polish immigrant, named Zygmunt Adamski, who had lived in the United Kingdom since World War II. He was a fifty-six-year-old coal miner at the Lofthouse Colliery. Adamski had left his home in Tingley five days earlier to shop for food. Adamski's wife believed the man had been kidnapped and tortured. Mrs. Adamski couldn't provide an explanation for why someone would have wanted to kidnap a coal miner unless the man were some kind of spy who had been tracked down, tortured for information he might have had, and then deposited on top of a coal tip in such a way that it looked very mysterious.

The coroner's subsequent medical examination revealed that Adamski suffered from heart disease, a condition so acute that his death was attributed to heart failure. But this, to Godfrey, was another mystery. If Adamski had suffered from a fatal cardiac arrest on top of the coal heap, he asked the coroner, how could he have climbed to the top of that heap without first suffering a heart attack? He could get no satisfactory explanation.

Perhaps Adamski had died prior to his being dropped on the coal heap, but then another mystery popped up. Godfrey examined the area around the coal heap and discovered that not only did Adamski not leave any footprints there, but there were no prints whatsoever, nor were there tire tracks or tread tracks to indicate that a front loader or other type of vehicle dumped the body twelve feet up. Perhaps the rain had washed away all of the tracks, one theory went, but even so, unless the area was completely flooded and new silt deposited all around, including at the base of the coal tip, there would be some residual footprints, tire tracks, or tread marks. However, there were none. It was as if Adamski had been floated through the air to the top of the coal tip. Interestingly enough, the area around Todmorden had been witness to strange sightings over the previous weeks with private citizens reporting glowing balls of light, or orbs, in the air.

At the official coroner's inquest, the jury found that Adamski had likely died from heart failure, a death from natural causes, and not a homicide. The coroner, however, could not identify the cause of the patterns of burns around the base off the deceased's head and neck, could only identify the chemical substance that comprised the ointment as "unknown," and did not explain the mystery of the state of undress of the victim. The coroner said that the Adamski death was the biggest mystery of his career. Godfrey said that he disagreed with the inquest's findings and argued that the death looked more like a homicide even though the perpetrator was mysterious and the police would have lacked motive or means. The coroner's inquest finding was legal, however, and there was no follow-up police investigation.

That would have been the end of the matter except for an event that took place a little over six months later in Todmorden, when Godfrey was on a routine patrol in the very early hours of November 28, 1980. It was 5 A.M., and Godfrey was following up on a report of missing cattle.

ALERT

If you come across a case where there are missing cattle or a missing cow, always ask witnesses or examine the site for yourself to see if there are any footprints around where the cattle were supposed to be. Act like a tracker. If there are no footprints, tire tracks, or hoof prints, chances are you have a real mystery on your hands.

As he drove, Godfrey was thinking about a recent visit to his doctor. While he had recovered fully from an injury suffered in the line of duty, his doctor said that he and his wife could never have children together.

As Godfrey arrived at the pasture from where they disappeared, he could not locate the cows. He didn't know it as he was heading back to headquarters, but the cows would eventually turn up after sunrise in a different location in a damp field but, strangely, without any tracks or hoof marks to indicate how they got there or where they came from. It was if they had flown out of their pasture to the new location. This was the other strange occurrence in a series of strange occurrences that would befall Godfrey. But Godfrey didn't know about what would eventually be discovered about the cattle as he noticed a light ahead of him on the road, which he thought might have a bus or a truck.

The UFO

To his astonishment, as he pulled up to the source of the light, it wasn't a vehicle at all, or at least not a vehicle that he could identify. He described it as a diamond-shaped object, very bright, hovering just above the road surface and spinning very rapidly. The motion of the object was so intense that it was creating a whirlwind effect, blowing the trees and bushes on either side of the road back and forth. There were leaves on the ground, wet from the rain, and Godfrey could see that the object was spinning right in the middle of them. He stopped his car and vaguely realized that he was hearing static on his police radio. He didn't know what the thing in front of him was, but, with the road blocked and his car stopped, he did know that he had to try to get a sketch of it made. So he took his clipboard, noted that it was just after 5 A.M., and began sketching the outline of the object when a bright flash, brighter than anything he had seen before, totally blinded him.

As his eyes recovered from the light and he could see the road ahead, he was suddenly aware that the object was no longer there. He was now driving his car, having no memory of his having put it back into gear, and he was in a different spot along the road. Had he jumped over the object?

He turned his patrol car around and headed back toward the spot where he had seen the object. It was gone. However, where it had been spinning, Godfrey noticed that the leaves covering the road had been spiraled out to the side as if a fan had blown them and that the road surface, which was wet from the rain, was completely dry. This, to him, was proof that something had been there and that he had not imagined the incident. He needed to get another pair of eyes on this before the rain covered up the dry spot.

He said that he contacted another police officer and together they drove back to the spot so the officer could confirm what Godfrey saw: that the wet road had a dry spot in the middle of it and that the leaves had been swirled out to the side of the road in a spiral pattern. Now with his sketch and at least one witness confirming the evidence that something had kept the rain from soaking the road in that spot, Godfrey headed back to headquarters, noting, for the first time, that his dashboard clock was fifteen minutes ahead of where it should have been. There were fifteen minutes missing from Godfrey's memory.

Godfrey Sighting Confirmed

Back at headquarters, Godfrey at first didn't file any reports about what he had seen. Rather, he waited until he found out that the police at Todmorden already had reports of the strange object. An officer in Halifax, Godfrey said, filed a report of a bright unidentified light overhead moving in the direction of Todmorden; another driver on Burnley Road had also seen the bright object and gave the report to the police. Therefore, what Godfrey had seen, he believed, had multiple witnesses, and he submitted his report of the encounter along with the corroboration of the other officer that had seen the dry spot in the road and the swirled leaf pattern.

Godfrey thought that he was submitting a police report in confidence, but he was surprised to find out that the police had given the report to newspapers. Soon Godfrey's sighting was attracting the attention of local UFO researchers and investigators, and Godfrey, who was making a career out of law enforcement, found himself the object of scrutiny and ridicule.

ALERT

In your pursuit of UFOs, you should be aware that nothing remains confidential for long. Witnesses who submit reports under confidentiality agreements are almost always revealed and subjected to intense scrutiny regarding their credibility and motives. Therefore, if you think that you are operating below the radar in your UFO hunting, think again, because eventually it will bob to the surface.

In Godfrey's explanation of the events of that day, he describes that he had a strange image of himself outside the car right after the bright flash. He had no conscious memory of it, but it was like a dream image that he could not shake. He also said that the soles on his police boots showed damage, as if they had been dragged along a hard surface.

The Hypnosis Sessions

Upon the suggestion of UFO investigators, Alan Godfrey underwent regression hypnosis, recovering images of his having been inside a spaceship, meeting at least one humanoid alien and robot-like small creatures with large heads—reminiscent of the Grays that other self-described alien abductees have described—and said that he already knew who his abductors were. He did not describe any invasive medical examination, but his recollection, even under hypnosis, was very spotty, as if whoever had controlled that event was still controlling his memory, screening him from disclosing all the details of the event.

Godfrey said that as he continued the sessions of hypnotic regression, the police command was uncomfortable. Even though they had confirmed sightings from their own department and by at least one civilian in the same area, and that the missing cows had mysteriously appeared in another field, the police were nervous. What was Godfrey going to discover, and why did he oppose the findings of the coroner's inquest in the Adamski death? Ultimately, they ordered Godfrey to cease all hypnotic regression sessions and forget about the incident. Not only did they tell him to terminate his own investigation into what happened to him that night during his missing time, they demanded he sign a national security letter in which he agreed not to disclose what happened to him about sighting the object.

ESSENTIAL

> Many people believe that hypnotic regression is the cure-all for lost memories. It's not. Memories, especially those of alien abduction or contact, can be subtly inserted into a person's memory by a hypnotherapist, even under the most benign of circumstances. Simply getting an acknowledgment that a client and the therapist will explore missing time in the context of an alien encounter is enough to induce this. The client may become conditioned into believing that he really encountered or was actually abducted by aliens, when nothing of the sort may have occurred.

Godfrey said that he had no choice but to sign the letter. However, the letter did not only mention the sighting of the unknown object and Godfrey's talking about the images he recovered under hypnosis, the letter also forbade Godfrey from talking about the Adamski case. Why were the two incidents linked, particularly when there was nothing on the surface damaging to national security about the Adamski case? It made no sense unless—and this is speculation—Adamski, like the missing cows, was a victim of an abduction. Maybe the entities that had abducted him did not know about his heart condition and he died of fright. In a futile attempt to restart his heart, they attempted their version of an electric shock treatment. That failed as well, and they hurriedly redressed the dead victim and deposited him on the coal tip. There were no footprints, of course, or tread marks, just like there were no hoof prints to account for how the missing cows got to the new field.

Ultimately, as well, the ridicule from fellow officers and from the public forced Godfrey to leave the police force. But in the wake of his decision to leave, a curious thing happened. Godfrey reported that his wife became pregnant, much to the surprise of Godfrey's doctors, who pronounced him miraculously healed from his injury. Was it a spontaneous recovery? What had really happened aboard that strange craft?

RAF Bentwaters

A little over a month after Alan Godfrey's strange encounter, one of Britain's most important, most documented, and most controversial UFO cases took place, a case still the subject of fierce debate today. This case is alternately referred to as the RAF Bentwaters incident, after the U.S. Air Force–controlled NATO nuclear weapons air base that the incident affected, or the Rendlesham Forest incident, where the events actually took place.

ESSENTIAL

U.S.-controlled facilities, like RAF Bentwaters, are considered U.S. military territory. However, Rendlesham Forest is British territory. Therefore, American military personnel are not allowed to carry weapons in Rendlesham Forest. The different jurisdictions, an American base and a British royal forest, allowed both the U.S. and UK governments to hand off the investigation of the Bentwaters incident to one another as if it were a hot potato.

Initially investigated by American military security agencies, the case attracted the notice of former British defence minister Admiral Lord Hill-Norton, who called for an investigation, and of Prime Minister Margaret Thatcher's office. It's reported that the prime minister commented to a query about the case that there are things "you have to keep from the people." Some researchers have said that news of the incident even reached Buckingham Palace and intrigued Prince Phillip, the Duke of Edinburgh.

There are still many confusing details regarding this case with respect to how it started, how many witnesses there were, what witnesses actually saw in the forest, and what was reported on radar. As the years go by, more witnesses are uncovered and more reports surface about the ways the U.S. Air Force Office of Special Investigations intervened within hours of the events to doctor the reports and get witnesses to change their stories. British Intelligence intervened as well, getting local witnesses to contradict what would become the official air force witness version of the story. But despite the conflicting reports and stories, the stories of the eyewitnesses relate an amazing event complete with physical trace evidence to document what the witnesses say happened.

The Christmas Sighting

The incident, stretching over multiple nights starting on Christmas 1980, began when members of a U.S. Air Force security detail noticed strange lights over RAF Bentwaters. Early the next morning the security detail left the base to look for the lights, which they thought were a downed aircraft in the forest. Rendlesham Forest is not part of the air base and is therefore part of Britain. Accordingly, for U.S. military personnel to enter the forest from the base, especially with equipment and weapons, is an extraordinary event requiring some sort of bilateral understanding. This entry into the forest, however, was deemed an emergency to search for what the detail thought was a downed aircraft. In the forest, however, what they discovered was no downed conventional aircraft.

FACT

During the months of November and December 1980, there was a major UFO flap over England, culminating in the famous RAF Bentwaters case, "Britain's Roswell," just after Christmas of that year. In 1980 the world was on edge because of the Soviet invasion of Afghanistan, bringing relations between NATO and the Warsaw Bloc to a straining point as President Jimmy Carter bristled with anger over the impunity of the Soviet Union's actions.

In the early morning on December 26, U.S. Air Force Staff Sergeant Jim Penniston of the security police was part of a contingent that left the east gate of RAF Bentwaters to go into the desolate Rendlesham Forest. Penniston described what they saw as bright lights over the trees, moving through the area in maneuvers that were beyond the capabilities of any aircraft he was familiar with. Then, coming upon a clearing, he reported seeing a brightly lit oval-shaped craft that had landed on the hard, cold, damp forest floor and was sitting on a triangular landing strut structure. Penniston described strange symbols, lettering or glyphs, around the base of the object. The rest of the security detail described being overwhelmed by a feeling of disorientation and confusion as they moved very slowly, as if through a dense but invisible field, toward and around the object.

Sergeant Penniston took out a small notebook and sketched the shape of the object and the symbols he saw along its body. He then approached the object and touched it. It wasn't hot at all, he remembered, which was strange because it was giving off so much light. Then the object rose off the forest floor and levitated through the canopy of trees, breaking off branches as it made its way to open air, at which point it flew off. The light show was over.

Early the next day local police went to the forest to investigate but found no traces of anything. Interviews with some of the local residents, however, revealed that on the previous night farm animals were all in an agitated condition and were behaving very strangely. Penniston also returned to the clearing where he said he saw the object and noticed three impressions in the hard sand that conformed to what he remembered about the shape of the object's landing gear. He took plaster casts of those impressions, which remain as physical trace evidence of what was in the forest that night.

The Charles Halt Sighting

On the evening of December 28, the lights returned. Deputy base commander Lieutenant Colonel Charles Halt and his boss, the base commander, were hosting a Christmas party when security personnel informed them that the lights in the forest were back. Charles Halt's first comment was "What lights?" When he was told that these were the lights from the UFO that had been seen the day or so before, he told his boss, base commander Colonel Ted Conrad, that he "would put this thing to rest" right away. Halt assembled a disaster response detail, including radios and generator-powered lights, and mobilized a detachment to enter the forest to find the source of the lights. He also took along his Lanier voice recorder to keep a voice log of what was happening should he need to write up a report on what took place. What he saw and recorded as the events unfolded was nothing conventional and was such an extreme event that Lieutenant

Colonel Halt would later say, "I wish I had never seen the thing or written a report about it."

Once in the forest with their equipment, Halt's security detail saw a flashing red light that, according to Halt, seemed to be dripping some kind of material. They followed the light through the forest as it maneuvered through the trees and watched it as it came to rest in a clearing outside of the forest. Halt specifically remembers that the light was so bright he could see the reflection of the light off the windows of a farmhouse in the distance, making it seem as though the house itself was on fire. Halt also distinctly noted the position of the light in the clearing as being different from the lighthouse beacon at nearby Orford Ness, a distinction that would be a major part of the controversy once the skeptics started to debunk the case.

Halt and his team watched the bright object in the clearing. Not having the clearance to enter onto private property, they could do little but approach it cautiously. Halt remembers hearing the farm animals making loud calls, apparently affected by the object. Then, as his group tried to approach it, the object suddenly split into five separate objects and took off. Halt, on his voice recorder, recounts seeing lights moving about overhead and moving through the woods. It was an incredible spectacle, the narration of which is all on Halt's recording.

Halt returned to base, put the voice recorder in his office drawer, and reported to Colonel Conrad, his commander, about what he had encountered.

The Investigations Begin

The previous incident and this follow-up incident had already attracted the attention of the Air Force Office of Special Investigations (AFOSI), which had investigators on the scene within a day.

The enlisted personnel in the two security details later said that they were ordered by AFOSI officers not to reveal completely the details of what they saw, only referring to the object as a light they couldn't identify. Staff Sergeant Penniston admitted later on that he did not turn over his sketchbook to AFOSI officers and did not tell them that he had made drawings of the object or of the symbols written on it. He said that he was ordered not to tell the base commander that an object had landed in Rendlesham Forest.

While the AFOSI was investigating, the British police and other units also dispatched agents into the field to gather information from local residents, one of whom told police that she saw the object the Americans had reported. The police then had their confirmation. Another group of plainclothes agents interviewed the local forester, Vincent Thurkettle, and advised him not to confirm anything the Americans said. Therefore, at first, he was a source for the skeptics even though he later, in part, recanted his debunking of the story.

FACT

People who say that the air force's involvement with UFO investigations ended with the shutting down of Project Blue Book are wrong. The air force continues to investigate UFO-related incidents to this very day. This is evidenced by their immediate involvement in the RAF Bentwaters follow-up investigation.

The British conducted radiation tests on the area where Penniston said he noticed the landing impressions. According to Nick Pope, an officer at the British Ministry of Defence, the area around the landing area registered ten times the normal background radiation. This fact was dismissed by skeptics and debunkers but was taken very seriously by higher-ups in the Ministry of Defence.

As the investigations heated up, the air force command suggested that Halt write up a formal report about the incident and his part in it, something that Halt now says he wished he had never done. The report was since released to the public, along with transcripts of his voice recording, and has become one of the most celebrated pieces of evidence in UFO lore. The information about the incident, the physical trace evidence, and the scientific analysis of the landing area and the broken tree limbs and bushes had such an impact that, even as the British tried to dump the investigation on the Americans and the Americans onto the British—each side claiming that jurisdiction belonged to the other—the seriousness of the incident was not lost upon both governments.

Ultimately, Admiral Lord Hill-Norton, commenting on the impunity of the craft coming into a restricted airspace where nuclear weapons were stored, called for a full investigation of the UFO phenomena. Researchers relate another story, explaining that the British Ministry of Defence was so concerned with this incident that they begged the United States to investigate it. Word of the incident and its anomalous physical trace evidence reached all the way to Buckingham Palace where Prince Phillip made inquiries about it. Also, with UFO researchers in the United Kingdom intensely pursuing answers for the Rendlesham incident, Prime Minister Margaret Thatcher provided a brief response to conceal the incident. At a reception after she returned from China, Thatcher responded to a question about an investigation of the Bentwaters incident from Lady Georgina Bruni. Thatcher answered: "My dear, there are things you just can't tell the people." And that just about says it all.

CHAPTER 8

Late Twentieth-Century UFOs

Beginning with the 1980 Cash-Landrum incident in Texas and culminating in the spectacular 1997 Phoenix Lights, UFO incidents in the late twentieth century were becoming more spectacular, attracting media attention, and resulting in some lawsuits. Both in the United States and Europe, UFOs not only made appearances, but they challenged air forces to intercept them and, in the end, provide lame explanations to the media and the public to account for the UFO incidents. While military personnel in high places sputtered for answers, triangular-shaped objects outran NATO's fastest jets over Europe. While ground personnel in Britain were stunned at the low-flying triangles, objects hovered over some of the RAF's most sensitive air bases, their presence cataloged by military and civilian observers. For UFO researchers, the heavily media-covered UFO encounters of the last quarter of the twentieth century provided rich data as well as recognition from the media that something—an unidentified something—was certainly in the skies.

The Cash-Landrum Incident

Just recently Americans applauded the efforts of Navy SEAL Team 6, ferried in by Task Force 160 helicopters operating out of the Joint Special Operations Command, to attack Osama bin Laden's compound deep in Pakistan. Few people know, however, that Task Force 160, the famed Black Hawk helicopter unit, was formed in the wake of President Carter's failed 1980 attempt to rescue American hostages from Tehran, Iran, after the fall of the shah. Even fewer people know that in the wake of that failure the military set up Project or Task Force 160 as a stealth helicopter-based unit to carry out operations of extreme secrecy and urgency.

This same Task Force 160 was at the center of a 1980 UFO incident in Texas known as the Cash-Landrum incident. This incident is one of the very few UFO-related cases that made its way into an American courtroom where it was thrown out on the basis of a judge's interpretation of federal tort law and the exigencies of national security.

A Lonely Road Outside of Houston

At about 9 P.M. December 29, 1980 (the night after Charles Halt's encounter with a UFO in Rendlesham Forest), Betty Cash, Vicky Landrum, and seven-year-old Colby Landrum, Vicky's grandson, were driving near Houston, Texas, when they spied a light in the sky. At first, Betty thought that it was a plane in a pattern over the Houston airport, but soon it was apparent that it was something else.

ALERT

A warning to novice UFO hunters is that if an object seems to be getting closer, no matter what you think it might be, don't stay out in the open. Betty Cash's experience, as do the experiences of others, exemplifies that sometimes UFOs can be dangerous because of radiation.

As they rounded another curve in the road, they saw the same light in the sky, only this time it was brighter and much closer. It clearly was not a plane. In fact, it was a large diamond-shaped object hanging in the sky and moving overhead toward them. As it got closer, the road was illuminated by the light from the object, and the occupants in the car could feel heat. The object was now just above the treetops. Through the windshield, Betty could see that the object seemed to be expelling flame and sparks from the base. Betty stopped the car.

At first, Betty Cash and Vicky Landrum got out of the car to get a better look at the thing above them, but Vicky got back in to comfort Colby, who was scared. Betty, however, stayed outside as the object came closer and had to shield her eyes from the brightness. She felt the intense heat from the flames of the object scorching her. She used her coat to protect her skin as she climbed back into the car, which also heated up from the flames.

The object rose in the sky, and Betty Cash started driving again. She said she could see helicopters around the object, escorting it or surrounding it as it flew away. She kept getting glimpses of the object and the formation of twin-rotor Chinook helicopters as the car drove back home.

The Symptoms Begin

Later that night, all three occupants of the car, witnesses to the object, started suffering from nausea, cramps, diarrhea, general physical weakness, and burning sensations on their skin and behind their eyes. Betty Cash suffered the worst of these symptoms, and as weeks went on she would also begin to suffer skin eruptions. Because she had stepped outside the car, she was the most exposed to whatever it was that was causing the symptoms, and over the ensuing weeks her condition worsened. The burning sensation did not go away, and her skin turned red and blistered. Patches of skin became scabby and her hair began to fall out. Vicky and Colby also experienced some of the same symptoms, but they weren't nearly as severe as Betty's.

Radiation Poisoning

Betty was concerned and checked herself into an emergency room, barely able to make it there on her own because of her weakness and near inability to walk. She was treated at the hospital but was released with little or no amelioration of her symptoms, which kept on getting progressively worse. A medical doctor, whom she had consulted about her deteriorating medical condition and because he was a specialist in treating patients with radiation poisoning, said that he believed Betty's symptoms were consistent with an exposure to radiation. Radiation would have weakened her immune system and left her prone to infections, which ultimately killed her in 1998. The deeper the doctor became involved, the more he became convinced that Betty was suffering from symptoms shared by some of the victims from Hiroshima. He said that he had spoken to a number of army veterans who told him that back in 1970s the army was experimenting with small nuclear reactors to power flying troop transports. The nuclear reactors had a tendency to overload, however, causing heavy radiation dispersal, and the army ultimately abandoned the project. The doctor became involved with Betty's case because not only was he a specialist in radiation poisoning, but he was trying to find out how a woman with no job involving exposure to radiation could have developed such an advanced case of radiation poisoning.

A Ray of Light in the Mystery

Vicky's and Colby's symptoms improved, and six months after the incident they attended a fair near their home when they saw a CH-47 helicopter on exhibit. Colby became agitated at seeing the helicopter, but Vicky approached the pilot, a member of the National Guard. Colby remembers that Vicky asked the pilot if he knew of a mission of helicopters escorting a strange object over the roads outside of Houston. The pilot said that he had been on that very mission, ordered to respond to an emergency call about a UFO. When Vicky said that she had been in the car that night observing the helicopters escorting the strange object, the pilot refused to talk to her any more. Colby later said that the pilot's silence was very telling.

FACT

Under black letter tort law, the burden to show that a defendant was responsible for your damages in tort falls squarely on the plaintiff. If a plaintiff cannot show to the satisfaction of the court that the defendant was responsible for and in control of the instrument that caused the damage, the lawsuit will not meet the minimum standard of a claim that will survive a motion to dismiss. In the Landrum case, unless Vicky could show that the army was responsible for those helicopters escorting or towing the flaming object, her lawsuit would be dismissed by the court as a "failure to state a claim."

The Lawsuit

In 1981, Vicky and Betty filed a lawsuit against the army, claiming $20 million in damages from injuries suffered as the object passed overhead. They were interviewed by the army to obtain information concerning any possible liability that the army may have had. The Pentagon dispatched an officer from the Inspector General's office to investigate the nature of the Cash-Landrum claims. He reported back to his superiors that he had checked all the bases from where the "army" helicopters might have originated and found that none of those bases had any craft in the air that night. Therefore, he concluded, the army could not have been responsible because it wasn't flying any helicopters. If there were no helicopters in the air, the army faced no liability under the federal tort claims act. And that, a court finally held in 1986, was the end of the Cash-Landrum lawsuit. Under tort law, the burden is on the plaintiff to prove that the defendant bears responsibility for wielding the instrumentality of the tort; in this case, the helicopters. If the plaintiffs couldn't prove that the army was flying the helicopters, the suit had to be dismissed for failure to state a claim.

UFO Hunters Investigate the Case

Thirty years later, the commander of the pilot's National Guard unit said that although he personally never authorized any mission regarding a UFO, investigators should look into a unit called Project or Task Force 160. This was the unit created after the failed attempt to rescue the American embassy hostages from Tehran. They would have been the only unit able to fly in complete secrecy and without the knowledge of the army Inspector General. This is because, technically, they were a nascent unit-to-be of what would become the Joint Special Operations Command, supported by the Intelligence Support Activities Command. The Intelligence Support Activities Command was not supported by the army, navy, air force, or marines but by a joint force reporting to the National Security Agency (nicknamed the "No Such Agency" for its low profile) and other intelligence agencies.

Could it have been, as the doctor who treated Betty Cash suggested, a nuclear reactor, not a UFO? Could it have been a reactor gone red hot that needed to be disposed of in the Gulf of Mexico without pesky local and federal environmental agencies getting involved? Or could a UFO that the military was experimenting with gone hot, or worse, could a UFO have gotten into trouble? At least one other witness, Detective Lamar Walker, saw the object and the helicopters as he rode on an adjacent road that night. Detective Walker said that he saw the same diamond-shaped object but that the helicopters escorting it had chains on the object, holding it up and carrying it toward the Gulf. This is a twist on the story because it means that Task Force 160, or whatever the unit was officially called, might not have been responding to a UFO but to a secret developmental technology for a weapon the military had that was melting down.

QUESTION

Why is the government so secretive about Task Force 160?
In April 1980, Operation Eagle Claw, President Carter's attempt to rescue American hostages in Iran, was aborted, in part because of command, control, and communications problems with the helicopters. Toward the end of his presidency, Carter was planning another rescue attempt, this one in January 1980. To facilitate this mission, the military created a special black-ops helicopter command called Task Force 160. If Task Force 160 was the unit involved in the Cash-Landrum incident, a unit that had to be kept secret so the Iranians didn't discover it, it was necessary that the army maintain absolute secrecy about the Task Force ferrying the flaming object across the road and into the Gulf.

The official mystery still lingers, but if Task Force 160 and the Intelligence Support Activities Command were involved, it makes more sense that there is an official mystery surrounding the case and a deep reluctance on the part of the Pentagon, especially in 1980, to disclose the existence of a super-secret black operations unit.

Hudson Valley Sightings

In 1981, a new flap of UFO sightings startled and then galvanized witnesses, this time just north of New York City and over Long Island Sound in Connecticut. Called the "Hudson Valley sightings," these began just before midnight on December 31, 1981, and continued well into the new year. They became the subject of an investigation by this country's top UFO researcher, former Project Blue Book consultant Dr. J. Allen Hynek.

The first sighting was by a very credible witness, a retired police officer living in Kent, New York. This witness saw a formation of lights arranged as the point of a triangle floating overhead. There was no engine noise, as would be heard if they were a formation of planes with prop or jet engines, or the sound of helicopter rotors. Instead, the lights seemed to emit a low humming noise, almost like a relatively quiet electric engine. The lights were red, green, and white and were heading toward him from the direction of New York City. At first he thought it might be a plane, the sound of whose engines would soon reach him, flying very low and possibly having difficulty. That was until he saw the object itself.

ESSENTIAL

One of the first questions to ask any witness claiming to have seen a UFO is "What did you hear?" Or ask, "Did the object make any noise?" This is sometimes the key factor in determining if the witness saw a plane or something else.

This was no plane, the witness must have thought, as he saw a large triangular structure that connected the lights at its edges. This was a rigid craft unlike any other conventional aircraft he had ever seen. What was almost just as incredible was that as this witness watched the giant triangle float overhead, hundreds of other witnesses in New York's Hudson Valley saw flying triangles as well, whether the same object or different ones.

Sightings in the New Year

The sightings continued through 1982, drawing more and more witnesses. As the news spread to communities along the Hudson River, people gathered at various spots to see the frequent displays of lights, hoping to catch glimpses of the triangular craft that the lights were attached to. Soon, news of the sightings reached New York City where residents along the West Side Highway claimed they could see some of the triangles, too. Some New

Yorkers even said they observed giant triangles over the Hudson River in broad daylight. The news finally began turning up in local Westchester County newspapers, drawing even more spectators to the area to scan the night sky for the lights.

As the numbers of witnesses grew and the lights kept coming, Dr. Hynek became interested in the case. He and local UFO researcher and science teacher Imbrogno assembled witnesses to get their sighting reports, focus on the most credible of those reports, and determine what common elements were among the descriptions of the lights and the object. To their surprise, Imbrogno has said, not only did some of the witnesses describe the lights and the triangular object in specific detail, some also described sightings of humanoid entities. The sightings continued throughout the ensuing year.

The Taconic Parkway Sightings

The reports of triangle sightings increased at an even greater rate, coming to a peak on March 24, 1983, when people said they were seeing the "mother ship." A subgroup of these sightings were reported by drivers who had pulled over to the shoulder on the Taconic State Parkway (which runs parallel to the Hudson River) near Yorktown, New York, where they phoned in reports to police in such numbers that dispatchers were overwhelmed. These sightings, sometimes called the Taconic Parkway sightings, were so voluminous and came in from so many different sources that UFO researchers have said they couldn't possibly have been mass hallucinations or an orchestrated hoax.

The Indian Point Sighting

For over two years, the Hudson Valley sightings were just that, sightings. The craft, one or more, simply flew by overhead, silently and slowly, without any indication that it was interacting with the witnesses. But that all changed in 1984 when New York State's Indian Point nuclear power plant faced a threat its builders never imagined it would face: an intrusion from an otherworldly craft. It's part of UFO lore and history that UFOs have been spotted around nuclear facilities.

On June 14, 1984, a UFO staged a brief flyover of the nuclear power plant, witnessed by three members of the facility's security police force. The second flyover was far more serious. On the evening of July 24, 1984, a security guard at the plant noticed an object coming over and said, according to an article by Vicki Cooper of *UFO Magazine*, "Here comes that UFO again," and alerted other security guards to the object's presence. The object, a large triangle- or arrow-shaped structure, hovered over the one working reactor, Reactor 3, for a full ten minutes at an altitude of approximately three hundred feet and sent the entire security apparatus of the plant into complete confusion. The plant simply had no defenses to prevent against a situation like this. This was a serious intrusion of highly restricted airspace that has never been explained by the New York State Power Authority, even though its director, Carl Patrick, acknowledged the event.

QUESTION

What happens when you do not receive an official explanation?
If you ask a question of an official source about an event and get no explanation, it means that the source is trying to hide something. The reasons for hiding information can be quite legitimate, such as national security. But, more often than not, the source, be it government or private, is simply too embarrassed to release the information. This is usually an important point to remember in all UFO investigations.

The Gulf Breeze Sightings

The story of construction executive Ed Walters and his November 1987 encounter with what he described as a UFO is one of great significance because of the controversy over the photos Walters took and the attempts of those to hoax the entire case. Like many UFO experiencers, Walters never sought publicity. Publicity sought him and changed his life in so many ways that he ultimately said he wished he'd never seen the thing or even reported it after having seen it.

The incident began one evening on November 11, 1987, when Walters saw a strange light in the distance over the tree line. He went outside his home in Gulf Breeze, Florida, to get a better look and was astonished when the light seemed to be getting closer. It was as if the light had spotted him and wanted to get a better look. In fact, that's exactly what happened when the light, now clearly a flying disk-shaped object, hovered over Walter's head and caught him in a bluish beam. Walters was paralyzed and felt himself being drawn up into the craft. He tried as hard as he could, but he was unable to break free until a neighbor appeared in the street, calling his dog, and the beam snapped off, releasing Walters.

The Encounters Become More Threatening

Over the ensuing weeks, the craft returned, sometimes with a humming sound that resounded in Walters's brain, summoning him to go outside and get beamed up. During this period, Walters was able to grab his Polaroid camera and snap photos of the craft. These photos would prove very significant when the Mutual UFO Network president, Walter Andrus, and photo expert Dr. Bruce Maccabee, agreed to analyze them. The Walters photos, some of which showed the craft emanating a blue beam, others revealing the craft over a tree, were as compelling as the Paul Trent McMinnville photos and the Rex Heflin Santa Ana photos.

FACT

To fake a photo with an old-fashioned Polaroid, an amateur has to stage the photo itself because the film-developing process takes place inside the camera. That's why when you see Polaroid photos of strange things, what you see in the print is usually what the camera saw and not something that was faked in the developing process.

Walters took his photos and his story about the UFO he saw to the local newspaper, submitting his material anonymously. But soon people, some of whom had also seen a UFO at the times Walters saw them, discovered who he was, and his story and photos began to get traction. As folks discussed, both pro and con, what Walters was claiming, Walt Andrus of the Mutual UFO Network (MUFON) saw something in the photos that he believed would be difficult to fake. He said that because Walters had taken the photos with a Polaroid camera, in which the developing process is inside the camera, it was highly unlikely that a person not skilled in the technology of photo fabrication would have been able to manufacture these photos. Dr. Bruce Maccabee agreed, and together Andrus and Maccabee approached Walters with a suggestion to provide him with a camera they would make hoax-proof by sealing in the film and accounting for every single frame. Walters agreed, and the photos he took of the craft were still compelling and not faked by doctoring the photos. That left the issue of setting up fake UFOs and photographing them against a background.

The Debunkers Attack

Walters was not without his detractors. There were many neighbors who said that Walters was doing it for the publicity—hard to imagine because he never sought publicity—or to promote his struggling construction business. Walters himself didn't make things any easier by describing incidents in which a robotic creature was beamed down from one of the craft to try to retrieve him and bring him back to the ship. He also talked about being summoned by a voice in his brain calling him by a strange name, Zehas, as if he were one of them. And these stories also brought his detractors out of the shadows.

The Debunkers Become the Hoaxers

Finally, Walters decided to move on. He published his book, *The Gulf Breeze Sightings*, in 1990, which did quite well, and sold his house. Then, whatever group was behind the debunking of Ed Walters tipped its hand. After the new buyers moved into Walters's house, they received a visit by someone claiming to be from air conditioning repair and maintenance, saying that he had to inspect the ductwork over the garage and make any repairs. It was part of maintenance agreement. The new owners let the man go to work, and he left without incident.

Shortly thereafter a self-described reporter showed up, claiming he was doing an investigative story on the Ed Walters UFO sightings, and asked whether he might take a look around the house, even if only to get the angles from where Walters said he saw the UFOs. The stranger went right up to the area above the garage and returned with a wooden model of a flying saucer that looked eerily like the flying saucer Walters had photographed.

FACT

When evaluating the worthiness of a UFO case, look for an extraordinary act on the part of a self-described skeptic or debunker to hoax the truth. When debunkers turn to creating false events so as to entrap a UFO witness, that's usually an indication that the witness story is likely to be true. In other words, the lengths that debunkers go to stretch or distort the truth to disprove a UFO claim is in direct proportion to the truth of the story.

It didn't take long for debunkers to display the photograph of the model alongside Walters's photograph of a ship to claim it was proof that Walters had hoaxed not only the photograph but the entire incident. However, when Bruce Maccabee investigated, he found out there was no such reporter and no such order for an air conditioning maintenance person. Absent any proof of the identities of the air conditioning repairman and the reporter, Maccabee argued, the entire sequence of events was part of a setup: plant the model, retrieve the model, and claim Walters was hoaxing. The debunking was a hoax, and Maccabee had debunked the debunkers. In so doing, he showed that when debunkers, or the government, go to extraordinary lengths to fake a hoax, there must be some truth behind the original UFO story.

Black Triangle UFOs over Belgium

At a 2007 press conference at the National Press Club in Washington, D.C., Major General Wilfried de Brouwer, former chief of operations for the Royal

Belgian Air Force (RBAF) staff, said that on March 30, 1990, restricted airspace over Belgium was challenged by an unidentified flying object that was shaped like a large triangle with lights at the corners. The Belgian air force had been on alert for UFOs for months because in 1989 a number of civilians in Belgian cities reported sightings of black triangles floating overhead. The air staff first tried to intercept the triangles, but could not, then agreed to work with Belgian police and local UFO organizations to put a squadron of F-16s on alert to intercept the black triangles the next time they appeared. And appear they did.

An Intriguing Sighting

On March 30, a little after 11 P.M., a civilian called the police to say a large black triangle sporting bright lights at each corner was hovering over his street. The police asked for radar confirmation, which they received, and alerted other radar bases. All the bases that were contacted confirmed the object on their radar. There was definitely something in the sky, something that wasn't returning a friend-or-foe signal via its transponder. They had to assume that it was a hostile. The RBAF dispatched two F-16s, at that time the most advanced interceptor in the NATO arsenal, to chase the triangle.

Visual Confirmation and the Chase

The pilots reported that they were able to see the triangle on radar and get an immediate lock on it with their weapons targeting systems. But, just like the 1952 flying saucer invasion over Washington, D.C., as soon as the jets got their radar lock, the UFO was able to break the lock. By this time a third fighter was airborne, and all three F-16s were able to get a radar targeting lock on the object, which then broke the lock again.

As the jets approached, the UFO flew away at speeds beyond the afterburner speed of the jets. No conventional object in the world was faster than an F-16 on afterburner, and the pilots were stunned. Then, the giant triangle dropped to about 300 feet over the city of Brussels, hovered there, and then sped off. The pilots returned to base.

A Repeat of 1952 Attempted UFO Intercepts

Major General de Brouwer, reporting the incident to the gathering of the press in Washington, D.C., in 2007, explained that on numerous occasions F-16s were dispatched to intercept these black triangles, but after repeated attempts, they were unable to close on them. In summary, he said, "the air force could not identify the nature, origin, and intentions of the reported phenomena." Although skeptics were quick to try to debunk the photos of the object and the reports of the pilots, General de Brouwer stood firm in his belief that this was a true UFO incident in which a huge craft was able to outrun, outmaneuver, and outfly the best jets NATO could deploy, even breaking what were thought to be unbreakable radar locks from multiple F-16s at the same time. It was an event that de Brouwer was unable to explain away.

The Cosford Incident

Just three years after the Belgian black triangle incident, a similar craft appeared over RAF Cosford and RAF Shawbury. As Nick Pope of the UK's Ministry of Defence (MOD) reported, on March 30 and 31, 1993, there was a series of UFO sightings in the United Kingdom involving hundreds of witnesses. Many of these witnesses were military personnel and police officers, the most credible of witnesses. The UFO flew directly over two RAF bases, highly restricted airspace, with complete impunity while the witnesses simply watched. Starting at 8:30 P.M. in Somerset, the craft was sighted again at 9 P.M. by a police officer in the Quantock Hills. The craft was so big that the police officer described it as looking like two Concorde jetliners side by side. At least one civilian in Rugley, Staffordshire, chased the object in his car as it floated overhead, and then came up on it near a field where he believed it had landed.

Flyovers in Restricted Airspaces

The craft passed over RAF Cosford, where it was observed by RAF security police, who filed a report. It was observed flying very quickly at about 1,000 feet. They described it as having two white lights with a faint light in the rear and making no noise whatsoever as it zoomed overhead. Later that night it was spotted by a meteorological officer at RAF Shawbury. This was an important sighting, Pope explained to reporters at a National Press Club conference in November 2007, because meteorological officers are the official weather analysts for the RAF who understand conditions and phenomena in the sky. If this had been anything conventional, this witness would have known it.

At this location, the officer said, the craft was moving slowly across the countryside at about 30 or 40 miles per hour. He saw the UFO fire a narrow beam of light along the ground in a sweeping motion—something that witnesses in Stephenville, Texas, would see fifteen years later—as if it were looking for something. While watching this, the officer heard and felt a deep humming sound and vibration. Then the craft seemed to retract the beam—not snapping it off, but pulling it back into itself—and sped away at a high speed, in the words of the witness, "many times faster than a military aircraft."

ESSENTIAL

You will find in your research that a common witness description is "the beam," a shaft of light, whether blue or white, that seems to scan the ground and is then retracted into the craft. In situations like these, it is likely that unless the beam is a sunspot coming from a police or military helicopter, the witness has observed an unconventional flying object.

Pope followed up on the reports of the UFO over the RAF bases when the information came to him at Whitehall, by ordering that radar tapes from nearby missile bases be sent to him. An expert from the RAF watched the tapes with him and both saw a number of radar targets that shouldn't have been there, but the RAF officer said that these were not conclusive of a UFO.

Ministry of Defence Follow-Up

There were more sightings the following night from all over Britain, particularly in Cornwall. These sightings might have been attributed to the re-entry into Earth's atmosphere of a Russian Cosmos satellite. However, given the re-entry trajectory of the satellite and the pattern of the witness sightings, some by police, Pope doubted that the satellite could have been responsible for all of the sightings, even though skeptics and debunkers jumped on that as the explanation for the entire affair on both nights.

One of the most interesting aspects to this case, Pope said, was that all of the files came to him at the Ministry of Defence at Whitehall from where an inquiry was made to the United States Department of Defense. The British asked the Defense Department whether the United States had been flying a top-secret craft over the United Kingdom on the nights in question. The United States responded by saying they had not and asked, having been informed about the sightings, whether the British might have a top-secret craft in the air that night. Neither side acknowledged any top-secret craft. Pope found this exchange particularly interesting in light of the U.S. Air Force's declaration that it had gotten out of the UFO business in 1969 with the termination of Project Blue Book. Yet, here it was, investigating a reported UFO in another country. Nevertheless, the RAF Cosford incident is part of Britain's great UFO mystery.

The Phoenix Lights

At the end of the twentieth century, residents of Phoenix, Arizona, and surrounding areas were witnesses to one of the greatest mass UFO sightings in history. The incident was covered by reporters around the world, and it spawned a controversy involving the former governor of the state, a witness to what he called a mysterious craft that night.

The Night of the Comet

It was March 13, 1997, the night of the Hale-Bopp comet. Residents in the American Southwest were gathered outside for a sky watch. That night, starting before 8 P.M., a configuration of lights in a triangular or arrowhead shape made their way from Henderson, Nevada, south through Phoenix and then to Tucson, Arizona. It was an incredible display of lights, floating slowly at a low altitude over the valleys and hilltops of Arizona. Another display of lights was visible at 10:30 P.M. Residents, particularly in Phoenix, were held in awe of the lights. Many residents, including Arizona governor Fife Symington, not only saw the 8:30 P.M. lights but observed a structured craft to which the lights were attached.

The Giant Triangle

According to the witnesses who spoke to MOD officer Nick Pope, the craft, which was described as similar in appearance to the giant triangle over Cosford and Shawbury, was startling. The craft was huge, multiple football fields wide, floating noiselessly only a few hundred feet above the trees and almost even with some of the houses high in the hills, and composed of a shimmering translucent substance with a satin-like finish that seemed to let the starlight through it. Governor Symington, in his appearance on History's *UFO Hunters*, said that as it floated over, it was so low to the ground that he could almost feel its presence as well as see it. He could see stars between the lights at the corners of the craft, but the craft was definitely a rigid structure that was unlike anything he had ever seen during his years in the air force or as the commander in chief of Arizona's National Guard and Air National Guard. He called it an otherworldly, peaceful experience as the craft passed overhead.

Other witnesses to the 8:30 P.M. lights reported similar experiences, some saying that they were so engulfed by a feeling of peace and serenity they weren't even astonished by the presence of the object. Some said that the craft was so close to their balconies that if they had a rock to throw, they would have hit it easily. These observations were made at less than fifty feet away and were specific in the way they described how the starlight seemed to shimmer through a hazy finish. What made it seem so otherworldly was the translucent nature of the rigid structure holding the lights in place.

Shock and Awe and Unaccounted Time

After the craft had passed over, some people didn't even acknowledge it to others who were in the same room or observing it from the same balcony. They just went back about their business. Other witnesses, such as Dr. Lynne Kitei, whose film documentary about the Phoenix Lights is one of the most comprehensive UFO documentaries ever made, said that for months afterward, her husband, who witnessed the event with her, wouldn't even talk about what he had seen. Dr. Kitei realized years later, after working with Dr. Bruce Maccabee on analyzing the still photos she took of the 8:30 P.M. lights, that she had experienced hours of missing time. During this time she had taken other rolls of film as well, film that she had forgotten about until Dr. Maccabee analyzed the background lights of the city to account for the passage of time.

The exact cause of the 8:30 P.M. lights, which were captured digitally on stills, on film, and on videotape, has never been determined. Covered by local, national, and international media, the lights remain a mystery not only because of their presence but because of the feelings and emotions they inspired in the witnesses. Debunkers have tried to argue that the lights were only a mass hallucination, but they have been unsuccessful in debunking the videos and the scientific analysis of the videos.

The 10:30 P.M. Lights: Ours, Theirs, or Flares?

The 10:30 P.M. lights are a different matter and have been a subject of great controversy. Different people, including Dr. Lynne Kitei, Dr. Bruce Maccabee, and well-known photo analyst Jim Diletoso, have all come to different opinions about the 10:30 P.M. lights, some arguing they looked like basic ground illumination flares that the Maryland Air National Guard said they dropped that night, and some saying that the light signatures on the video bear no resemblance to flares. The flare story, witnesses have said, was simply a cover story promulgated the next day by the air force to explain the entire event.

According to the timeline of events, as the 8:30 P.M. and 10:30 P.M. lights appeared, witnesses called not only the 911 dispatch, which quickly became overloaded, but the local Luke Air Force Base to find out whether the military had planes in the air that night. Governor Symington also called his commanding general of the Air National Guard and Luke Air Force Base to find out if the military was sending low-flying craft over residential areas. He said that the military told him they had no planes in the air. Luke Air Force Base also told callers there were no planes in the air that night.

The following day, however, Luke announced that the Maryland Air National Guard was conducting a ground illumination flare exercise at 10:30

P.M., called Operation Snow Bird, and that should have explained the entire event. Even if it explained the 10:30 P.M. lights, it did not explain the 8:30 P.M. lights. And, witnesses said, why wait an entire day to figure out that planes were in the air from Luke? Other witnesses said that the only place over which flares could have been dropped was the Goldwater Test Range on the other side of a small mountain range. Yet the videos some people showed indicated that the lights appeared in front of the mountains, not behind them, which meant that either flares were dropped over a residential area— a military no-no—or they weren't flares at all.

FACT

One of the most confusing debates regarding the Phoenix Lights is the insistence of debunkers that the 10:30 P.M. lights were flares. There's real disagreement about this, but worse, most debunkers don't even talk about the 8:30 P.M. sightings of the rigid structured craft. If the 10:30 P.M. lights were flares, perhaps they were a deliberate ruse to detract from the sighting of the craft at 8:30 P.M.

The National Guard Tries to Put the Matter to Rest but Fails

This matter was made all the more controversial by a concession the National Guard made to witnesses three years later. In 2000, the Air National Guard staged a flare drop to prove to witnesses that the lights were the same. However, Dr. Lynne Kitei, who filmed both sets of lights, was able to show that the illumination signatures from the flares and the signatures from the 10:30 P.M. lights were absolutely different. Hence, she concluded that the 10:30 P.M. March 13, 1997, lights were not flares.

Skeptics still pounded the stories of witnesses and tried their hardest to debunk the videos. However, professional analysts like Dr. Bruce Maccabee and Jim Diletoso argued that their frame-by-frame scientific processing of the videos showed that the 8:30 P.M. lights were not flares and were not satisfactorily explained away either by the debunkers or by the air force. The 10:30 P.M. lights still remain a matter of debate even between professionals, but these, too, have no resolution.

The Heaven's Gate cult was a UFO quasi-religious cult based in San Diego, California, founded by Marshall Applewhite. They believed that human souls would eventually be joined with the extraterrestrials, who had originally planted them in human form on Earth. Applewhite believed that a spaceship inhabited by the extraterrestrial overlords was hiding in the tail of the Hale-Bopp comet and convinced his followers that the appearance of the comet was their immediate chance to release their souls to join the extraterrestrials. The method of release he prescribed was suicide. Thus, Applewhite and his followers committed suicide in order to unite their souls with the ETs onboard the spacecraft supposedly hiding in Hale-Bopp's tail.

Whatever the opinion, what is clear is that the Phoenix Lights, coming on the same night as the Hale-Bopp comet and the mass Heavens Gate suicide in San Diego, California, and the mysterious disappearance of President Bill Clinton after he claimed an ankle injury is not just one of the most curious UFO sightings; it is probably the most intriguing and lingering cases of a UFO presence since 1952's flying invasion over Washington, D.C.

CHAPTER 9

Major UFO Sightings in the Twenty-First Century

The turning of the new millennium marked a change in the way UFO sightings were reported by the media. Even during the latter half of the twentieth century, the media looked upon UFO sightings with a high degree of ridicule, called the "snicker factor." Tainting their coverage with the ridicule of a human interest feature story or downright derision, correspondents treated UFO witnesses as if they were delusional, crackpots, or simply charlatans trying to hoax the public for their own benefit. Toward the end of the twentieth century, that attitude began to change, especially after the Phoenix Lights. Then came the major cases of the twenty-first century, and things began to shift on a larger scale. What caused this shift? It was the attitude of the government and officialdom, which denied that events were taking place even though those events were right before the eyes of the public. As pundits have said over and over again, it's not the crime or the event, it's the cover-up. And in these events, it was more about the denials than about the sightings.

Chicago O'Hare Airport Sighting

The November 7, 2006, sighting of an unidentified object directly over United Airlines Terminal C at Chicago's O'Hare Airport was more of a wake-up call to the media and a watershed event in media coverage of UFOs than it was an actual UFO event. To this day, nobody has been able to figure out what the members of the United Airlines ground crew actually saw except that it was in restricted airspace and could have interfered with flight operations over one of the nation's busiest airports. The event, however, made national news as a UFO story because the media was so intense in its uncovering of the FAA's attempt to bury the story. A reporter for the *Chicago Tribune* that covered the incident became a hero in the UFO community, though the reporter, Jon Hilkevitch, didn't see himself as a UFO hero.

The Strange Object over United Terminal C

The incident began at 4:30 P.M. when a United Airlines ground crewman was about to push back United Flight 446 to Charlotte from jetway gate C-17. Standard crew procedure when moving a jet with a small tractor is for the tractor operator to look up into the cockpit to make sure the pilots' hands are off the controls. This time, as the tractor operator looked up into the cockpit, he could see through the windshield that there was an object, which he described as a silvery metallic disk, hovering over the terminal. The tractor operator advised the cockpit crew of an object directly above them. The pilot and copilot both looked up and saw the object as well. These transmissions were picked up on the radio, and as many as ten other members of United's ground crew heard the conversation and looked up to see the object. No one knew what it was, only that it was something that had to be reported to air traffic control because it posed a potential collision condition in restricted space.

The FAA Must be Notified of Any Potential Collision Condition

As required by FAA regulations, United's ground crew advised the tower of the potential hazard. The control tower crew said they were unable to see the actual object because their job was managing runway traffic. They advised incoming flights to steer clear of United Terminal C because of a

UFO report at the airport. Thus, a UFO report was released into the official radio traffic between tower and aircraft.

The ground crew then reported that the disk-shaped object suddenly shot up straight through the cloud layer over the airport, punching a hole in the clouds. Witnesses said they saw a doughnut-shaped hole through which clear sky could be seen. The hole lingered for a few minutes.

The Follow-Up to United Airlines Ground Safety

Subsequent to the incident, the United Airlines ground safety personnel sent e-mails to the ground crew witnesses asking them to describe what they saw and recount the entire incident. Again, this type of follow-up for a potentially hazardous airport condition is standard operating procedure and is required by law. After the exchanges of e-mails, however, United Airlines did not follow up in a way satisfactory to the witnesses. The United ground crew witnesses reported the UFO sighting to the *Chicago Tribune*'s transportation reporter Jon Hilkevitch, who followed up with both United and the FAA.

ESSENTIAL

It's almost a rule of thumb that the UFO stories that are not self-described UFO stories but stories about something else get the most UFO coverage. The O'Hare Airport story was about a safety issue, not about a UFO. Yet it became one of the biggest UFO stories of 2007. Even today, no one knows what the object was over the United Airlines terminal at O'Hare. However, the witness stories of the presence of an unidentified object posing a threat remains as a fact in evidence.

The ground crew members sent Hilkevitch copies of the e-mails and the sketches of the object they sent to United. But both United and the FAA, whom Hilkevitch also contacted for the audio tapes of the radio traffic, initially denied that any incident took place. Hilkevitch informed both of them that he had copies of the e-mail exchanges and e-mails from United and could obtain the radio transmission transcripts through a Freedom of Information Act request. Both United and the FAA released the information, which Hilkevitch published in a *Chicago Tribune* article in January 2007. The story was picked up by other media, and Hilkevitch became something of a media personality himself, getting coverage on national television news media and making his own appearances. Moreover, the news of an apparent UFO sighting so excited the American public that the *Chicago Tribune*'s website received over one million hits, an astounding number for what was actually, according to Hilkevitch, simply a story about a potential collision hazard at the local airport.

The Media Assessment

Jon Hilkevitch said in interviews that he was never intending to write a story about a UFO sighting. UFOs weren't his beat. He was writing a story, as the travel correspondent, about a collision alert at a local airport. The object posing the collision threat happened to be something witnesses could not identify. However, in the aftermath of Hilkevitch's 2007 coverage, UFO researchers saw that the media itself seemed to have changed its opinion about UFOs. Seeing the amount of interest and web traffic that the story generated, other media outlets began to cover UFO stories in greater depth and pay more attention to them. Whether they took them seriously or not is a matter for conjecture, but starting in the twenty-first century, the media seemed to be paying much more attention to reports of UFOs from credible witnesses.

The Stephenville Lights

The small city of Stephenville, Texas, bills itself as the cowboy capital of the world. In the heart of the Texas cattle ranching area south of Dallas and Fort Worth, Stephenville is also a dairy capital. But in late 2007 though early January 2008, a series of UFO sightings rattled the town and drew the attention of the national media.

First reported by Angelia Joiner of the *Stephenville Empire Tribune*, the stories were picked up by the AP's Angela Brown. According to Joiner, a private pilot, the town constable, a machinist in Dublin, Texas, and hundreds of other residents saw a large flying triangle with bright lights at its corners similar to the craft seen over Phoenix over a decade earlier. A very intriguing video from the constable's police unit video camera shows a large object in the distance moving slowly in the sky, too slowly for a conventional aircraft.

Mysterious Beams of Light

Footage from a nighttime surveillance camera on light-collecting night shutter mode showed a beam of light snap on from above the camera frame, sweep back and forth across the ground, and then snap back up. This film, broadcasted on History's *UFO Hunters*, although intriguing, proved nothing. However, a mother driving her teenaged daughter and her friends back from cheerleading practice witnessed what she said was the same event as she stopped at a railroad crossing. This witness saw not only a beam of light in afternoon twilight but the actual craft, a large object with windows or lighted portholes along its side, floating above the railroad tracks and sweeping the area with its beam.

FACT

Ever since some of the early American UFO sightings, witnesses have reported beams of light emanating from unidentified flying objects. Whether these are sensors, tractor beams, or simply versions of searchlights, no one knows. But because so many witnesses have seen them, they have become almost commonplace.

The Experiment: Testing the UFO Theory

When *UFO Hunters* got to town to interview witnesses, we found that the stories of sightings matched each other so closely that we set up an experiment. We arranged the witnesses in the places where they said they were standing when they saw the object in the sky and floated a lit balloon over the area. Sure enough, from a position over the town's center, all the witnesses at the same time radioed in that they could see the balloon. While it might not have proved that they had seen a UFO, it did show that from their respective positions they all could have seen something in the sky at the times they reported their sightings.

The Air Force Flap

After the sightings in late 2007 and early 2008, residents called local air bases to find out if the military had any planes in the air on the nights in question. Witnesses had said that after the UFO passed over, it was followed by a flight of F-16s. The military said there were no planes in the air. However, on January 24, the air force reversed itself, saying that a flight of F-16 Fighting Falcons was on a training mission in the area at night. The air force reversal, like the air national guard reversal in Arizona over ten years before, prompted witnesses and residents to argue that a cover-up was under way. In order to corroborate the air force and the witness stories, MUFON radar expert Glen Schulze collected FAA radar tapes from the area and compared them to the UFO flight locations and trajectories observed by the witnesses and the course of the F-16s. In some cases, the objects and F-16s were in the same area, as some of the witnesses observed, but the tapes also showed objects traveling at 2,000 miles per hour and also traveling very slowly, too slowly for an F-16, which would have fallen below stall speed.

ALERT

In Stephenville, as in Phoenix and the O'Hare Airport incident, there was an initial denial that anything had happened. The air force said that no jets flew over Stephenville. But, twenty-four hours later, the air force reversed itself with an improbable story of a squadron of F-16s in the air that night. First reports are usually the truth. Subsequent reports usually cover up the truth. Therefore, look for the reversal of a story as an indication that the first disclosure contains an element of truth to it.

What were the objects over Stephenville? It's a case that's still under investigation, but it awakened local residents to the possibility that there were more than just F-16s in the air.

The Kokomo Boom

This possible UFO sighting—some absolutely say they saw an incredible display of two UFOs in what looked like an air duel—made it all the way to the National Terror Alert notifications posted from Homeland Security. The notice referred to the April 17, 2008, 10:30 P.M. boom that shook houses and jolted Kokomo, Indiana, residents out of their homes and into the street to find out what had exploded. For some, there was a dazzling display of a string of lights in the sky and a huge explosion. For others, it was the roar of fighter jets from a nearby air base.

The Earth Shook and Houses Rattled

The alert started when 911 dispatch centers received calls of a loud boom. Some say it was a sonic boom; others, particularly air force veterans, say it wasn't. The 911 dispatcher alerted the sheriffs' units in Howard and Tinton counties to the report of a plane crash outside of Kokomo. The sheriffs' officers responded but found no crash site. Nor did local fire departments, also dispatched, find any crashed aircraft, and the FAA reported no missing aircraft.

At least one resident, an air force veteran who was responsible for handling both ground illumination flares and anti-air-to-air missile chafe (flares that draw missiles away from planes), said that he ran out into the street seconds after the boom and saw a huge orange ball in the sky. Next to it he saw what he believed to be a string of lights coming on in succession in an absolutely straight line as an object that was holding the lights in place was rotating. Then he saw the orange orb descend, and the lights slowly went out as, he believed, the craft rotated and the lights turned to the other side. He said the lights he saw were not flares because they hovered too long in the air, the line was too straight connecting the lights, and there were no planes in the area dropping the flares. He said that for either F-16s to be using chafe or dropping flares, they would have to be so close to a target that one would hear the roar of their engines. The witness heard no jets while watching the lights.

Other residents who saw lights reported that after the lights had gone out or gone away, they saw F-16s flying a crisscross pattern in the same area of the sky. They said they thought it looked like the fighters were looking for the source of the lights or chasing them away.

The Witnesses Follow Up

One of the sheriff's officers who was dispatched to look for a crash site called the local air base and was told that the tower had closed at 10:15 P.M. and that there were no planes in the air that night. He also checked with many of the Indiana Air National Guard pilots, who told him that none of them were in the air that night. They also reiterated that for more than two F-16s to be scrambled for an intruder alert, the entire base would have gone on alert and reservists would have been called out of their homes for maintenance and fueling. That was the kind of thing you couldn't keep secret, they said. But the base was closed and there was no alert.

The Experiment

The town of Kokomo was left with a mystery. What was the cause of the boom and the lights? In a follow-up experiment over the summer of 2008, *UFO Hunters* assembled a loud air-powered concussion device and assembled many local witnesses to try to identify the decibel level of the boom they heard. They graphed the sound pattern of the test booms to see if they could match the boom of an F-16 breaking the sound barrier. In the test, none of the witnesses except one could identify the resulting boom as the sound they heard on the night of April 17. However, one analyst said that if the F-16s were close enough to the ground, below a ceiling of 1,000 feet, the resulting boom would be highly concussive, enough to shatter windows. One explanation, therefore, was that an F-16 on a training mission to evade air-to-air missiles—despite denials from the air base—broke the sound barrier in a restricted area as he dived toward the Earth after releasing antimissile chafe. The phosphorescent chafe was the source of the light, and the jet's breaking the sound barrier as it pulled out of its dive was the source of the loud boom.

FACT

Author and UFO researcher Stanton Friedman's theory, called, "ABA," means that for a skeptic, there is a prejudgment that any argument, no matter how implausible, is better than the ET hypothesis. Friedman says that the skeptic's mantra is "anything but aliens" because to admit that there is a possibility of an extraterrestrial hypothesis is to suggest that some flying objects may well be unidentifiable.

Sometimes people cling to conventional explanations because they are more plausible than an appearance of a UFO. This was the case in this event, even though the air base, the pilots, and the FAA all reported there were no planes in the air that night.

The Needles, California, Crash

Just a month after the Kokomo boom, Needles, California, was the scene of a brief media frenzy. A report of a crash landing of an elliptical object along the banks of the Colorado River and an immediate military retrieval—shades of the Kecksburg incident—drew media from around the area. There were two primary witnesses to this event: a man who lived on the Colorado River who called himself Riverboat Bob, and the retired security chief and director of operations at the Los Angeles International Airport (LAX), Chief Frank Costigan of the LAPD.

Costigan, as credible an observer as there ever could be because of his years directing operations at LAX, said he was out in his backyard at 3 A.M. when he saw an illuminated object fly overhead from Lake Mojave. It seemed to slow down and sank below the tree line toward the Colorado River. As it descended, it lit up the ground. Then it disappeared. Closer to the scene was Riverboat Bob, who saw the glowing object come down into the riverbank and witnessed the sky crane helicopter lift it out of the brush while it was still glowing and fly it away. It all happened quickly and would have been over but for the presence of a military or paramilitary unit that entered the town the next day.

The Arrival of the Men in Black

Dave Knox, owner of local radio station KTOX, said that while he was driving to work he saw a group of unmarked military-type vehicles. Once at the station, he received reports from local folks that they had been questioned by what he called "Men in Black" and advised not to talk about any rumors of objects coming down. KLAV news correspondent and host of *Coast to Coast AM*, George Knapp, arrived in Needles from Las Vegas to investigate the UFO story. According to Knapp, the presence of the paramilitary unit, which was heavily armed, spooked the town's residents. Why were they questioning local people? Why were they so interested in who saw the object come down?

Who were the Needles Men in Black?
These men revealed that they were from a hitherto unknown unit attached to the Nuclear Regulatory Commission and based at Area 51, and they were responsible for making sure nuclear materials didn't get out into the public.

Another mystery was the intense presence of personnel from Area 51 that landed late at night in the local Bullhead City Airport in Arizona. Witnesses said that they saw what looked like commercial aircraft, white with a red stripe along the side, landing in Bullhead. These planes belong to an outfit known as Janet Airlines, and they are the official transport vehicles for personnel at Area 51 flying out of McCarran Airport in Las Vegas. If Janet Airlines planes landed in Bullhead City, they were on a mission that, circumstantially at least, seemed related to the Needles crash.

Riverboat Bob Flees for His Safety

Riverboat Bob said that when stories began to circulate about a Men in Black unit in town, he took off downriver on his boat and stayed out of sight until the vehicles left. George Knapp said that he confronted the paramilitary unit, whose members told him they were from an agency out of Groom Lake that he'd never heard of but were tasked to recover nuclear material.

No one discovered what the actual object was that the military retrieved, but Frank Costigan said that it might have been a vehicle that should have landed along the test range in Lake Mojave and overshot its target. In the year following the Needles crash, though, the military surveillance of the town continued with residents saying that military helicopters flew over the town every night. Is the town still under surveillance because of the 2008 UFO crash?

Bucks County UFOs

During the first half of 2008, municipalities in southeast Pennsylvania, from Philadelphia north through Montgomery and Bucks County and all the way to the Delaware River, were part of a UFO flap that attracted media across

Pennsylvania, New Jersey, and New York. The sightings of lights in the sky and a structured craft began when people in the area around the Bucks County seat of Doylestown reported seeing a light in the sky that was brighter than a star. As MUFON state chairman John Ventre reported it, people were calling 911 about a light that they could not identify that was moving in a way that stars didn't. These witnesses were also curious about the way the light seemed to change color, going from bright white to blue. That certainly was unlike any star.

John Ventre's chief investigator, Bob Gardiner, took reports from witnesses in the Philadelphia area who said they'd seen strange lights over the city and made inquiries at air traffic control at the Philadelphia International Airport. Their radar tapes on the nights in question corroborated what the witnesses reported, thus providing a radar confirmation to the visual sightings. As Bob Gardiner told an assembled audience at a Bucks County MUFON conference in fall 2008 at Bucks County Community College in Newtown, the FAA tapes provided confirmation that there was something in the skies over the area that people saw.

A Strange UFO over Levittown

Perhaps the most interesting incident in the Bucks County flap was a homeowner's sighting in Levittown on successive nights right over her backyard. As in the Doylestown sighting, homeowner Denise Murter first spotted the strange light when she was looking out a window into her backyard. The light was far brighter than a star, was moving across her field of view, and was changing color. She thought that it was a plane flying very low, but there was no noise. She watched it as it moved very slowly, much slower than a plane, until it passed overhead.

On the next night, the Levittown witness had gone out to let her dog out late at night when she saw the same light. This time the light was much lower and moving much more slowly. It was fascinating, and she just stared at it in amazement.

The Strange Beam, Again

She walked outside and saw that the light was coming down from a large structured object noiselessly gliding right over her yard. It was triangle-shaped and so close she felt it could have landed. But instead the object was passing a bright beam over her yard, sweeping across trees and bushes. Then it focused its beam on a tree right by her back door while Murter simply stared at it. As she watched the beam, a white substance, almost like snowflakes, began swirling around the beam, floating around without gravity and playing all over the branches and the leaves in the bright light that bathed it. No children's fantasy cartoon could have been more beautiful. It seemed like only a few minutes before the craft snapped up the beam and sped away, leaving the witness in awe of what she had just seen.

FACT

Another commonality among UFO witnesses, especially those who describe some sort of interaction with a UFO, is a sense of awe so overwhelming that the witness completely loses track of the passage of time. Some UFO researchers call this "temporal dislocation" because it's not automatically tied to a UFO abduction event but still results in the witness's inability to account for time.

Once back inside the house, though, Murter noticed that what she thought was only a few minutes was actually over an hour, a period of time she could not account for. She had no strange feelings of having forgotten or having been told to forget anything, just a feeling that more time had passed while she was consciously awake than she could account for. She went to bed, hoping that whatever it was had left. But, to her surprise, that wasn't the end of her experience.

The Effects of the Beam

The next morning Murter awoke and went out into the backyard. What she saw shocked her. The tree next to which she had been standing and that was covered by the beam had a white substance on it. What was even more astounding was that the part of the tree bathed in the beam with the white snowflakes was brown and heavily aged. The leaves seemed dead, as if the tree had become old and damaged. The part of the tree untouched by the beam was still vivid green and full of life. The same was true for other parts of her yard. Alongside the tree she saw a dead robin. She thought it was funny—just the other day she saw a robin in that tree that looked like a very young hatchling or fledgling still in its nest. Could it have been the same bird now completely aged, as if it something had pushed it through an entire life cycle in the space of time it was in the beam? Just as the witness had noticed that an amount of time had sped by that she was unaware of, could whatever that object was have speeded up time?

The Analysis of the Foliage

Murter contacted John Ventre and Bob Gardiner, who, weeks later, came out to the Levittown property to collect soil and foliage samples. They took samples from the tree that had been hit by the beam and control samples from elsewhere in the yard, also noting the time of the incident and the witness's experiences. They noticed that in the tree, half the foliage was green and living while the other half was completely dead. That observation combined with the witness's statement that just the day before the entire tree was still alive told them that some anomalous event had taken place. Unfortunately, it had rained since the event so that whatever samples they took were not fresh, but it was worth taking them to BLT Research Team, a scientific research firm whose soil and field analysis of crop circles was well known in the UFO community.

The BLT Research Team, named for its founders John Burke, William Levengood, and Nancy Talbot, analyzed the plant material Gardiner and Ventre submitted. Although they found no otherworldly material on it, perhaps because of the passage of time and the rains that the material had been exposed to, they did find the substances boron and magnesium only on the branches hit by the beam. Boron, according to Ventre, although not otherworldly, didn't naturally occur on the foliage and was, in itself, an anomaly. The team at BLT was also intrigued by the witness description of the aged branches right next to the living branches, aged in a single night.

The Bucks County UFO flap has continued on and off for over two years with sightings all across the state of Pennsylvania and into neighboring Mercer and Hunterdon counties of New Jersey. There have been videos taken and still photographs of the lights from observations as far south as the Commodore Barry Bridge near Essington and the Philadelphia

International Airport to Oxford Valley Mall in Lower Bucks, but no explanations. Of course, there has been no shortage of skeptical commentary and even derisive comments by some in the media, but for the folks in the Philadelphia and Bucks County area, they say they know what they saw.

ESSENTIAL

Because all residue from contacts between anomalous objects and organic materials tends to degrade quickly, the Delphos, Kansas, soil sample notwithstanding, if you are collecting soil or material samples from a UFO scene, get to the scene as quickly as possible before rain or snow wash away any residual chemical compounds.

UFOs over New York and Other Major Cities

The late Stanley Fulham, a retired Canadian Royal Air Force officer who once worked at the North American Air Defense Command, predicted in his book *Challenge of Change* and on a number of video interviews that a group of UFOs would invade Earth's major cities on October 13, 2010. It was a bold prediction, he admitted, but he said that he had been in contact with channelers who were in contact with an alien presence. That presence predicted that alien fleets would start showing themselves in 2010 over American cities.

During World War II, Fulham was shot down and held in a German POW camp where he heard tales of the foo fighters and said he saw his first UFO. After the war he served in NORAD and spoke to many others in NORAD, who told him they routinely tracked UFOs entering the atmosphere but were told to keep silent about them. In one instance, Fulham revealed, a NORAD officer scrambled fighters to intercept the UFO. The fighter pilots said that the object was huge, hanging 1,000 feet up and motionless. When the fighters approached, the object streaked away and stopped again. The fighters couldn't approach it. The prevalence of UFO sightings like this was so intense among NORAD personnel that Fulham wanted to explore the phenomena further. That's what prompted him to contact the channelers, a group called the Transcenders, who predicted a coming apocalypse presaged by the mass appearance of UFOs.

FACT

One of the best-kept secrets from the public are the UFO sightings—on radar, on camera, and visually—that are made by North American air defense personnel and by NASA. Sometimes called "fast walkers," these strange radar hits appear in the upper atmosphere on a course that seems too directed to be the course of a meteorite. NORAD and NASA personnel have been ordered not only to disregard these sightings but to not report them to any agency that might release them to the public.

With Fulham's prediction of October 13, 2010, already in print, but not generally known to the public, news organizations that had gotten hold of his 2008 book *Challenges of Change* about the Transcenders saw Fulham's prediction of UFO sightings over major cities such as New York and turned him into an overnight media sensation. Fulham predicted, based upon his conversations with the Transcenders, that the twenty-first century would be a period when the inhabitants of the UFOs, whether interdimensional beings, time travelers, or extraterrestrials, would disclose their own existence and, through that disclosure, begin to alter the ways governments controlled their populations.

CHAPTER 10

NASA's UFOs

Now that the space shuttle has been retired, and NASA's planned manned missions will be hitching on Soyuz spacecraft, an era has seemingly come to a close. However, the mystery of what, if any, UFOs U.S. astronauts observed in space since the 1960s still lingers. The number of radio conversations between astronauts and mission control describing "bogeys," or strange objects maneuvering in space near orbiting space capsules or lunar modules, is overwhelming. Famous astronauts, such as Gordon Cooper and Edgar Mitchell, have said flatly that not only are flying saucers real but that the government knows about them and is working with them. Other NASA employees have said that the agency doctors photos it takes to airbrush out or digitally erase images of UFOs. If true, these are startling revelations. NASA's beginnings, though, were toward the end of World War II when the United States first took custody of the most important German rocket scientists, a brain trust that became the backbone of the U.S. space program.

The Roots of NASA: Nazi Scientists and Extraterrestrials

If there was a book entitled *The Everything® Book about NASA*, probably the first chapter would deal with the fact that the key NASA scientists who worked on the American rocket program from the late 1940s well into the formation of NASA's famous astronaut programs were Germans. The Germans were at least fifteen to twenty years ahead of the Allies in their advanced rocket science. According to German scientist Hermann Oberth, who wound up working as part of a Pentagon science brain trust, "We were helped by people from other worlds." If Hermann Oberth was speaking the truth, then maybe the Germans had made extraterrestrial contact, and that was one source of their technology.

Even recently, some researchers into the history of the Roswell crash have pointed to stories circulated by the military that it was Nazi technology responsible for the UFO incident at Roswell, and maybe even Kecksburg and Needles. This subject may be hotly debated, but what isn't debated are the historical facts. The American military rocket program was restarted after the German scientists were brought to America along with most of the Nazi technology, and that technology helped jump-start NASA into space exploration.

Advanced Luftwaffe Aircraft

The Germans had already experimented with jet engine fighters, which they actually deployed toward the end of the war; rocket planes whose purpose was to dive on American bombers from the upper atmosphere; jet-propelled flying wings; intercontinental bombers, which would almost make it across the Atlantic; and submarine-launched ballistic missiles aimed at New York City. The Germans were at least fifteen to twenty years ahead of the Allies in their advanced rocket science. According to German scientist Hermann Oberth, who wound up working as part of a Pentagon science brain trust, "We were helped by people from other worlds." It was an astounding statement by a German scientist who helped develop the rocket and missile programs. If Hermann Oberth was speaking the truth, then maybe the Germans had made extraterrestrial contact, and that was one source of their technology.

The Vril

Late nineteenth-century author Edward Bulwer-Lytton's 1897 novel *The Coming Race* (later called *Vril: The Power of the Coming Race*) was about a force called the Vril, similar to chi or *Star Wars*' the Force, that was an extra-terrestrial power imparted to a master race. The Vril Society was a group of Russian women who believed, based on the novel, that the Vril were really the Aryan race. The Nazis seized this idea and transformed the Vril into the Thule Society. They believed that the Aryans were descendants of an alien race from a distant planet and were the inheritors of UFO and extraterrestrial secrets. These theories, although a pseudoscience according to German immigrant Willy Ley, have gone into UFO lore as the source for the German Wonder Weapons and their supposed UFO secrets. These secrets, allegedly, became part of the American space program immediately after the war.

FACT

The idea for the Vril Society originated with Madame Helena Blavatsky, whose writings about spiritualism in the nineteenth century were part of the "New Age of Spiritualism" that swept Europe and the United States, attracting such devotees as presidents Pierce and Lincoln. The founders of the Vril were a group of Russian women, all of them psychics, led by Maria Orsic, who claimed to be in contact with a race of Aryans from the planet Aldebaran.

Astronaut Sightings

Although it rarely, if ever, reaches the newspapers, there has been a long history of astronauts who've sighted UFOs. Even before the program began, astronaut-to-be Gordon Cooper said that he personally witnessed and saw a photograph of a UFO landing at Edwards Air Force Base. He remembered that the film canisters were removed from the camera and secreted away, never to resurface. Cooper said that he remembered the commanding officer, as the strange craft was landing, telling the personnel at the base to remember exactly what they saw, even if they were told never to talk about it.

The Edgar Mitchell Revelations

Astronaut Edgar Mitchell said he was personally told by those in government service (he will not name them) not only that UFOs were a real phenomenon but that the government knows about them. According to Mitchell, the U.S. government has had dealings with the intelligence controlling or guiding those UFOs, whether they are from another planet or another reality. Mitchell's statements about the reality of UFOs evolved from early suggestions he made indicating that he believed UFOs visited Earth to his statement that he had been told (by members of the U.S. government) that UFOs had actually been in contact with the military. His disclosure of this revelation was a major bombshell on a British radio talk show.

Scott Carpenter of NASA also said that at no time were the astronauts in space alone. They were always under constant surveillance by UFOs. This was an incredible statement because it asserted that UFOs weren't just something seen on radar or seen from the ground. They were around planet Earth and, despite NASA's official denials or reluctance to talk about them, involved with the space program.

Mercury

Mercury astronaut Donald "Deke" Slayton said that in 1951, when he was testing a P-51 fighter in Minneapolis, he spotted an object above him. It was a clear, sunny day, and at first Slayton thought he was looking at a kite. Then he realized that kites don't fly at 10,000 feet, the estimated altitude of the object. Then, as he climbed and approached to get a better look, he thought it might be a weather balloon. But as he got closer, he realized he was looking at a disk-shaped object. He tracked it, cruising at 300 miles an hour, when the object suddenly sped away, making a hairpin turn at a high speed, and disappeared.

An X-15 test pilot, Major Robert White, also saw an object that he could not identify. Not knowing what it was, he said in a subsequent interview with *Time* magazine that, "There are things out there."

Gemini

Probably the astronaut with the most UFO sightings is Gene Cernan, who first spotted a UFO that accompanied him and his crew on Gemini IX. He also saw a UFO as he orbited the moon on Apollo 10 and again on Apollo 17.

He told the *Los Angeles Times* that he believed the objects he saw belonged to "someone else's civilization."

Gemini astronauts James McDivitt and Ed White saw an object shadowing them as they flew over Hawaii. The object looked nothing like anything they had ever seen before because it had long appendages sticking out of it. McDivitt took photos of the object, but those photos have never appeared in public.

And finally, James Lovell on Gemini VII reported to Houston that, "We have a bogey at ten o'clock high." Houston suggested that Lovell was actually looking at his booster rocket. But Lovell responded that they had "several" and that they also had the booster rocket in sight at the time they saw the bogeys. It is a radio transmission that was recorded and made public.

QUESTION

Where are the Gemini VII recordings?
Early on, the NASA feeds were wide open and available to anyone with a radio who could find the correct radio frequency. However, when NASA controllers realized that UFO sighting reports were going out to listeners around the world, they began scrubbing the radio transmissions, filtering them through the Goldstone relay so that only approved conversations were released.

Apollo

Many Apollo astronauts have sent messages about strange things they've seen on the moon, from UFOs to evidence of structures to highways to at least one transmission saying that something was shooting at the astronauts. NASA spokesperson Dr. James Oberg has said publicly that it's all nonsense and mass hysteria because no astronaut has ever talked about UFOs, and the alleged reports of transmissions about UFOs are bogus. However, UFO researchers still persist in presenting evidence of radio transmissions from astronauts and statements from astronauts that they've seen UFOs, especially on the moon.

Apollo 16 astronaut Charles Duke describes in a transmission to NASA that he can see "domes" and "tunnels" on the lunar surface. Whether these are natural formations that look like domes and tunnels or are artificially constructed domes and tunnels is a matter of debate. Astronauts usually agree to a security oath that precludes them from talking about UFOs or anomalous things they see on missions.

In an Apollo 17 conversation with NASA, the command module pilot said that he saw a bright spot on the lunar surface that turned gray. The Apollo astronauts were clearly startled by what they saw. The capsule commander was told when he saw the flashing light to go to KILO. This means to switch to code to describe what he's seeing because NASA knew these conversations were monitored. What, UFO researchers ask, might be the flashing light on the surface of the moon? Then the command module pilot said he saw the flashing light again over the edge of a crater and was again startled by what he saw. He had not switched to code at this point, and the CAPCOM (the person at NASA communicating with the command module pilot) suggested that the flashing light on the lunar surface could be the Russian Vostok probe. But the Vostok probes were only in Earth's orbit, not moon probes.

The Doctored Lunar Photos

Related stories about NASA and lunar exploration are told by two individuals. Donna Hare worked for NASA and appeared on *UFO Hunters* with John Schuessler, director of MUFON and a former NASA employee. Hare said that when she was working in the photography division, downloading images of the lunar surface, she saw an image with a structure on it, which she took to be a craft. She watched as a photo specialist airbrushed out the anomalous image. He said that it really didn't belong in photos that NASA was releasing to the public, and it was his job to make sure nothing like this got into the public domain.

Another story comes from an air force veteran named Karl Wolfe, who told his story in *UFO Magazine*. He worked at an air force facility as a technician in charge of repairing various photo imaging machines. He once received an emergency call that one of the image printers in a secure and classified section of the base had broken and that it was urgent that it get repaired right away so it could print out what it had received from the satellite. This was a weekend when the regular technician was off, so it was up to Wolfe to fill in and get the machine repaired.

He said that he was allowed into the secure section where he saw people roaming around in civilian clothing: individuals from different countries. He didn't recognize any of them. He said that when he got to the machine, he realized that he would have to take it back to his workshop because he couldn't make the repairs on site. The airman trying to print the lunar images had to accompany him back to the workshop, where the two of them got the machine working again.

Suddenly a stream of lunar images began printing, and Wolfe noticed that the images contained structures on them—buildings—as if they were some sort of industrial complex. But whose was it? The airman, not knowing that Wolfe didn't have the security clearance to see the images, simply said something along the lines of how amazing it was and that no one knew there was this type of structure on the moon. When he saw the shocked look on Wolfe's face, he realized that he was talking to someone without a security clearance, and he was suddenly in a lot of trouble. He swore Wolfe to secrecy, but after twenty-five years, Wolfe finally told his story to *UFO Magazine* and on television.

The stories of Donna Hare and Karl Wolfe, told from different perspectives, all indicate that they saw something anomalous on the moon. The stories corroborate, to some extent, some transmissions of the Apollo astronauts that they either saw or encountered anomalous things on the moon. Maybe the transmissions are apocryphal, as Oberg argues, or the product of mass hysteria, but there are so many of them. Astronauts themselves have come forward to say that they've had experiences with UFOs in space, and overlooking the body of these revelations would be a mistake.

The NASA Report on Lunar Anomalies

One of the most interesting documents on the Internet is NASA's study of 500 years of lunar anomalies. These notations are contained in *NASA Technical Report R-277, Chronological Catalog of Reported Lunar Events*, available online at *www.astrosurf.com* and from the U.S. government as a print publication. The reported incidents date back to New England preacher Cotton Mather's sighting of strange lights around the moon. The report includes accounts of the British Astronomical Society's sightings of activity on the moon and articles in New York newspapers about the sudden appearance and disappearance of structures on the lunar surface. Readers of the report can find anecdotal evidence that observers have been seeing strange things on or around the moon for half a millennium. Combine this with stories of the astronauts from all of the space programs and it certainly sparks the imagination.

UFOs and Extraterrestrial Artifacts on the Moon

Even though video images, the return of moon rocks to Earth, and statements of Apollo astronauts all attest that there was a moon landing in 1969 and that there were a number of missions on the moon, conspiracy theories still abound. Some people believe that the moon landings were a hoax, and others believe that extraterrestrials discovered on and around the moon drove astronauts away. It's also believed that the moon vibrated, as if it were a hollow bell, when rods were fired into it to get a seismic reading. There are plenty of misconceptions about the moon that linger to this day, including how the moon got there in the first place, why top-secret photos of the lunar surface picked up images of factorylike structures on it, and why some astronauts were apparently recorded talking about some intelligent life forms firing on them while they explored the lunar surface.

NASA has been very aggressive about dismissing the moon-landing hoax stories. These began with the television show *Conspiracy Theory*, posing its theory that U.S. astronauts never made it to the moon and the moon-landing videos and photographs of humans on the lunar surface were all faked. The conspiracy theorists argued that the U.S. government set the whole thing up to trick the Soviets into believing that it had made it to the moon first, thereby winning the space race.

Yet other theories have been posed that the United States faked the moon landing at a movie studio to cover up the real space exploration program, which was far more advanced and had already created a fortified base and manufacturing facilities on the moon. Why would the United States spend money covering up a moon landing when it already had facilities there? The conspiracy theorists contend that the United States wanted to keep its activities secret from the Soviets during the Cold War. They believe that government officials were keeping the relationship with extraterrestrials secret from the general public and were busy secretly exploiting what resources they could mine on the moon as part of an international cabal. Even if these theories don't make sense, the anecdotal evidence from NASA employee Donna Hare implies that *something* was concealed.

Retired NASA official John Schuessler has said on television that inside NASA are groups of individuals who have a "special access" clearance. These individuals are involved in any handling of UFO or extraterrestrial-related information and/or the suppression of that information.

Are there any real, ascertainable facts about the possibility of extraterrestrials living and working with their spacecraft on the moon? For one, it is now believed that based on water samples analyzed from lunar soil there is a vast amount of liquid water on the moon, most of it either at the bottom of craters or underground. If water is present, and if the moon is bombarded by bacteria-bearing meteorites, then there could be rudimentary bacterial life underground.

The seismic study of the moon, if what it points to is true, suggests a hollow moon. Those who want to extrapolate from that suggest that the moon might have been an intelligently constructed satellite, in a permanent orbit around the Earth with one side always facing away to conceal the activities going on there. NASA's report of various structures on the moon that have been observed over the centuries may point only to misidentifications of natural structures highlighted in strange ways by light, or simply through jumping to conclusions.

Why Was Lunar Exploration Abandoned?

In another series of conspiracy theories, proponents argue that from the time NASA's Apollo program was first proposed, the plan was to build settlements on the moon to harvest the minerals there. If that was the case, why was this effort, costing billions of dollars over the course of the Apollo program, ultimately abandoned? Was there nothing on the moon except moon rocks? What was the purpose in having the Apollo astronauts ride around on lunar rovers and plant flags only to abandon the moon for the Chinese and the Indians to establish their bases on it thirty years later? What really went on moonside?

Perhaps, say some NASA conspiracy theorists, explorers were driven off the moon. ETs had been there before and had driven off the astronauts from Earth. Were there road structures on the surface, as at least one NASA Apollo transmission indicated, and did aliens fire on astronauts to keep them away from their facilities? What is known is that after eleven crewed missions, manned lunar exploration was simply abandoned. Some say that the message wasn't just what was found on the moon but an actual attack on Apollo 13.

"Houston, We've Had a Problem"

It was a heroic mission for both the Apollo 13 crew and the NASA personnel who helped them get back to Earth after an explosion in an oxygen tank vented gas and made the navigation system unreliable. The crew couldn't land on the moon and certainly could not have made a U-turn in space to head home. They had to use inertia to continue their journey to the moon and then use the moon's gravity to swing them around the moon and head back to Earth. In so doing, they had to abandon the Apollo service module and use the lunar module as their return vehicle.

QUESTION

What will China and India find on the moon?
Both the People's Republic of China and India are planning manned lunar missions. Will they find the treasure trove of water and minerals that has eluded NASA? Or will they find pockets of extraterrestrial colonies that will drive them off the moon, which is what some UFO researchers believe happened to NASA? Only the next twenty years will tell.

The entire world followed the story of the Apollo 13 crew from the time the tank ruptured on April 13, 1970, until they splashed down in the Pacific on April 17. But what was the real cause of that tank rupture? ET conspiracy theorists suggested that it was either a direct warning from ETs or an accident that occurred while Apollo 13 was being surveilled by ETs. The remaining lunar missions to finish out the series were simply completed with ET compliance so as to continue the cover-up of the presence of an extraterrestrial base on the moon, possibly a fortified observation base or relay station.

Every conspiracy theory is really speculation, an extension of opinion beyond fact-based conjecture into the realm, in some cases, of pure fantasy. However, was there ever a real plan to fortify the moon, to turn it into a type of military base so that the United States could occupy it? The answer is absolutely yes.

Project Horizon

Project Horizon was the official U.S. Army plan to fortify the moon and turn it into a military installation as well as an outpost for exploration. The plan was conceived in the mid 1950s and was proposed in 1957 by the new commander of the army's Office of Research and Development, Lieutenant General Arthur Trudeau. Trudeau was a hero of the Korean War, famous for his valor during the Battle of Pork Chop Hill. His troops were left almost abandoned atop a hill, surrounded and bombarded by North Korean troops. Trudeau was ordered to retreat, but he disobeyed the order and refused to leave his men behind. He grabbed the first helmet he could get his hands on and led his men back up the hill, firing back at the enemy as he went, to relieve the siege and bring his men back.

FACT

The story of how General Arthur Trudeau got his third star was told by author Philip J. Corso in *The Day After Roswell*. Corso was serving as a military staffer at President Eisenhower's White House when he learned that CIA director Allen Dulles wanted Arthur Trudeau fired from Army Intelligence. Corso said that he rounded up other staff officers and appealed to President Eisenhower to save Trudeau's career. When that didn't work, they want to Senator Strom Thurmond, who intervened forcefully on Trudeau's behalf.

Once the war ended, Trudeau, an army engineer by training, was posted to the command of Army Intelligence (G-2). There he again caused controversy by revealing that a CIA-run West German spy ring under former Nazi Gehlen had been penetrated by the East German Stasi and was filtering information back to the Soviets. The CIA was led by Allen Dulles, who demanded that Trudeau be disciplined. However a group of army officers appealed to members of the Senate as well as directly to Eisenhower, stating that Trudeau should be rewarded rather than disciplined. Senator Strom Thurmond bluntly told the White House that the Senate would not confer any more elevations of officers to general rank if Trudeau was punished. Eisenhower agreed and Trudeau was given his third star but removed from Army Intelligence and posted to the backwater command of Army Research and Development and Foreign Technology.

At Army R&D, Trudeau discovered the plans for what was known as Project Horizon, the establishment of a military base on the moon. By 1957, it became Trudeau's first campaign. He argued that it was an incredible engineering feat that would require the establishment of an entirely new army command, drawing upon the personnel from everything from the Army Corps of Engineers to the Quartermaster Corps and field artillery. The plan was secret and not widely circulated. Not even the senator from Ohio and former astronaut John Glenn knew of the plan's existence. It was revealed to Glenn by Trudeau's former deputy, Lieutenant Colonel Philip Corso.

The creators of Project Horizon argued that the United States needed a new front in the Cold War. They suggested that if the Soviets got to the moon first, they would fortify it and be able to fire missiles at America at will or cow us into submission with a nuclear threat. For an artillery officer like Trudeau, the moon was the high ground that had to be taken and could not be left to the enemy.

In his bestselling memoir *The Day After Roswell*, Colonel Corso suggests another rationale for Project Horizon, one fictionalized by the television science fiction series *Space 1999*, which ran from 1975 to 1978. In this scenario, the moon base was not a fortified base to outflank the Soviet bloc from above but a base to deny aliens' unfettered use of the moon to attack Earth. During an ongoing war with an extraterrestrial species, the fortifications on the moon could monitor incoming UFO activity and effectively target the alien spacecraft, serving as Earth's first line of defense.

Corso also suggested that such programs as Reagan's Strategic Defense Initiative, better known as Star Wars, were also ultimately aimed at monitoring and shooting down UFOs as they were outflanking enemy missiles. These programs were designed to be able to target enemies at launch from above, shooting them down before they re-entered the atmosphere. The real purpose, Corso suggested, might have been a defense against UFOs.

Life on Mars

Legends about Martians and life on Mars have abounded for hundreds of years. Mars has been the subject of motion pictures, comic books, novels, and television shows such as *My Favorite Martian*. H. G. Wells's *War of the Worlds* (1898) was the first modern science fiction satire about Martian life invading Earth and defeating its most powerful empire, England, by rendering its weapons useless. The simplest of Earth's life forms, a virus, was used to attack the Martians' systems. Because the aliens had no natural defense against the virus, it killed them. *War of the Worlds* became the model for science fiction invasion films from the 1940s through today. The story was so powerful that, in 1938, the Rockefeller Foundation funded the Orson Welles Mercury Theater of the Air broadcast of a radio drama based on *War of the Worlds*. The radio play changed the landing zone to a small rural farming community just outside Princeton, New Jersey, called Grover's Mill. The radio broadcast was said to have been so frightening that, despite announcements that this was a radio drama, people believed the simulated newscasts were real news and supposedly panicked in the streets.

Years later it was revealed that the street panic did not really happen. The panicked response was reported in newspapers as part of a social experiment conducted by the Rockefeller Foundation to see how human beings would react to news of a panic set off by a fictional Martian invasion. The results of that experiment found their way into the famous Rand Corporation study of extraterrestrial contact in 1968, which suggested that humans may panic but advised that a central repository for the study of UFOs be created.

Despite the earlier thoughts that Mars was a cold, desolate, waterless, and lifeless world, new theories have emerged that Mars might contain significant amounts of water. Also, based on data from the 1976 Mars Viking lander, Martian soil might contain the basic protein building blocks of life. When the results of an experiment from the lander were first discussed in the 1990s, the results of the Viking soil samples were dismissed as bad data. However, three years ago scientists revisited the data and revealed that perhaps the Viking lander experiments did actually find building blocks of life or the residue of organic activities on Mars.

Compelling evidence for prehistoric life on Mars, four billion years ago, was discovered in a Martian meteorite that landed in Antarctica 13,000 years ago on the Allan Hills ice field. This meteorite contained forms of single-cell bacteria almost like the single-cell bacteria found on Earth today. This discovery had two major implications. The first and most obvious was that life existed on Mars four billion years ago when the planet had a warm, wet atmosphere. It is evidence, though still refutable, that Earth is not the only planet to contain life. If life existed elsewhere in our own solar system, might it still exist, and if so, where and what form would it take?

The second stunning implication is that the development of life on Earth might have been jump-started by an injection of life from Mars on this meteorite. In other words, if Earth's bacteriological ancestry comes from the bombardment of Earth's oceans from Mars, then we earthlings might technically all be Martians.

Exoplanets

Exoplanets are planets that exist in star systems other than our own or are star-free drifting planets. These planets, depending upon whether they are in a habitable zone, might be capable of sustaining life. Exoplanets are the subject of major studies by NASA and academics because the potentially huge numbers of these objects may indicate that there is a heavily populated universe, with some neighbors close enough to visit—if hyperlight transportation or a suitable propulsion system can be achieved.

The search for and study of exoplanets dovetails with the study of exobiology, the search and analysis of species on Earth that live in some of the most hostile environments imaginable. NASA devotes financial resources to this because expanding the definition of what life is leads to a better understanding of the parameters of what might constitute extraterrestrial life. For example, if the single-cell forms of bacteria discovered in Martian meteorites is real evidence, then the argument about whether Earth is the only planet in the universe that can sustain life is proven wrong. If four billion years ago, before life on Earth evolved, there was life on Mars, and that life strongly resembles the origins of bacteria on Earth, might it have had a similar evolution as life on Earth? Might that life have migrated deep beneath the Martian surface where water was abundant? If so, might there be sentient or even sapient life on Mars?

The search for exoplanets and exobiological life forms also led NASA researchers to an astounding discovery made only recently. NASA scientists discovered life on Earth that was based not on carbon but on silicon. Since it is known that there is an alternate track of life based upon another substance, could that life form be adapting to a changing climate on this planet? Might there be more advanced forms of silicon-based life if not here then out there? The recent and exciting discoveries of planets in other star systems, and maverick planets floating through the galaxy having been set free from a star system, offer immense clues to the potential of extraterrestrial life.

Exoplanets and Ancient Civilizations

If you look at the remains of ancient civilizations of Egypt, Mesopotamia, and North and South America, you'll come upon strange structures and the organization of villages. These communities seem to reflect the configuration of constellations that would have been seen thousands of years ago from those locations. There are native villages that resemble the configuration of stars in Canis Major, for example, and artifacts that capture the image of Sirius, the Dog Star, in Canis Major. Why is this star so important? Sirius is the brightest star in the heavens, and it presages the coming of summer. As it rose in the sky, ancient peoples knew they had to get their crops in the ground. For the Egyptians living in the Nile River flood plain, it meant the floods would deposit silt, nourishment for the crops.

Studies of these ancient civilizations and their mirroring of the configurations of star systems also prompted many researchers to hypothesize that human civilization might have been seeded by explorers from planets in these star systems. Because new discoveries of exoplanets in the habitable zones of distant star systems hold out the possibility of civilizations on these planets, it may be that space-faring explorers from these civilizations either established colonies on Earth, jump-started sapient life on Earth, or seeded Earth biologically with strains of DNA. If any of these theories, collectively called the "ancient alien hypothesis," are true, then the whole of human history has an extraterrestrial origin. The secret may well lie in what can be discovered about exoplanets and anomalous life forms on planet Earth.

SETI

If skeptics want to argue that institutions do not have any belief in life out there in the universe, the existence and financial support of SETI, the Search for Extraterrestrial Intelligence, belies that completely. SETI's self-described mission is to "explore, understand, and explain the origin, nature, and prevalence of life in the universe." SETI manages arrays of radio telescopes that systematically search specific parts of the heavens in organized grid patterns to see if there are any artificially generated radio signals. This radio telescope array presupposes, of course, that extraterrestrials are broadcasting on a radio band instead of in some highly advanced type of yet-undiscovered signal. However, because the search points are many light-years away, the radio telescopes are not just searching through space, they're searching through time. The signals they may pick up could have originated hundreds of millions of years ago when these signals were in a radio frequency. And these signals may not have been deliberately sent.

Imagine a civilization on a planet orbiting Sirius or Zeta Reticuli B that sends a scout craft, probably robotic or piloted by android-like creatures, to scan solar systems for signs of life. Imagine further that as they near the position of Earth at the edge of the Milky Way, they pick up RF signals from a planet. Not knowing what life forms exist on planet Earth, they know that there has to be some sapient life, because how else could the technology have been created to generate these signals?

SETI works on this principle. Maybe the directors of SETI adamantly argue that there are no ETs on Earth or flying saucers landing here. But they do believe that life exists out there in the universe. Therefore, they hope to find trace evidence of that life by picking up the radio signals that any civilizations in a distant star system might have generated. Thus, you don't need UFOs to figure out if there is life out there. Better, the very existence of SETI indicates that folks in academic and public institutions believe that extraterrestrial life exists. If they didn't, why would they be looking for it?

CHAPTER 11

The Science Behind UFOs

Just thinking about the presence of UFOs, that humans might not be alone in the universe, can be mind-boggling. Once you've wrapped your mind around that concept, try thinking about how UFOs got here. Would they use advanced versions of the same technology available on planet Earth, or something close to what science fiction authors and shows have posited? Some of Earth's brightest thinkers, from Nikola Tesla and Guglielmo Marconi to Stephen Hawking, have looked at the science behind interstellar travel. From light-speed travel to wormholes to ion drives and dark energy, there are many different ways to accomplish interstellar travel, and perhaps it's closer to being realized than you think.

How UFOs Get to Earth

What about the nuts-and-bolts technology of UFOs? With star systems many light-years apart, what kinds of propulsion systems could get an alien craft to Earth? Stanton Friedman and others suggest that flying saucers might not be flying thousands of light-years through space. They may be scout ships traveling here from nearby planets or even from the dark side of the moon. Others suggest that UFOs are always here, hiding beneath the oceans at bases so deep in trenches that the most sophisticated equipment can't locate them. Or, the unthinkable: The government knows they're here and simply can't do anything about it, except observe them and stay out of their way, because that is the arrangement President Eisenhower agreed to with the extraterrestrials.

A more mundane explanation might involve the propulsion systems themselves. Don't think that because humans rely on jets and rockets or even pulse jet or nuclear power plants that this is what the UFOs would have to use. Professor Michio Kaku and futurist Charles Ostmann both suggest that advances in nanotechnology are such that it is not at all far-fetched for extraterrestrial propulsion systems to be as tiny as a small jet engine yet hundreds of times more powerful. Fuel also might not be an issue if UFOs from highly advanced technological civilizations are able to use the dark energy of the universe itself as a fuel. Recycling existing energy, transforming it, and increasing its power might be a basic intergalactic propulsion mechanism in use for thousands of years by space farers.

The concept of hyperlight speeds offers another example of the ways space travelers can cross large distances without spending eons in space. Science itself posits that as one approaches the speed of light, time actually slows to zero. That means that at the speed of light, time for the traveler does not pass, though time does pass for those the traveler has left behind. In this way, space travelers also travel into the future. Michio Kaku (*Physics of the Impossible*) has also pointed out that even when astronauts travel at almost 20,000 miles an hour, they are moving more slowly than folks on Earth. Therefore, they are actually traveling into the future on their journeys as well as through space.

Further, if space travelers developed a way to travel faster than the speed of light and make the passage through a wormhole at hyperlight speeds, they may not be crushed by the huge gravitational forces. In fact, black holes or wormholes might be the freeways of the universe, very valuable crossings allowing space commuters to move back and forth in ways that are simply beyond our comprehension.

ESSENTIAL

Speculation aside, there has been practical science and invention associated with the possibility of otherworldly creatures. For example, the entire field of exobiology focuses on the search for exotic life forms on Earth living in inhospitable or extreme regions that might mimic the conditions on distant planets. Just recently, scientists discovered a life form that was silicon-based and not carbon-based. This means that there is potentially an entirely different track of life on our planet in parallel with our own carbon-based evolution. Scientists have also discovered microbes on meteors that fell to Earth millions of years ago into the primordial chemical soup of our oceans—ones that might have seeded life on Earth.

There is science behind this. Stephen Hawking, the great modern theoretical physicist, has said that not even a black hole can destroy matter. Theoretically, matter can emerge on the other side of a black hole.

Early UFO Prototypes

One early candidate for UFO contact, a self-admitted contact, was inventor Nikola Tesla, who, at the end of the nineteenth century, was experimenting with particle beam energy and the wireless transmission of electricity. During this period, Tesla believed he had contacted radio transmissions between planets. He also believed that extraterrestrials were speaking to him and encouraging him to develop new inventions.

Although very few people believed that Tesla was in contact with extraterrestrials, there is no doubt that Tesla's inventions were far advanced and way beyond the technology of his day. For example, Tesla invented the first remote-controlled robotic model boat, proving that radio waves could control electrical motors. He offered the U.S. Navy a plan for a remote-controlled torpedo and even foresaw the development of robot soldiers. His proposals to the navy for weapons development were torpedoed by the navy's other technical advisor, Thomas A. Edison, long a Tesla adversary because of Tesla's advocacy of alternating current instead of Edison's direct current.

QUESTION

What started the feud between Edison and Tesla?
According to Tesla's biographers, when Tesla first came to the United States it was to work with Thomas Edison. Edison put Tesla to work on the repair of a large steamship engine. The ship was scheduled to leave after the weekend, and Edison couldn't fix the problem. He said to Tesla that if he could repair the engine so the ship could sail at the beginning of the week, Edison would sign a check, give it to Tesla, and let Tesla fill in the amount. For the penniless Tesla, this was even more than he could ask for. He worked for over forty-eight hours straight and finally repaired the engine. When he approached Edison for his check, Edison simply laughed at him and said, "You didn't think I was serious, did you?" Thus began the end of their brief relationship and the beginning of a feud.

Tesla's antigravity experiments were so advanced that toward the end of his life he believed that he had cracked the code for developing machines that could defy gravity. Although he attempted to secure funding from the United States for the development of antigravity, his efforts were futile. He turned to the Soviet Union, who awarded him a $25,000 grant, a grant that aroused the suspicion of the United States. Tesla's comprehensive notes on the nature of antigravity devices were stored in his two-room suite at the New Yorker Hotel in Manhattan. Upon his death on January 7, 1943, federal agents entered his room, took possession of his notes, had them stored by the Office of Alien Properties, and microfilmed them. They then sent his antigravity notes to General Nathan Twining at the Air Materiel Command at Wright Field. The bulk of Tesla's notes were turned over to the Tesla Museum in Belgrade, Yugoslavia, in 1952.

QUESTION

Who invented radio, Tesla or Marconi?
While the short answer is both, the real dispute is who invented radio first. According to original U.S. patents, Marconi's European broadcast qualified him as the holder of the patent. But Tesla challenged it based on his earlier experiments. Tesla's challenge went nowhere until the outbreak of World War II when Marconi sued the U.S. government for patent infringement in the manufacture of military radios. The U.S. Supreme Court resolved the lawsuit simply by awarding the patent to Tesla and thus removed Marconi's standing as a plaintiff. Now the answer is that Tesla is recognized as the inventor of radio.

Marconi's UFO

The Italian inventor Guglielmo Marconi, although known, along with Tesla, as the creator of wireless transmission of radio waves, was also fascinated by the concept of antigravity and by craft that could employ antigravity mechanisms to levitate and even leave Earth's atmosphere. Like Tesla, Marconi developed particle beam weaponry. Marconi demonstrated it by stopping cars on a highway by sending a beam to interfere with their ignition systems. Such weapons are in use today by highway patrol officers to stop fleeing cars in high-speed chases. Marconi was also said to have created a secret city in the Andes where he developed a flying saucer, using a combination of the Bernoulli effect combined with his antigravity technology, that could lift out of Earth's atmosphere and travel as far away as Mars. Marconi had become a very rich man through his inventions and was capable of funding his own research and building the secret city in the Andes that has become the source of much speculation and wonder.

The Bernoulli Effect and the Coanda Effect

A basic example of the Bernoulli effect is lift, such as the lift of an airplane wing or airfoil. Air, or any fluid medium, traveling faster over the top of the wing because of the wing's shape creates lower air pressure than air traveling under the bottom of the wing. This difference in air pressure creates an upward motion from the bottom of the wing called *lift*, and it is the principle that lets airplanes fly. Translated into flying saucer technology, by forcing air down over the top of a disk-shaped craft so that the air below it moves more slowly, the craft should rise. The practical application of this is the structure of flaps on an airplane wing. By lowering the flaps, even as the plane slows down, the attraction of the air being forced over the wing to the ground creates additional lift and keeps the plane airborne during slower-speed landings.

ESSENTIAL

The U.S. Air Force and the Canadian Royal Air Force both looked at flying saucer designs in the 1950s, especially the Avrocar. But flying saucers were so unstable, needing complex computer-managed stabilizing systems to keep them aloft and directed, that the design development was abandoned, just as the Germans had abandoned them in the 1930s.

The Germans experimented in the 1920s and 1930s with disk-shaped craft that took advantage of the Coanda effect and antigravity simulation and were able to demonstrate the possibility of flying saucers. Briefly, the Coanda effect explains the properties of lift through a liquid medium by demonstrating that faster-flowing liquid over the top of a surface reduces the pressure while slower-flowing liquid—or air—underneath the same surface increases the pressure and thus allows for lift. These man-made flying saucers were thought to be early designs of airborne craft that the Nazis hoped to use in warfare. However, they were highly unstable and difficult to navigate. Their existence, which was well known to Army and Army Air Force Intelligence during the war, was initially thought, in some military circles, to have been responsible for flying saucer sightings. But that theory was quickly dismissed, as was any thought that the Horten brothers' flying wing was the crashed craft at Roswell (another unusual design that resembled the crescent-shaped craft Kenneth Arnold observed over Mount Rainier in 1947) because it was a conventional airfoil made of balsa wood and powered by conventional jet engines.

Antigravity and the Electromagnetic, Gravity-Defying Envelope

If transforming lead into gold was the dream of medieval alchemists, then antigravity devices are the dream of modern theoretical engineers. Long explained by UFO researchers as a mechanism for the way UFOs seem to hover in midair or move so slowly that conventional aircraft would stall at those speeds, antigravity and the antigravity envelope is the technology presupposed for the way flying saucers fly through the atmosphere. One of the theories behind the Roswell crash—one of many—is that the new radar technologies in 1947 interrupted the craft's antigravity envelope so as to cause it to lose its navigational ability and crash into an arroyo or another craft.

Corso's UFO Sightings at Red Canyon

Lieutenant Colonel Philip Corso, in *Day After Roswell*, told the story of his time in service at the Red Canyon Army Missile Proving Grounds in New Mexico. There he was given the order to shut his missile-tracking radars down at specific times. If his radar operators missed that time by even as little as a minute, their radars would pick up strange craft on their scopes—craft not authorized to be in that restricted airspace. Corso said he was told to forget about what he saw and tucked it away, but years later he thought about what effect his radar beams might have had upon the strange objects' ability to defy gravity with no apparent conventional propulsion system.

Experiments in Antigravity

In one experimental theory, Dr. Franklin Felber suggested that by accelerating a mass in space to almost 60 percent of the speed of light, the mass would repel other objects and create an antigravity slipstream that would actually increase its speed. As the object approached the absolute speed of light, the intensity of the beam would increase so that at a certain point the object itself would exist within an antigravity bubble sucked through space and time. The trick would be, of course, to propel the object to over half the speed of light initially—no small feat, unless a nuclear reactor operating in the space vacuum was the means of propulsion.

Nuclear Propulsion and Ion Drives

Thought to be clearly in the realm of science fiction, but presupposed by Project Horizon, was the possibility of constructing deep-space propulsion systems outside Earth's gravity, probably on the lunar surface. Current technology already allows for launching small nuclear reactors into space, which has been possible for almost half a century, and assembling a large nuclear reactor in Earth's orbit is not beyond current technology, either. Such a reactor, revved up to generate enough propulsion, probably an ion drive, would, over a long enough run, bring its payload up to 60 percent of light speed, even accounting for the increase in mass. At those speeds, which have already been achieved in particle accelerators and colliders, you would be able to see what the effect on gravity would be. Currently, one of the unmanned spacecraft on NASA's Dawn mission, powered by an ion drive—releasing ion particles into space so as to drive the craft forward—is rendezvousing with the large asteroid Vesta in the asteroid belt between Mars and Jupiter.

Element 115, Temporal Distortion, and Dark Energy

One of the most science-based—or pseudoscience-based, depending upon one's opinion—theories about UFO propulsion came out of the Bob Lazar story at Area 51. Bob Lazar, whose work at Area 51 as a propulsion engineer is still a matter of controversy, explained to retired CIA pilot and test pilot John Lear that he was led past a room into which he could see through a window that a candle was flickering. He was told to watch the candle, and the flame suddenly stopped flickering as if it were frozen in position. He asked why the candle stopped moving. He was told that it was still flaming but that time had stopped around it. From the outside of the temporal envelope it looked as if it had been frozen. But inside, the candle was still moving in its own temporal envelope. And this, he was told, was part of the secret of UFO propulsion.

Element 115

As John Lear explained on *UFO Hunters*, the alien craft has a device, powered by element 115, an element that is yet to be synthesized, which is bombarded with protons to bump it up to element 116. It immediately decays and in so doing releases an immense amount of energy. That energy doesn't drive the craft through space; it draws space and time around the craft. In so doing, the craft is pulled through space and time traversing incredible differences in no time at all because time ceases to be a factor in the journey. Time stands still for those onboard, and they are able to arrive at their destination at the moment they left even though time outside the slipstream might have passed. This is why the candle seemed to stop flickering in the room that Bob Lazar observed.

Examples of Temporal Distortion

As incredible as this temporal distortion sounds, there is real testimonial/anecdotal evidence to support the idea. Many witnesses—from some of the witnesses who watched the 8:30 P.M. lights over Phoenix to police officers who've encountered UFOs to the air force security detail at RAF Bentwaters to the witness in Levittown, Pennsylvania, who watched the snowflake beam in the tree by her house—have explained that, for them, the passage of time seemed to have been distorted. At least one police officer said that when a huge flying triangle floated over his police car, shutting down its engine and the police radio, he thought it took only a couple of seconds for the craft to pass over. In fact, it took almost fifteen minutes, fifteen minutes during which the dispatcher could not raise the officer on his radio because it was shut down. Then, miraculously, the car started up on its own. If a car engine shuts off, normally it does not start spontaneously on its own.

One can argue that car engines and lost time are not accidental. What is really happening is that because time itself has stopped or slowed down to a crawl because of the incredible power source of the craft, human beings who find themselves swept up along the fringes of the temporal distortion slipstream simply lose time, just like the candle.

Temporal Distortion Effects on Living Organisms

Trees and some life forms also lose time; for example, the Levittown robin simply aged overnight from a young fledgling to an old bird. And the beam that engulfed part of the tree simply sucked not the life out of it but the time out of it. Such may be the power of the propulsion system that powers this one particular type of craft.

Dark Energy—Zero Point Energy

There is a theory among physicists that there is an invisible energy driving the universe apart. You can't see it, but scientists are conducting experiments to measure it. One group of researchers, working in secret, is trying to harness this dark energy, or zero point energy, as a source of power for potential spacecraft. Rather than carry fuel with it, a craft able to harness the very energy of the universe itself would have limitless fuel and be able to travel anywhere at the speed of the expansion of the universe. However, as one physicist has said, "With all the spacecraft we've recovered, we still haven't recovered a zero point energy propulsion system."

Wormholes

If you remember the television series *Star Trek: Deep Space Nine*, you'll remember that one of the commercial advantages of the space station was its proximity to a stable wormhole connecting different quadrants in the galaxy. Wormhole jumps constitute one theory of interstellar travel that enables craft to cover vast distances by utilizing the connectivity of a wormhole between two distant points in the galaxy.

The problem is that black holes have such intense pressure that they would crush anything crossing the hole's event horizon. But what if a craft could travel at hyperlight speeds so as to move through the black hole before the pressure destroyed the craft? Theoretically, according to Stephen

Hawking, the craft would emerge on the other side of the black hole. This is another way that craft could cover vast distances, perhaps even distances in time or through dimensional portals.

Biological Propulsion Systems

On the fringe of UFO theory is the concept of a biological propulsion system for some spacecraft. UFO contactees have revealed that, during their times aboard extraterrestrial craft, they were introduced to different types of propulsion systems, a number of which were thought to be biological in nature.

This might mean that the craft was actually a living organism or at the very border between life and machine. This craft may interface with its android or robot pilots through the kind of headpiece that is an advanced version of what scientists are experimenting with today. These headphones have electrodes that are directly connected to the parts of the human brain that control movement and carry impulses from the pilot's brain to the craft's navigational systems. In army combat helicopters, a version of this headpiece exits in which the movement of a pilot's head or eyes can control the craft.

Some contactees have said that they've seen biological symbiants who drive the craft and who are in biological contact with the ship's pilots. In a version of mental projection, creatures are able to visualize coordinates and project the ship there; coordinates are communicated to the ships by the pilots. There has never been any scientific evidence to support this, only the anecdotal reports of those who say they've been aboard.

CHAPTER 12

Extraterrestrials and Otherworldly Beings

Among the group of witnesses who have reported seeing UFOs are a large subgroup who claim to have seen not only the spaceships but the creatures inside them. This group of ET witnesses includes not only self-described abductees but contactees and crash retrieval personnel, as well as casual witnesses. Bystanders at the Roswell Army Air Field in 1947 reported seeing the alien bodies, as did members of the 1948 National Air War College. Contactees, however, have been the most descriptive and have reported all types of otherworldly figures, from Nordic human types to strange, claw-equipped beings floating on beams of light. The array of different types of strange-looking beings, most of whom, when communicating, describe themselves as extraterrestrial, is indeed vast. Floating orbs, for example, have been described as intelligent beings, too. The list is long, but without any official manifest of alien creatures, there are only witness descriptions, including one from George Washington.

How Do You Know They're Extraterrestrials?

Technically, you can't be sure what the otherworldly beings are that witnesses say they've seen. You can only go on what abductees and contactees have said. For example, Betty Hill told her therapist Dr. Benjamin Simon that the entities that abducted her and her husband, Barney, told her that they came from a planet in the star system Zeta Reticuli. She even drew a copy of the star map to illustrate what she saw in (what she said was) the spacecraft where she was taken.

Travis Walton does not recall any specific conversations with the creatures who beamed him up to their ship, because there was no conversation. However, he does recall that when he left his hospital bed and went down a corridor into a control room or navigation room, he saw a three-dimensional star map projected over his head. This was an indicator that, whatever these creatures were, they navigated among the stars.

QUESTION

Can angels be otherworldly beings?
By definition, reports of angelic encounters or encounters with entities claiming to be angels certainly can be called encounters with otherworldly beings if by "otherworldly" you mean not human in its common meaning. Spirits and ghosts, if they exist, can also be considered otherworldly beings. Maybe ghosts and spirits reside in a different dimension and can be called interdimensional beings. It all depends on how you define the nature of the creatures that some people have reported seeing.

Descriptions of the creatures who piloted the different types of craft in question abound, and some of the descriptions have the ring of authenticity. For example, the best descriptions of the creatures from the Roswell crash come from at least six eyewitnesses: a maintenance man at Walker Field in Roswell; a firefighter from Roswell; Lieutenant Walter Haut and Colonel William Blanchard, both from Walker Field; Captain Philip J. Corso at Fort Riley; and Lieutenant Colonel Marion "Black Mac" Magruder at Wright Field.

Betty and Barney Hill, Betty especially, gave a detailed description of the entities that abducted them. Travis Walton, too, described two types of beings on the craft that he said he was taken to. The different beings seemed to be in a supervisor/subordinate relationship, but they were clearly different species.

You can also look at the description of the creature that Eve saw in the Garden of Eden in Genesis as otherworldly, and you can look at the Bible, even if only for the sake of argument, as a description of humanity's otherworldly origins. The description of the serpent takes on a new meaning when doing this, as does the description of the creatures that the prophet Ezekiel describes, who referred to him as "Son of Man" and instructed him on the message he had to bring to the House of Israel. There is also a large contactee movement of individuals who have claimed to have seen a variety of beings in addition to the Grays that the Roswell witnesses said they saw.

There is a history of self-described witnesses of extraterrestrials or otherworldly creatures dating back tens of thousands of years, including the petroglyph and pictographic images inscribed upon or carved into rocks in the American Southwest and in the Middle East.

The Grays

Witnesses have seen different types of what they say are alien species, varying in size, demeanor, shape, color, and resemblance to what you would call a life form. The most prevalent of these otherworldly species are the Grays.

Some witnesses, especially those in the military who encountered strange-looking beings as part of their official responsibilities, have described the most common type of alien as a "Gray." The descriptions vary, however, but there are broad similarities among the witness descriptions.

Roswell Witness Descriptions

The most prominent Roswell eyewitnesses describe living or dead Grays with the following characteristics. The creatures had larger-than-normal, lightbulb-shaped heads, lightbulb-shaped large eyes that are sometimes described as completely black, tiny or no apparent ears, and a slit for mouths. These creatures had longer-than-normal arms and were very spindly. They stood only about four to four-and-a-half feet tall. The creature's skin tone was described as a grayish pink, reminding at least one witness of an insect with a humanlike face called Child of the Earth. This large insect is very common in the American Southwest.

Among the eyewitnesses to this creature was a firefighter whose truck responded to a crash report in the Roswell desert. His crew was probably the first official response to the crash. He saw dead aliens and one that was still moving. When one of the living aliens was brought back to Walker Field, the home base of the 509th Bomber Group of the army air force in Roswell, a civilian maintenance man who was standing outside of a hangar having a cigarette noticed the commotion. He saw the alien carried on a stretcher right past him and into the hangar. He said the alien looked almost human, but from its distinctive facial features he could tell that it was not human. He said that it communicated with him that it was dying.

FACT

Alpha Boyd said that when her father was diagnosed with terminal lung cancer, he finally took her to a secluded spot where they could not be overheard and told her the story of seeing the live, but seriously injured, ET lying on a stretcher. He said that after the debris retrieved from the crash in the desert had been stowed in the hangar, a group of army officers surrounded him, roughed him up, and threatened him with death if he ever revealed what he saw. Another officer at the base intervened and said there was no room for roughness. The secret would be kept by all good Americans. And Alpha's father kept it until he revealed it to her.

Philip Corso at Fort Riley

As the wreckage was shipped overland to Wright Field in Ohio, it made a stop at Fort Riley, Kansas, the home of the U.S. Army's 7th Cavalry, where the drivers rested for the night. The shipment was stored in the old veterinary stables at Fort Riley, where the on-duty officer that night was a young captain named Philip Corso. Corso was making his rounds when he saw one of his team members guarding the stables, now used as a warehouse.

The sentry informed Corso that there was a highly secret shipment sitting inside the building. The scuttlebutt was that this shipment came from a crash in New Mexico and that it was very strange. Corso told the sentry, whom he knew very well, to keep quiet about it while he inspected the secret material.

Corso said that he was shocked at what he saw. Under a tarp in a clear coffinlike container and immersed in liquid was the body of a creature. Corso describes the creature in his book *The Day After Roswell* as a child-sized figure with a large lightbulb-shaped head, a slit for a mouth, no nose or ears, but with very large black eyes. The arms and hands, which were longer and spindlier than those of a correctly proportioned human child, were very thin, and the hands had only four fingers. Corso said he was chilled by the sight of the creature, not because it looked especially gruesome, but because it looked vaguely human even though he knew, as he later said, "it was not of this world."

Black Mac Magruder Sees the Alien at Wright Field

From Fort Riley the shipment went to Wright Field. Authors Tom Cary, Don Schmidt, and Stanton Friedman all agree that Wright Field would have been the initial place where strange or exotic material would have been taken. Wright was the home of the Air Materiel Command led by General Nathan Twining, the air force officer who received Tesla's notes on antigravity and who was deep inside the loop of the news of the Roswell crash. At Wright Field the initial analysis of the Roswell material began, including biological testing on the living alien. At Wright Field as well, the initial army air force and then air force—because the services separated as of August 1947—created study groups to determine the issues supporting policy about the nature of this crash at Roswell and whether it posed a threat to national security. This policy became formulated for recommendation up the chain of command to the head of the air force, ultimately reaching President Truman. To that end, the air force asked the National Air War College class of 1948 to visit Wright Field for a purpose not disclosed to them at first but pertinent to the military.

One member of that class was Lieutenant Colonel Magruder, a hero at the battle of Okinawa. World War II veteran Magruder, after years of silence, finally described to his children what he saw on that day at Wright Field, the day when he saw the extraterrestrial, an experience that affected him so deeply he remembered it vividly even on his deathbed. He said that after seeing some of the Roswell crash debris, he was led into a room where he could view a strange figure behind glass. The figure had long, thin arms; a thin neck; and an oversized head. It was more pinkish than gray and had larger eyes than normal; very small, almost nonexistent ears; and a slit for a mouth. The creature, because it was clearly alive, moved in a wavelike motion with its long arms hanging disproportionately low. Magruder referred to the creature as "Squiggly." Squiggly, he said, was not a human being even though he looked remarkably close to one. It communicated with Magruder, informing him that he was alive, not from this world, and that those around him were experimenting on him. They were conducting tests on him that were going to kill him. Magruder, who would four years later be one of the advisors at the Pentagon during the July 1952 invasion over Washington, D.C., said that he believed the entity he saw, the Gray, was one of God's creatures and that what the air force was doing to him was a crime.

ALERT

On one of the nights of the flying saucer invasions over Washington, D.C., according to Magruder's son, a black military-style limo pulled up to the Magruder home, picked up his father, and took him away to a secret location. Magruder eventually told his children that he had been taken to the Pentagon to listen to the radio transmissions between the interceptor pilots and flight control as they tried to get radar locks on the flying saucers.

Magruder was visited at least every year by government agents in dark suits who questioned him about the events, reminded him of his secrecy oath, and asked him whether and to whom he might have disclosed the secret information. Toward the end of his life, Magruder told the men in suits never to speak to him or contact him again. He was a marine, he said, and marines follow orders. When a marine makes a promise, the marine keeps that promise, and to keep questioning him was an insult not just to him but to the entire corps.

The Hills' ETs

In 1962, Betty and Barney Hill described their experience with entities they called the Grays to their psychiatrist, Dr. Benjamin Simon. Their descriptions, which could not have been influenced by any of the Roswell witnesses because none of them ever went public at that time, comported with the prior descriptions. They described the creatures that accosted them on the road and dragged them to the clearing in the woods as small humanoid, but nonhuman, creatures who seemed to work for other strange creatures on the craft where they were taken. In the years after her story came out, Betty Hill became a featured guest on many television talk shows, particularly in the Northeast. She often brought with her a model of the head of the alien to show the television audience what it looked like. Skeptics said that because either Barney or Betty had seen an episode of *Outer Limits*, featuring a similar-looking alien head, that this image had influenced one of them who then influenced the other. But Betty adamantly maintained this was not the case and that she had seen the Grays on the road in front of their car on the night they said they were abducted.

The small Grays have been described both by abductees and contactees as workers. Philip Corso described the small Gray from the Roswell crash as an android or biological robot. He said it had no digestive system whatsoever and was connected electronically to the navigation controls of the spacecraft. Those who described the small Grays at work also described larger Grays, literally called "Large Grays," who seemed to be their supervisors. These larger creatures looked just like the smaller ones, except that they are approximately six feet tall and operate as if they're not bees in a hive.

The Nordics

In numerous interviews, Travis Walton described two types of creatures that beamed him aboard. He said that when he was lying on a type of hospital bed, those who attended to him were small Grays. However, the creatures he encountered in the navigation room looked exactly like tall human beings. They were wearing helmets, which partially disguised and concealed their faces, but in their general appearance, except for their eyes, which seemed a different color than human eyes, Walton said that these creatures were in most respects human. They didn't speak to him, only gestured, which he believed was a function of the headgear they were wearing. But they seemed benign, if not benevolent, and were the creatures that made sure he got off the ship and back home.

FACT

The Nordics showed benevolence toward Walton. Travis Walton said that the Nordic or humanoid creatures must have realized that Walton was not someone they wanted to keep onboard, because as soon as they encountered him, they strapped him down and then transported him back to Earth.

Others who have encountered similar creatures called them "Nordics" because of their tall stature, their human appearance, and their blond hair and blue eyes. Witnesses said that these extraterrestrials were indeed benevolent. The Nordics described future catastrophes on the planet and warned contactees, much like the ETs who appeared to the prophet Ezekiel, that unless human beings changed their ways, the planet was headed for destruction.

General George Washington's vision of an otherworldly entity at Valley Forge was, in some respects, a Nordic being because of her tall stature and her completely human appearance. Washington himself took her for an angelic spirit because she was robed in white, but her ability to prophesy and her overall benevolent demeanor has led some UFO historians to suggest that Washington had encountered a Nordic. This is in contrast to the orb in the forest that he saw and the green-suited figures who surrounded it. They were under five feet tall—Washington himself was six feet—and might have seemed more like Grays who served the Nordics.

The Reptoids (the Biblical Serpent)

Imagine millions of years ago, as Earth's climate began to change with the coming Ice Age and the many species of reptiles began to die off, that some

species of reptiles, in search of a more hospitable and sustaining environment, sought shelter under the earth. These reptilian species at first inhabited caves, but as the air grew colder, those who were fortunate enough to
survive did so by finding passages in caves that led them closer to the hot
center of the earth.

QUESTION

Why is Genesis so heavily populated by otherworldly beings?
If you look at the book of Genesis as a science fiction novel, for the
purposes of argument, you'll find a whole host of unearthly creatures
there. Not only does Genesis describe the actions of the Creator, but
it accounts for the spirit beings who serve the Creator, the Reptoids
who subvert the Creator's creation, and those who fell from the
heaven, or Nephilim, evil creatures who interbreed with the children of
Adam and Eve and who, eventually, must be destroyed in the Flood.
As science fiction, is Genesis describing what might be the invasion of
Earth by extraterrestrials?

Over the course of millions of years, the surviving reptiles gradually
developed a social structure, a rudimentary means of oral communication,
sapience, and, just perhaps, the ability to advance technologically. After
waiting beneath the earth for generations, eventually some of the species
ventured back toward the surface and might have found that the Ice Age
had passed, allowing them to repopulate the surface. Now imagine that after
the passage of another million years, these reptiles saw the appearance of
humans, a strange bipedal species that looked nothing like they had ever
encountered before. If you can imagine that these human beings had been
genetically manipulated to serve extraterrestrial overlords, for which they
had been rewarded with mastery over the earth, then imagine further that
the reptilian creatures felt threatened and sought to subvert the interlopers
they saw. If you can suspend everything you were taught, you have just witnessed another version of the serpent in the Garden of Eden story in the
opening books of Genesis.

Or in another scenario, perhaps there is a multiplicity of realities, planes
of reality on multiple universes. In the most perfect of physical realities,

these planes do not intersect. Timelines on one plane simply exist regardless of timelines on another plane. However, physics is not perfect, and planes do cross. When they intersect, particle interactions between them can open portals through which matter, maybe in the shape of life forms, can pass through. If there are spots on Earth where these portals are more likely to open than others, thereby allowing life forms to move from one plane to enter another, perhaps the reptilian beings inhabit a totally different reality and enter ours through portals.

Regardless of which scenario seems more attractive, witnesses around the world have said they have seen bipedal reptile creatures, seemingly able to communicate with each other, that are hostile to human beings. At least one researcher has suggested that the reptile beings, or Reptoids, are running a breeding program to create hybrid human/reptiles through a form of *ex vitro* fertilization. In this way, the argument runs, reptiles plan to reinhabit the earth using the hybrids as their servants. It is a bizarre scenario.

The Mantis Beings and Insectoids

Contactees have described insectlike beings resembling mantises or giant ants and have said they've seen these creatures aboard ships. Another story, hailing out of S4, the secret base near Rachel, Nevada, and Dulce, New Mexico, are stories of insect beings working with human beings on advanced biological projects. According to the lore of security details at both S4 and Dulce, guards have to be especially trained and hardened against the shock of seeing mantis beings or insectoids for the first time because the human system finds large insects repellant. As one story goes, a guard who had not been fully trained encountered a mantis being in an underground corridor at S4 and went into such a state of fear-driven shock that he died of a heart attack. Since then, only selectively trained security personnel are allowed anywhere near where the mantis beings are working.

Orbs or Light Beings

People who have seen orbs floating in the sky or even near them aren't sure about the nature of this phenomenon. And crop circle researchers and cattle mutilation investigators have entirely contradictory views about orbs. Are orbs small craft, inanimate mechanical devices used for surveillance, manifestations or projections of energy, or actual living beings? Where do orbs come from? Are they extraterrestrial, extradimensional, or a part of the life force of planet Earth? No one really knows. All there is to go on are a variety of witness descriptions that go all the way back to George Washington, who saw a greenish orb in the forest at Valley Forge where his troops were wintering while the British occupied Philadelphia.

Orbs and Foo Fighters

Foo fighters, the phenomena that Allied pilots observed during World War II, were certainly orb-like. These orbs displayed no overt hostility even though their intrusive nature and close approach was considered a hostile activity. They were neither friend nor foe, but an American B-29 bomber shot one down over the Pacific in 1945.

Detachable orbs were parts of triangular craft appearing over the Hudson Valley, New York, as well as Phoenix, Arizona. However, witnesses couldn't determine their nature except for watching them move from point to point on triangles.

Marley Woods Orbs

Orbs have been appearing at a UFO site in the Ozarks for almost seventy years. They not only pop up during the day and at night, but they seemingly interact with human observers. Researchers in the area have interviewed local residents who have been attacked by orbs. It's thought that the orbs attacked people perhaps for trespassing on land that the orbs dominate. Some were confronted by orbs while trying to drive them away from observing local children. In one chilling witness description, a mother reported that she saw an orb in front of her child while the child was playing, clearly frightening the child. The mother screamed at the orb to get away, at which point the orb turned and floated over to her, getting very close. That told researchers that, at least in this instance, the orb seemed not only to be intelligently controlled but was in full communication with the human beings in its proximity.

In another story from this Ozark community, an orb was seen heading into a stable where a horse was in a stall. When the horse's owner rushed into the stable after the orb left, he found the horse, in his words, "microwaved dead," apparently exploded from within. Limbs and organs were gruesomely splattered all over the walls of the stall. Was this an accident, or did the orb attack the horse with an energy burst?

ESSENTIAL

Researchers in this community have found that two people standing side by side were not able to see the same orb. When one person asked the other to stand in front of him, the orb appeared. This told the researchers that the orbs were somehow able to enter our reality through a transparent or translucent tunnel or portal, reinforcing the theory that orbs were not of this dimension but were able to enter it freely.

Indiana Orbs

In the American Midwest during the past decade, there have been many orb sightings, and individual witnesses have said that the orbs presented a dark presence. Indiana MUFON investigator Glenn Means said on *UFO Hunters* that he interviewed many individuals who told him that when orbs appeared, they felt a sinister mood come over them as if they were in the presence of another life form whose intentions were not at all neutral.

ALERT

Many psychics have said that when they've encountered orbs they're filled with an ominous sense of alarm, because the orbs they see are not benevolent. Attempts to communicate with them have proved unsuccessful because they are either remotely controlled or incapable of doing anything more than observing or releasing energy.

The questions linger about orbs. Are they natural phenomena, energy manifestations, craft, or simply light beings? You can't dismiss them as purely natural phenomena because of so many eyewitness encounters with them and what seems to be their ability to communicate in some way with human beings. For the time being, at least, they've been classified by many contactees as extraterrestrial life forms, but that may well change if it turns out they coinhabit the planet with humans.

Extraterrestrials on Planet Earth

There is an entire area of UFO investigation into the possibility that human beings are not the only sapient life form on the planet. Dolphins have exhibited the kinds of group behavior and benevolent actions, individually and collectively, that bespeak of not only an advanced sense of self but a sense that they can differentiate between a rudimentary right and wrong. While all animals are protective of their young to some extent, dolphins have shown through pod behavior that they're protective of other species as well, particularly of humans in trouble in the water or threatened by sharks.

Beyond humans' mammalian relatives, however, there is a theory that hundreds of thousands or even millions of years ago, Earth was seeded by an extraterrestrial population. Records of this seeding may exist in religious texts, folklore, the oral histories of ancient societies, or even ideographs or hieroglyphics carved into ancient monuments. Great megaliths themselves may be records of the work of ancient extraterrestrial builders assembling places for their workers to measure stars and agricultural seasons.

Ancient Aliens Might Still Be Among Us

If extraterrestrials came to Earth as ancient aliens, one line of reasoning goes, why would they have ever left? Perhaps hidden among humans are aliens who look like humans or who can camouflage themselves just enough to pass for human but whose abilities surpass ours. Contactees from the 1950s and early 1960s like Frank Stranges, Howard Menger, and George Adamski suggest this very thing. They pointed out that extraterrestrials like Valiant Thor, who allegedly met Vice President Richard Nixon, simply walked in and out of the Pentagon completely undetected. Photos of Valiant Thor show that he looked like any 1950s character from a television commercial or soap opera. Yet, according to author Frank Stranges (*Stranger at the Pentagon*), Val Thor, as he called him, was from the planet Venus.

Howard Menger, too, wrote of aliens who walked among us, visitors who contacted him to foretell of events that would happen. Other contactees have also revealed to those who follow them that some extraterrestrials have worked themselves into positions of power and inserted themselves behind public figures. In this way they have been able to manipulate events on Earth for their own purposes and, hopefully, for the benefit of humans.

A Plurality of Species

If there is one extraterrestrial species on planet Earth, there might be others. Is it conceivable that different extraterrestrial species have embedded themselves in different countries, almost like an extraterrestrial intelligence agency? They may be here to keep planet-extinction wars from taking place. They might be making sure that nuclear weapons don't go off accidentally, interfering with the very things that might cause a planetwide devastation, and leveling the playing field among nations. If so, what is the intent of all this. Why the interest, or why would any extraterrestrial species even care about Earth? This raises the larger questions about human origins, evolution, and, assuming for the sake of argument that humans are not a cosmic accident, what the purpose of our existence may be.

Are Humans the Extraterrestrials?

In analyses of ancient meteorites that fell to Antarctica from Mars, scientists discovered proteins that are the building blocks of life. These meteorites predate life on Earth but indicate that life existed on Mars when the climate was wetter and warmer. The discovery also raises the strong possibility that life here originated from Mars, thus making humans, ultimately, Martians. It also raises the possibility that because other meteorites, not from Mars, carried bacteria to Earth, the bacteria began to colonize in the primordial soup of Earth's nascent oceans. Earth itself could be a true melting pot of life forms from other planets in the galaxy or even the universe.

Are religious texts indicators of humans' off-planet origins? Genesis 6:1–4 says that the first humans were planted here by their Creator, but already here were the Nephilim, literally "the fallen" or "those who have fallen from the sky." Researchers in the area of ancient aliens suggest that the Nephilim, whose children mated with the children of Adam and Eve, the first humans, were either a native species who landed here first and populated the planet before humans arrived or were another alien species who came here after Adam and Eve. The mingling of the two species hybridized human beings, which was why, in the story of the Flood, Noah was saved because he was 100 percent human, completely pure of Nephilim DNA.

Niburu

Author and scholar of ancient civilizations, the late Zecharia Sitchin (*The Twelfth Planet*), has suggested that humanity was a worker race created by a race of extraterrestrials called the Annunaki. The name also means "those who came down from the stars," and in traditional histories of Sumer and Babylonia, the Annunaki were deities or children of deities. However, Sitchin suggests that the Annunaki were actually a race of extraterrestrials who arrived here to mine the planet's plentiful natural resources. But they were too few in number or maybe just downright lazy, and, with their advanced technology, they seeded existing species with just enough of their DNA to grow a new species called humanity.

Humans were created to harvest the planet, obey the rules set down by the Annunaki (their overlords), and in return enjoy a bountiful existence. However, because a native sapient species, the Reptoids, attempted to subvert and give humans the ability to challenge the authority of their overlords, the Annunaki relegated them to crawl and be crushed under the heels of human beings, and banished humans from paradise to work by the sweat of their collective brow and bear children with extreme pain. This was how Sitchin and other ancient alien researchers interpreted the biblical stories of creation.

There is another theory, however, one promulgated by the late Nobel Prize winner Sir Francis Crick, discoverer of DNA, who suggested that life may have been brought here deliberately, seeded here by an advanced extraterrestrial civilization colonizing hospitable planets in the universe. What better way to establish remote colonies of your own civilization than to seed them with DNA so as to guarantee the survival of your race? You don't even need manned space flight to do so, especially if you have discovered that asteroids or meteors traveling through space can host dormant bacteria carrying your DNA. Simply infect these celestial nomads with your own bacteria by impacting them with robot spacecraft (a technology NASA is already developing) and let them travel. If that was the case five billion years ago, Earth may be a colony of another highly advanced or extinct human species.

ESSENTIAL

Panspermia, both accidental and directed, also known as the theory of exogenesis, is the hypothesis that life began off planet Earth and came here via meteorites during the early bombardment around four billion years ago. Accidental exogenesis presupposes the existence of life forms called extremophiles, life that can exist in the extreme conditions of outer space. Scientists have found evidence that some bacteria can certainly exist in outer space on comets or asteroids. These bacteria colonized here after falling into the hospitable protein-rich environment of Earth's oceans and formed the primordial soup out of which primitive organic life evolved.

Human Alien Hybrids

A theory promulgated by many UFO researchers, especially those dealing with individuals who say they've been abducted by aliens, is the theory of hybridization. Based on testimony delivered under regression hypnosis or even conscious memory, some self-described abductees describe medical procedures in which their egg or sperm cells are extracted during their time onboard the alien spacecraft. At later dates, when they say they've been returned to the craft, they remember being shown organisms and told that these human-looking creatures, with some strange facial and other physiological features, are their offspring. The late Barney Hill, in particular, described a procedure in which sperm was extracted from him. He developed physical symptoms around his genital area, which made him very nervous. Under hypnosis, he described a procedure in which his abductors placed a suction device over his genital area and extracted semen from him.

Still other researchers have described a hybridization process in which alien hybrids are used to breed with humans to create successive generations of hybrids that look human but have alien DNA. This process,

182

reminiscent of breeding generations of species that contain just the right genetic material, a version of eugenics, might well be a way for an alien species of exoplanetary civilizations to colonize Earth. They do it not by physical invasion, as in *War of the Worlds*, but by an invasion of alien DNA, implanting their seed genetically through successive generations of inter-breeding of the species until their species has taken hold. This raises the question that if there are aliens among us, are we the aliens or have the aliens been visiting us for generations in order to hybridize us into a ver-sion of their own species? If the alien hybrid theorists are correct, then successive generations of human children displaying increasing enhanced mental, telepathic, and athletic abilities might not be the results of normal evolution but enhanced evolution spurred by an extraterrestrial eugenics program.

CHAPTER 13

Crop Circles

Crop circles—strange, highly organized, and ornate geometrical designs imposed upon a grain field—have been perplexing UFO researchers as well as New Agers and spiritualists for over forty years. They have turned up in grain fields all over the world. They have been hoaxed, commercialized by farmers and landowners, and subjected to scientific testing. They are an important part of the UFO subculture because if found to be a true anomaly, they speak to a strange presence. Some groups that congregate around new crop circles each season act like worshippers, looking for a message in them. Many try to interpret them by calculating the mathematics of the designs to see what message an other-worldly entity might be sending. There's no denying, however, that some of the crop circles are truly beautiful and attract adherents from all parts of the UFO and New Age communities.

The Phenomenon

A crop circle is a large pattern or design imposed upon a field of grain such as wheat or barley. The stalks of grain are flattened in such a way that the direction of the flattening creates the pattern. Some of the designs are extremely intricate and detailed and have, according to some of the scientists and mathematicians who have analyzed them, mathematical relationships among the different points of the design. A crop circle is actually a formation with different subformations contained within the main pattern. The formation does not destroy the flattened grain or break the stalks; it presses them into the ground as if a hairbrush or comb had organized them into place.

Crop circles, a phenomenon that has been around for over forty years, were first recorded in the late 1960s and early 1970s in at least twenty-five different countries around the world. Crop circle research is one of the most exciting areas of UFO research and experience because, if real, they might well represent real physical trace evidence of an otherworldly presence. Crop circles have been photographed, debunked, hoaxed, visited by spiritualists, and examined by biologists, mineralogists, and chemists for decades. Yet despite all this scrutiny, there is still debate over whether these impressions in grain fields are hoaxes perpetrated upon gullible UFO true believers or actual phenomena imposed by some force of energy, whether extraterrestrial or spiritual or both, for reasons not fully understood or appreciated by human beings.

ALERT

Visitors to crop circle sites say they have seen orbs hovering over fields, and after the orbs have disappeared the crop circles appeared. Groups of crop circle enthusiasts have also claimed the ability to imagine a complex design, focus on that design collectively and intensely, and watch that design imposed on a field of grain by one or more orbs.

The man-made explanation for crop circles notwithstanding, there are crop circle researchers who point to documented crop circles before hoaxers, like the Englishmen Doug Chorley and Dave Bower, came forward to announce their crop circle making. Crop circle researchers also point to the existence of crop circles in countries where Chorley and Bower or other hoaxers have never been. Accordingly, they argue, some crop circles might have been hoaxed, but the majority of them are real.

Hoaxing Crop Circles

In 1991, Englishmen Dave Bower and Doug Chorley announced publicly that since 1978 they had been making crop circles in grain fields using improvised plank shoes or by stomping down grain in circular patterns. To the initial dismay of crop circle researchers and enthusiasts, Doug and Dave—as they came to be known by UFO researchers and skeptics alike—demonstrated how in an hour they were able to stamp out a design in a grain field. Had crop circles only been a UK phenomenon and had crop circles not been discovered in fields prior to 1978, the controversy might have ended right there. But despite Doug and Dave's assertions and the chortling of skeptics, crop circles turned up in Canada, the United States, and all over Europe. Elaborate crop circles turned up in Switzerland, too, formations that were not claimed by any pranksters.

Subsequent to Doug and Dave, who have since died, and their demonstration of how to create crop circle formations, pranksters around the world, some seeking to hoax the media and lure UFO enthusiasts into believing that man-made formations were extraterrestrial, began stamping out formations, some far more elaborate than others, in fields in the United Kingdom and in eastern Europe. In Hungary, for example, two crop circle pranksters, students involved in a project, were prosecuted and fined for destroying a field. In the United Kingdom, another prankster was found guilty of trespassing and destruction of property.

These hoaxes are in stark contrasts to experiments in projected consciousness at sites where visitors gathered and collectively imagined the same design. By concentrating on that design, they said, they were able to control balls of plasma energy to impose that design on the subject field. There was no stomping down any grain, but simply the imposition of a vision upon the field. Does this constitute a hoax, a man-made crop circle, or the communication of human beings with a higher energy source manifesting itself as a ball of plasma energy?

The Business of Crop Circles

The crop circle craze, even after Doug and Dave, became so intense in the mid-1990s through 2000 that farmers in whose fields these formations appeared opened the fields to tourists and experiencers, charging admission fees for the privilege. Some businesses contracted with farmers to use their fields for crop circle creation, while crop circles that seemed to have no man-made origin became the subjects of advertisements and art and design. In the years since crop circles became a worldwide phenomenon, a robust debate has raged between proponents and opponents of their otherworldly origin.

The Science of Crop Circles

Proponents of the otherworldly reality of crop circles are adamant that Doug and Dave, though self-acknowledged hoaxers, were actually put up to the task. It's thought that government-affiliated disinformation specialists were behind the hoaxers, because the reality of crop circles was becoming more apparent and reaching more people year after year. Because so many people were traveling to crop circle locations and bringing serious scientific investigation and analysis to the phenomena, governments, fearing that a real disclosure might break through, engaged Doug and Dave through third-party cut-outs to step forward and announce their hoaxes. However, crop circles have continued to appear subsequent to Doug and Dave's passing, and real scientists have evaluated the soil and grain shafts inside the crop formations with some startling results.

FACT

As one member of the U.S. clandestine services once suggested, cloak and dagger is not always James Bond. Most undercover operations are no more complicated than an agreement between a government or military operative under an assumed name who contacts an individual or individuals to perform certain acts and take responsibility for them. Usually, this involves making the target look like a fool so as to undermine the target's credibility. In the case of Doug and Dave, it was to undermine the otherworldly beliefs of UFO researchers who were honing in on crop circles as examples of a UFO presence.

The Mathematics and Geometry of Crop Formation Designs

The elements of the most visually compelling crop circle designs are not randomly arranged. Hoaxers' designs, while apparently quite intricate in some cases, do not have the disturbingly precise geometric and mathematical relationships that "real" crop circles display upon analysis. For example, in an article in *Science News*, Professor Gerald Hawkins of Boston University demonstrated that shapes in crop circles are scaled mathematically to one another so that outer and inner circles are exactly proportionate to one another. This type of exactness and precision is not found in nature. When measured, these mathematical relationships defy the design relationships in hoaxed circles, especially the demonstrations where formations were stamped out in an hour or less. Designs are designs, but relationships between elements of the designs require far more precise measurement, especially since once the grain is tramped down it can't be raised again for a do-over.

In other mathematical examples, although separated across the formation, measurements of triangles and circles showed that one element could fit precisely inside another one if the design was moved over, so as to be multidimensional. It was as if the design was a static representation of something that was multidimensional. Again, eyeballing that type of precision is next to impossible for amateur stompers. Hawkins also noted that there were precise numerical ratios among the shapes in the designs, including their circumferences, diameters, and lengths of the sides of a triangle. This further suggests that it would be beyond the ability of hoaxers to have created these ratios by sight. And because the formations are so large, absent a precise layout on graph paper, which Doug and Dave did not even attempt, there would be no way to scale these ratios among design components to the size required. In many cases, the designs make no sense unless observed from the air, which is why many crop circle researchers came to believe early on that these were markers or messages for spacecraft.

Physical Trace Evidence Anomalies in the Crop Circle Grain Shafts

Perhaps some of the most important scientific work on crop circles was performed by BLT Research Team and written up by W. C. Levengood in

1994 ("Anatomical Anomalies in Crop Formation Plants," *Physiologia Plantarum*). Professor Levengood states categorically that the anatomical alterations in the actual structure of the plants in crop formations are unique. They differ substantially from the structure of crushed and randomly flattened shafts in hoaxed formations. His analysis was prepared by comparing the physical trace evidence of the structure of plants inside of formations with Levengood's control sample, those outside of formations. He found specifically that there were "structured and cellular alterations" in plants in the formation, which were manifested, he wrote, in transformations to the plant nodes in the form of swelling and changes to the outer skin of the plant. There were also changes in the way the plant seed germinated. On a microscopic level, there were changes to the plants' cells themselves. Levengood theorized that the effects on plants in the crop formation resulted from their being exposed to a heat-based, high-energy plasma in concentrated form.

FACT

New York businessman John Burke, researcher William Levengood, and researcher Nancy Talbot created BLT Research Team, the paramount scientific research organization in crop circles, UFO trace evidence, and other types of paranormal events. Their work on such cases as Delphos, Kansas; Bucks County, Pennsylvania; and the Betty Hill dress have helped provide scientific background for events that might otherwise be purely anecdotal.

There were also higher levels of magnetite inside the crop formation. The magnetic field was such that birds tended to fly around the crop formation rather than fly directly over it. It has not been determined if this was due to the high levels of magnetite in the plant shafts or not. It is important to note, however, that none of these transformations to the plants occurred in the hoaxed crop formations either by Doug and Dave or by others.

The Physics of Crop Circles

In his 1998 article "The Physics of Crop Circles," BLT researcher John Burke wrote that the biological evidence of plant alteration within the formation was truly consistent with heavy exposure to plasma. Plasma, he wrote, is "electrified air," which, when passing through a magnetic field, such as Earth's, swirls magnetized material into a spiral. You can see this by running magnets over iron filings. Further, when the spiraling occurs, there is an emission of microwaves. The effects on the plants in the field, the swelling of the flattened shafts, the explosive nature of the plant nodes, and the altered cellular structure are also consistent with exposure to microwaves.

Burke reasons that because plasma transmission is a common feature of Earth's ionosphere and can travel 90 percent of the distance to the planet's surface in the form of lightning, a negative charge on the planet's surface might cause it to travel the remaining 10 percent to the ground. He examined the areas in England and the United States where crop formations occur. Burke found that in the United Kingdom, the substrata in that part of southern England was a chalk-based aquifer in which water traveling through the calcium carbonate was stripped of one of its electrons to give it a negative charge, thus attracting the lightning. In the United States, the aquifers were limestone, also creating a negative charge as water flowed through them, also attracting plasma.

Accounting for the shapes, however, is not as straightforward, Burke wrote, until one realizes that the most common shape inside the crop circle formation is a spiral. A spiral is the most common shape in a plasma-generated (microwaved) field. The other shapes, such as straight lines, rectangles, and triangles, he reasoned, could also be accounted for by understanding that plasma behaves like an "excited fluid." An excited fluid creates many dynamic shapes, including geometric patterns with straight lines.

QUESTION

Who's making the crop circles?
If Doug and Dave can't account for every crop circle, and if John Burke's plasma instrumentality theory is correct, who's controlling the plasma? British crop circle researchers conducted a focused-conscious experiment in which they imposed a design upon a field. Other witnesses have observed balls of light, orbs of plasma energy, hovering over crop circle fields, and still others have observed UFOs. Could it be that otherworldly entities can manipulate and focus plasma energy the way a group of British researchers did so as to create designs? If so, what about the hidden codes embedded in the geometric shapes?

UFO researchers using this type of science-based approach to the formation of crop circles have also reasoned that the shapes themselves, shapes composed of spiral flattened grains, may have been formed into the odd geometric shapes with precise mathematical relationships among them by an intervening force. In other words, the plasma attraction to the calcium carbonate aquifer in areas of crop formations is not a cause, in their opinion, but an instrumentality, a natural force acted upon by an external force, much like an artist may use a piece of charcoal for a sketch. There is nothing mystical about the mark that charcoal leaves on paper. The mystical element is the actual sketch. So it might be that crop circles are created by formation with some external element manipulating or shaping the direction of the plasma impact on the surface of the ground so as to create the shapes in the grain.

Eyewitness Testimony

Eyewitnesses and experiencers have said that they have been able, in collective focus sessions, to imagine designs that have then been imposed upon the grain field. Either some intelligent force, they suspect, picks up the collective telepathic signal and translates it into a crop formation design, or perhaps the human collective itself is the base force at work. Whatever the mental energy is—and the human brain transmits electrical energy—it manifests itself as a directional force to the balls of plasma, the orbs, that impose the design upon the field of grain.

Of course, there is always the extraterrestrial or interdimensional explanation. According to this explanation, there are otherworldly forces on the planet, forces that interact with human beings but manifest themselves in the form of electrified air or plasma. They are able to shape themselves into balls, like the foo fighters from World War II or balls of light in the Midwest, and are attracted to human energy. The greater the human energy, the greater the attraction. Therefore, UFO researchers assert, it may be that the strange electrical and magnetic reactions humans and their electrified objects have to plasma balls are themselves instruments of otherworldly creatures. These relationships could be at least a collective element in the entire range of seemingly anomalous events—events that occur when humans experience the appearances of balls of light. In other words, these truly are alien encounters, but the aliens themselves use the instrument of plasma balls to facilitate their connection with humans and Earth.

ALERT

Just because you've located a crop circle doesn't mean that the land is yours to enter. Most crop circles are on private property, sometimes property on which the owner is raising livestock as well as grain for that livestock. This means that entering someone else's land, even for the benevolent purpose of photographing a crop circle, is still trespassing under the law of almost every state in the United States. Therefore, always get permission from the landowner or someone authorized to give permission before entering the land. It will save a visit from the local sheriff and the hostility of the landowner.

Where to Find Crop Circles

Crop circles are part of the yearly landscape in the United Kingdom as well as in the grain fields in Canada. But they are also found in the Netherlands and in grain-producing eastern European countries as well as in the United States. For a quick tour of historic as well as current crop circles, you can visit *www.cropcirclesecrets.org/links.html*, which will also put you in touch with crop circle research organizations around the world.

CHAPTER 14

Cattle Mutilations

Cattle mutilation is one of the most misunderstood aspects of the entire UFO field. There is a lot of argument over what constitutes a mutilated cow and why there would be such a thing in the first place. The standard description of a mutilated cow is that a farmer or rancher discovers the animal lying on its side, dead, with its eyes, udders, or genitals removed; its rectum cored out; tongue and soft tissue removed; and body completely drained of blood. These wounds, however, are made with surgical precision so delicate that to blame it on predatory animals, such as coyotes or birds, makes no sense. Finally, not only is the downed cow drained of blood, but predators give the dead cow a wide berth. Flies won't even perch on a mutilated cow. It is as if there is a chemical emanating off from the animal that keeps scavengers away.

The Crime Scene and Locations

The nature of the cattle carcass notwithstanding, one of the strangest aspects of a cattle mutilation crime scene is that there is no evidence of any external presence in the form of footprints or tracks. Mutilated cattle have been discovered in mud, snow, and soft dirt. If there had been any human causality evident, one would have seen footprints leading up to the downed animal. Farmers and ranchers who have discovered their animals mutilated often say that they arrive on the scene in the morning and that the cow in question was alive the evening before. In the absence of pouring rain or fresh snow, where are the footprints?

ALERT

If you have the opportunity to visit a cattle mutilation site to inspect the downed animal, remember, don't touch the carcass with your bare hands. Police and veterinarians don't know what method the perpetrators in a cattle mutilation case used to knock over the animal. If it is some powerful chemical, strong enough to keep scavengers away, it might be strong enough to harm human beings in high concentrations.

The situation is even stranger when the mutilated cow turns up in another pasture, away from the rest of the herd. Sometimes they're found on the other side of a fence, yet there are no tracks. In one particular case in Colorado, a rancher accounted for the entire herd the night before it began to snow. The next morning, he discovered a cow on the other side of a high fence. Not only were there no human footprints, but there were no hoof prints. The cow didn't walk to the location where it died because it would have left tracks. The cow couldn't have climbed over the barbed wire fence, and there were no tractor tread marks or tire tracks, meaning that there was no presence of any apparatus. Stranger still, there was only one impression of the cow in the snow. Had the cow staggered before it fell, been dragged, or even bounced as if it had been dropped from a height, there would have been some indication of it in the snow. But there wasn't. The only impression of the cow's carcass was directly under the cow, and it was an exact fit. How did the cow get there?

Even if the cow in question had been knocked over by human beings, it would have moved in the snow. The lack of movement could have only meant that either the cow was motionless from some drug, like ketamine, when it was tipped over, or the cow was dead before it hit the ground. Yet the veterinarian's necropsy could not find any unnatural cause of death. In fact, it could not find any cause of death. There were no trace chemicals, no virus infection, no poison, and no external force. The rancher himself explained that he could always tell a sick cow from the way she walked and hung back from the herd. This cow was not sick before she died. It was a mystery.

FACT

If there is a rule that nothing disappears or appears without a trace, then cattle mutilations certainly defy that rule. For every death, there is a cause of death. In cattle mutilations, however, the cause of death is either so subtle that veterinarians and toxicologists can't find it, or the cause of death is alien to human science, which doesn't have the tools to ascertain what it might be.

Even though the fresh snow on the ground added an extra element of mystery to the crime scene, this scene was typical. An owner discovers his animal motionless and all alone in the field, various organs excised, drained of blood, and shunned by any predators. The veterinarian cannot discover a cause of death, and the sheriff and any other investigating state officials are completely flummoxed. Perhaps, in some of these cases, a court will blame the death on teenagers or some ritual group or witches, but the crime scene contains none of the signs of ritualistic theater. There are no candles, no implements, no signs such as the pentangle or pentagram inscribed on the ground or on the cow's carcass. Nor are there any footprints on the ground. There is simply no cause of death or any evidence of a human presence around the animal.

The Forensics

Over the years, county, state, and federal authorities, including the FBI, have performed crime scene analysis and medical investigations into the causes of death. The patterns have been largely consistent from mutilation scene to mutilation scene, and they include:

- A lack of any footprints or tracks around the animal. It appears to have been dumped, sometimes from a height, in the area where it is found.
- Some of the animals have broken bones, fractures consistent with the animal's having been dropped from a height.
- There is an impression or crater under the animal that precisely conforms to the shape of the animal.
- Excision of the soft tissue including the eye, udder, tongue, lips, and anus. These excisions are performed surgically with a cutting tool that leaves no bruising around the wound. The tongue has been removed from deep in the throat.
- No coagulation of blood around the wounds so as to cause scabbing or bruising. This means that the animal was already dead when the excisions were made because the blood had stopped flowing.
- Many of the animals are often completely exsanguinated, or drained of blood.
- Lack of any predatory indications on the animal. No tooth marks from coyotes or foxes, no signs of scavenging by birds, no insect deposits on the animal.
- Avoidance of the carcass by other animals, including predators and scavengers, who avoid the carcass completely.

Witnesses sometimes report seeing aerial lights in the area prior to the discovery of a mutilated animal. At least one sheriff has reported having witnessed the presence of glowing orbs over a field the night before a mutilated animal was discovered there. And other cattle in the area seem skittish around bright, whirling, and colored lights.

In these cases, there is a complete lack of any evidence of ritualistic observances around the animal. No candles, implements of torture or cutting, designs or signs, or any evidence of human presence have been found.

Laboratory studies were unable to pinpoint a cause of death. Where there were blood samples taken, there were sometimes unknown substances in the blood that seemed to have been introduced after the animal had died.

ALERT

A milk- and calf-producing cow can be worth over $20,000 to a rancher, which is why, especially for a small ranch or dairy farm, the loss of a single cow can be devastating. Imagine a rancher who has lost over twenty cows from his small herd. It's not only a criminal act to kill another's cow, it's an economic crime as well.

In some cases, organs, such as the heart and the liver, were reported missing from the animal. In other cases, however, the organs were present but had been reduced to a white, mushy pulp. No explanation was found for the condition of these organs. In some cases of freshly discovered mutilated cattle, there was no blood left in the system, while in other cases, veterinarians said that the blood had pooled at the underside of the animal and dried.

Many of the mutilated animals belonged to the same herd, meaning that whatever was responsible was seeking animals of the same genetic pattern. Also, in some cases, the cows were pregnant and the calves had been surgically removed from the womb. In all cases, however, the telltale signs of a mutilation were present: the removal of the tongue and soft tissue from the mouth, the coring of the rectum, the removal of the eyes, and the removal of the sexual organs.

The Progression of the Cases

The first officially recorded animal mutilation was in 1967 in Colorado. The victim was a horse named Lady. However, cattle mutilations go back to the late nineteenth century in England and the 1960s in Pennsylvania. By the late 1980s, cattle mutilation reports had spread from Colorado to New Mexico, Texas, and to Montana and the Dakotas.

From the first case of Lady to cases breaking out across the American West's cattle country, the reports of farmers and ranchers have been the same. A cow that seemed fine one day turns up on its side the following day without any indication of a human or mechanical presence and with its soft tissue removed. Reports of strange lights in the sky or clandestine helicopters abound, but there is no official explanation, despite a number of official investigations.

The FBI, for example, said that while some of the mutilations might have had human causes or have been copycat crimes, others simply provided no evidence whatsoever as to the cause. The FBI concluded that the cattle probably died from natural causes even though the nature of those causes was not determined in the necropsy.

An investigator for the U.S. Forest Service concluded, upon a review of the Lady case, that one could speculate that a high level of radiation near the death scene might have been responsible for the horse's death, but he could not be definitive. He said Lady's death was one of the "strangest cases" he had ever investigated.

FACT

As discovered on *UFO Hunters*, mutilated carcasses turn up in pastures almost every month in places like Colorado, Wyoming, and New Mexico. Police now take them as routine, log them, and the rancher must turn to his insurance company for any relief.

Cases progressed from Colorado to the Dakotas to New Mexico, especially in the area around the Archuleta Mesa in Dulce, New Mexico, sparking all sorts of rumors about alien/human collaboration into a hybridization of the species or the creation of an entirely new species. However, no definitive evidence beyond speculation or uncorroborated anecdotal testimony has emerged. This has sparked many theories about the causes of cattle mutilation and who might be behind it.

The Theories

The many theories behind cattle mutilations range all the way from simple natural causes and predators (misdiagnosed by investigators) to ritual slaughter by covens or Satanic worshippers to juvenile crimes such as cow tipping. Others believe that extraterrestrials are harvesting organs for their own purposes, or that government agencies and pharmaceutical companies are involved. All of these theories have their proponents and opponents, but, as in many other areas of UFO-related cases, there is some science underpinning the theories.

Natural Causes and Predators

Some veterinarians have argued that cows have died from various virus infections, even though they look normal to the nonmedical eye. They fall ill and collapse, and predators such as birds climb inside the eyes and eat them out. Other predators, specifically coyotes, crawl up inside the rectum, core it out by leaving the hide and hard tissue, and consume the soft tissue. All the rancher sees is the remains of the cow after rigor mortis sets in and the blood has settled into the ground. However, ranchers and farm owners dispute this vigorously, saying that after raising cattle for generations on family-owned farms, cattlemen know when an animal is sick. They also know how predators attack a dead cow because they see it more often than they want to and know the trails that predatory animals leave. Moreover, they argue, when predators attack a carcass, they leave tracks and paw prints. Mutilated cattle have no tracks or prints around them, thus eliminating the natural causes and predator theory.

Cult Activity and Ritual Slaughter

The theory that groups of neo-Satanic worshipping cults enter onto a farmer's land to perform rituals over animals they slay was initially a popular law-enforcement theory during the New Age movement in the 1970s. As attractive as this theory was, it was unsustainable on the basis of evidence because cows simply don't walk up to strangers in a field at night and wait to be slaughtered. Cows run away from strangers. It takes more than a random visitor to inject a cow with a chemical like ketamine to knock it over. Besides, ketamine will leave traces in the tissues during a necropsy.

Even more important for crime scene investigators, however, was the lack of any ritualistic trappings at the scene. Neo-Satanic worshippers are theatrical and often leave evidence to show that they have marked a territory. One would find candle drippings, marks of cutting tools, chains or other binding implements, and, above all, the actual signs of a ritual presence such as the pentangle or pentagram along with significant numbers, such as 666. Absent these markings, there would be no point in conducting a ritual slaughter. Therefore, specialists in ritual-related crime scene investigation quickly eliminated ritual slaughter as one of the causes of cattle mutilation.

FACT

Law enforcement agencies from the FBI to the local sheriff love the ritual slaughter theory because it allow them to close the books on a case without the messy details of having to find a perpetrator to charge with the crime. With ritual slaughter as a cause, investigators can pull together disparate facts into a conventional theory, look for Satanic groups in the area, and conduct routine questioning. If there are no suspects, they can wash their hands of the case.

Cow Tipping

As a prank, groups of teenagers have been known to enter onto a farmer's land for the purpose of knocking over a cow and then leaving. The point is not to hurt the animal or deprive the farmer of a living but to get in and get out quickly. These types of pranksters leave all kinds of trails or footprints, often make more noise than they want to, and are usually identified and quickly apprehended by law enforcement. They are not and do not have the skills or wherewithal to be cattle mutilators and are not out to kill any animals.

Extraterrestrials

This is a popular theory that still has many adherents. Believers cite the lack of any footprints or tracks around the animal, the precision of the cutting and removal of organs—as if an advanced surgical device was used that is beyond human technology—the stealth and suddenness of the attacks, and eyewitness reports of strange lights or orbs hovering over a cow pasture at the time a mutilated cow is discovered. The rationale behind the extraterrestrial theory is that the ETs, for their own purposes, are harvesting bovine organs for stem cell purposes or for developing serum to culture hybridized human sperm and egg cells. Absent an abducted mother, bovine serum, used in current *in vitro* fertilization procedures, is ideal for such culturing and would be a natural medium for ETs to use, especially if they had artificial wombs for gestation purposes.

Government, the Military, and Pharmaceutical Companies

One of the more popular theories, also backed up by some witness testimony, is that there is an unholy alliance among the government, the military, and the big pharmaceutical companies to harvest organs and soft tissue and serum from cattle for a number of purposes. At its most basic, as Nancy Talbot from the BLT Research Team suggested, the government is testing a variety of herds for bovine spongiform encephalopathy, or what is commonly called mad cow disease. This is also the theory of author Colm Kelleher (*The Hunt for the Skinwalker*) with coauthor George Knapp and cattle mutilation researcher Charles Oliphant. Rather than purchasing heads of cattle, which would be a tip-off to consumers that the government is concerned about the health of the nation's beef stock, the government contracts for the active retrieval of cattle, conducted by clandestine domestic military operations, to retrieve samples. Pharmaceutical companies could then test the cattle and develop a vaccine to prevent mad cow disease.

FACT

Recently, researchers in Japan have developed techniques to combine human nucleic DNA with that of a host animal to create stem cell banks that can be used for donor-specific and organ-specific replacement organs, such as new heart valves. While this is a breakthrough, it has raised so many ethical questions that the rules for crossbreeding and harvesting embryonic tissue have to be rewritten.

Other theories of government involvement concern testing cattle for traces of radiation from above-ground nuclear testing decades ago. By testing the soft issue, the areas where grass-feeding cattle would store radioactive material, the government can determine how quickly the radiation levels are dropping in the soil.

While this seems mundane enough, there is an even more incredible explanation. Advanced by some researchers and conspiracy theorists, the military and the pharmaceutical companies, perhaps in collusion with extra-terrestrials, are trying to develop a hybrid species of living organ banks. Initially, the military may want a storage facility of hybridized organs for organ replacement on the battlefield. However, the commercial medical possibilities for this technology are limitless. Imagine being able to replace any organ in your body with your own hybridized stem-cell-generated organ. There would be very limited or no rejection and an endless supply of hearts, kidneys, and livers, all specifically grown to the unique biology of the recipient's body. Research into this possibility would yield enormous profits, benefiting both the military as well as consumers.

The Dulce Hybrid

Retired New Mexico State Police officer Gabriel Valdez made an appearance on an episode of the History Channel's *UFO Hunters* in connection with their visit to Dulce, New Mexico. The staff of *UFO Hunters* was to investigate the theory that the United States government, possibly in collaboration with extra-terrestrials, was maintaining or had maintained an underground research facility inside the Archuleta Mesa on Apache Nation tribal land. During his appearance, Gabe Valdez discounted an extraterrestrial theory but told the story of his coming upon a mutilated cow with a black or unmarked helicopter hovering overhead. Helicopter transport of cattle might be the way cows were retrieved for mutilation purposes and then redeposited. This could be the case, especially if a sling were rigged that did not involve a human presence on the ground and if the rotors were silent. Valdez said that his police unit frightened away the helicopter. When he examined the mutilated cow, he found that it was pregnant and that the fetus was still in the womb. When a veterinarian opened the womb, he found a strange-looking calf fetus with the body of cow and the head of a human being. Valdez revealed a photo of that strange fetus, which was shocking, indeed.

UFO Hunters were at a loss, initially, to explain the rationale behind a creature that might have been the result of interbreeding between the egg cells of a cow and the sperm of a human. The fetus itself was taken away, sequestered, and any genetic testing was not made public. To this day, it's not known what the purpose of that interbreeding was—if indeed the animal was the result of interbreeding—but Nancy Talbot of BLT Research Team theorized that it was possibly an experiment to see if a vaccine could be developed for humans for the debilitating effects of mad cow disease. Just how much of the American cattle stock might be infected and whether the government and pharmaceutical companies were covertly trying to develop a vaccine outside of congressional oversight is not known.

The Senators

Suspicions about congressional concern over experiments in crossbreeding species and hybridizing human and bovine embryos were fed not long after the *UFO Hunters* episode aired when United States senators Mitch McConnell, Lindsey Graham, and Charles Grassley introduced a bill in the U.S. Senate amending Title 18, the Federal Penal Code, so as to make it a crime to interbreed humans and animals. If the government had been up to something, clandestinely conducting an interbreeding or hybridization program in collusion with pharmaceutical companies and with the participation of the military, the introduction of the criminal code amendment in the Senate might well have cast light on that activity. The investigation into this continues.

Cattle mutilation is still a problem in the American West, with ranchers and farmers losing their livelihood to the parties who are perpetrating these crimes. Not only are these crimes of criminal trespass, criminal vandalism, and cruelty to animals, they are driving some cattle ranchers and farmers out of business. Still, the United States government and law enforcement agencies have no answer.

CHAPTER 15

The Military and Pilots Versus UFOs: Famous Cases of Air Encounters

There is a long history around the world of pilot encounters with UFOs, military air encounters with UFOs, and actual dogfights between the military and UFOs. After the 1952 Washington, D.C., flying saucer invasion and the 1952 UFO intrusions over the NATO combined fleet in the North Sea, unidentified flying objects continued to monitor and interfere with aircraft. In some cases, pilots reported that the strange craft seemed to track them and then disappeared before the pilots left the area. In other cases, pilots almost panicked when they believed a UFO was on a collision course and would not retreat. And in yet other cases, military pilots were dispatched to intercept, lock weapons on, and shoot the UFOs down, often with harrowing results. Pilot encounters and dogfights read like scenes out of a science fiction movie, but to the pilots involved they were all too real.

The Mansfield, Ohio, Case

This 1973 case out of Mansfield, Ohio, was incredibly striking. This military encounter has been mentioned in a number of official UFO studies, including the famous Rockefeller panel on UFO investigations. The panel found that the multiple sightings from credible witnesses required that the military investigate this case more fully to try, if possible, to find a conventional explanation. To date, none has been proffered.

On October 18, 1973, at around 10:30 P.M., a U.S. Army Reserve Huey helicopter was flying out from Cleveland and passing over Mansfield, Ohio, when members of the crew noticed a red light in the sky above them. No one took notice of it until the light started to come toward them on a collision course. Captain Lawrence Coyne, in command of the helicopter, took the control from his left-seater, Lieutenant Arrigo Jezzi, and put the helicopter into a steep dive to avoid a collision. As they descended at full power, the crew could see the craft in detail that was coming toward them.

According to their descriptions, it was a flying cylindrical-shaped object that looked like a craft with a slight dome on top. It was large, gray, and metallic, and it seemed to have a line of windows or portholes along the dome. The object had a red light in front and a white light in its tail section, clearly visible as the object rushed toward the helicopter. Then, even as the crew braced for what they thought might be a collision, the object stopped dead in the air and hovered, a maneuver a conventional object could not make.

FACT

The importance of cases like the Mansfield, Ohio, case is that multiple witnesses from different locations, especially from the ground, confirmed the occurrence as being in the same place at the same time. Thus, investigators did not have to rely on just one set of witnesses from one location but could triangulate the location of the anomalous object so as to confirm that the different witnesses were seeing the same thing.

With the object hovering just below them, the crew recalls that the flying cylinder lit up the helicopter with a green pyramid-shaped beam. The beam played along the fuselage of the helicopter, starting at the nose, then shone through the windshield into the cockpit, illuminating it in an eerie green light. For the next few seconds, the craft kept the helicopter in its beam. Then it turned and flew off over Lake Erie, its white taillight still visible. As it flew over the lake, it seemed to turn itself off and disappear.

The helicopter crew thought at first they were the only witnesses to this strange sight, but ground witnesses saw the entire event. Occupants of a vehicle on the ground reported interference with its engine as the craft scanned the helicopter. Multiple witnesses from three different locations—ground observers, observers in a vehicle, and the crew of the helicopter—all confirmed the same basic incident, thus making it one of the most credible U.S. military air encounters in the 1970s.

Tehran Airport

Today, retired Iranian Air Force general Parviz Jafari is a hero and sought-after speaker among UFO historians and researchers. His encounter with a triangular UFO over the skies of Tehran on September 19, 1976, represents one of the most dramatic stories of a dogfight with an otherworldly craft in history. He has told his story to newspapers and has been a guest on the History Channel's *UFO Hunters*, but the story, often repeated, never loses its frightening aspect and confirms that there is a presence in the skies that cannot be controlled. Further research into General Jafari's story revealed that intelligence reports about his dogfight with the UFO made it all the way to the desk of the then-president Gerald Ford and probably to a briefing with president-elect Jimmy Carter. There are records of that report.

ALERT

During the eight-year war against Saddam Hussein's Iraq, Jafari was a member of the Iranian general staff and supervised the defenses against an Iraqi invasion. His deployment of troops and use of air power blunted the Iraqi invasion and forced an eight-year stalemate that saved the Iranian government. For that strategy, Jafari became a military hero, and his story about his dogfight with a UFO has become very popular in Iran.

The Dogfight over Tehran

The story, as Parvis Jafari explained on *UFO Hunters*, began when he was a squadron leader. On the night of September 19, 1976, Jafari was advised that at least one Soviet MiG fighter was near the Iranian border and flying uncomfortably close to Iranian airspace. An Iranian U.S.-made F-4 Phantom fighter was already near the border to observe and intercept, if necessary. Jafari advised the pilot not to cross the border into Soviet airspace, but the pilot radioed back that he was observing a very bright, almost as brilliant as sunlight, triangular object that was heading toward Tehran. Attempting an intercept, the pilot lost the use of his instruments and radio and veered away from the object. When his radio communications returned, he informed his base that the object was still there but had interfered with his ability to navigate because his instruments had gone dead. At that point, Jafari was scrambled to intercept the object, still heading for Tehran.

Jafari told the assembled press at the 2007 National Press Club UFO conference that he made visual contact with the object but was so blinded by its brilliance that he couldn't make out its exact size. It dominated the sky, and its dazzling blue, green, and orange flashing lights captured Jafari's attention. The object kept a fixed distance from Jafari's Phantom jet as he shadowed it in a southerly direction. Then he noticed that a smaller object flew away from the larger object, almost like an aircraft taking off from an aircraft carrier, and headed toward him. He said that he interpreted the approach of the smaller object as a hostile threat and immediately armed his weapons control panel to launch an AIM 9 air-to-air missile. As he did so, his weapons panel went dead, he lost instrumentation, and his radio failed.

Jafari took evasive action, diving as steeply as he could, but the object followed him. It was on his tail on one side of his plane, but, suddenly, without any apparent movement, it turned up on the other side of his plane. Jafari said he experienced moments of missing time as his plane headed into his dive. Then he noticed that the object broke off and pulled up back toward the larger object, at which point Jafari's instruments came back and his weapons system returned to his control.

Jafari pulled out of his dive and headed back toward the larger object to keep it in sight. Then he noticed that another smaller object flew out of the large object and headed toward him. Again, Jafari tried to activate his weapons panel, and again the weapons panel died, as did his instruments. His radio was filled with static. He radioed his base that he was breaking off his intercept. He veered off, and his instruments came back to life. He was vectored toward Mehrabad Airport, but he could still see the object that had approached him. Now it was heading straight toward the desert floor, where it landed. Jafari carefully descended and flew over the object's landing site, noting its position for his report. Then he continued to Mehrabad, where he radioed the tower of his approach.

ESSENTIAL

You can hear Parviz Jafari tell the story of his frightening encounter in his own words at *www.youtube.com/watch?v=KJydT3AZ370*.

As he approached Mehrabad for landing, Jafari observed a fourth unidentified object, this time a cylinder, overhead. The tower observed it, too, as their radio communications went offline, and a commercial airliner spotted it as well. The airliner lost radio communications as the object passed overhead.

The Follow-Up Investigation

The following day, Jafari returned to the landing site of the object he'd seen. It was near an oil refinery. The craft was no longer on the ground. Again, he noted what he had observed the day before and the disappearance of the object on the following day.

Jafari said that upon his return to headquarters, he was interviewed not only by superior Iranian Air Force officers in the Iranian Air Force but by at least one American in civilian clothes, a person he took to be an intelligence agent. He was also interviewed by American military personnel. Apparently the U.S. Defense Intelligence Agency filled out a detailed follow-up report of the entire incident, calling it one of the best reports for its detailed observations and the criteria for documenting a UFO encounter.

The report circulated within classified units of the Department of Defense, and, as discovered at the 2007 National Press Club conference, the report made it all the way to a briefing document submitted to President Gerald Ford in 1976. At the conference, researchers, who had recovered the document from the National Archives, circulated a report of intelligence briefings that reached President Ford. The report of Jafari's encounter was on that briefing document. The existence of that briefing alone contradicts the air force's contention that it had abandoned investigations into the UFO phenomenon. In fact, the air force continued its pursuit of UFO investigations through the 1970s and into the 1990s because it was actively investigating RAF Bentwaters, RAF Cosford, and probably the Phoenix Lights. In all likelihood that investigation continues today.

Oscar Santa Maria Huertas and the Peruvian UFO Dogfight

Another speaker at the 2007 National Press Club conference was former Peruvian Air Force fighter pilot Oscar Santa Maria Huertas. Santa Maria Huertas is one of the only pilots since World War II to have opened fire on a UFO that intruded into protected national airspace. On April 11, 1980, air traffic personnel in Peru, near the border with Chile, a neighbor who had fought a war with Peru, picked up a large object in Peruvian airspace near the border with Chile. They assumed it to be a Chilean spy balloon and scrambled a Soviet-manufactured Sukhoi SU-22 fighter to intercept and destroy the balloon. At the controls of the SU-22 was the then-lieutenant Santa Maria Huertas, who, in full view of a formation of 1,800 military personnel on the ground, closed in on the object.

He saw the object hanging motionless in the air only a few hundred feet away from him. He told a riveted audience at the National Press Club that it was a solid object with a blue dome, looking like a lightbulb split in half, with a wide metal base that made everything shine. He said, "When I approached and saw it completely, I realized that it lacked nozzles, wings, windows, antennae, nothing at all. It was a very smooth surface above and below."

He got the object in his guns' sights and opened fire with 30 mm machine guns, hitting the object directly with at least sixty-four rounds. He saw the rounds hit, piercing what he thought was the object's skin. But there were no explosions, no spray of impact, no ricocheting bullets.

In response, Santa Maria Huertas told the audience, the object in his sights accelerated rapidly, beyond the speed of his fighter, and climbed much higher. Santa Maria Huertas cut in his afterburner, going supersonic, and chased the object, now attempting to get a radar lock on it with his air-to-air missile firing mechanism. But before he could get a lock, the object stopped dead in the air, forcing Santa Maria Huertas to take evasive action to avoid a collision. Then the object climbed again as Santa Maria Huertas got back on a pursuit course. At that point the object stopped, defying all laws of aerodynamics, and began to pursue the SU-22 to an altitude of over 60,000 feet, beyond the SU-22's ceiling. At that altitude, the plane would stall, flame out, or lose all maneuverability. Santa Maria Huertas said he realized he was low on fuel and could no longer engage the object that could outclimb, out-run, and outmaneuver his fighter. It seemed impervious to direct hits with 30 mm rounds. He broke off the engagement and returned to base.

QUESTION

How did Santa Maria Huertas know he'd hit the object with his machine guns?
The fighter pilot could tell by the trajectory of his tracer rounds that he was hitting the object. The rounds didn't bounce off the object but were absorbed by it, something Santa Maria Huertas had never seen before.

The object did not pursue the Peruvian fighter but remained motionless in the air in full view of the ground for hours. This dogfight, unlike previous air-to-air maneuvers between jet interceptors and UFOs, was the only documented modern engagement where a fighter fired on the object. Santa Maria Huertas told his National Press Club audience that never had he imagined that gunfire as intense as his would have no effect whatsoever on an object. The object seemed to absorb the impact as if the rounds went right through it, but he could not see the tracer rounds coming out the other side. His rounds just disappeared. He had no explanation for what could have happened.

Air France Sightings

The Channel Islands between England and France were witness to two incredible UFO sightings by three different pilots in just over a decade. The first sighting was by Air France Captain Jean Charles Duboc on January 28, 1994, during Flight 3532 from Nice, France, to London, England. Captain Duboc, crossing the French coast toward Paris, said he spotted a very large UFO over Paris at 1 P.M. during a period of excellent visibility. Other members of his crew also saw the object. In fact, it was the steward who notified the cockpit crew of the sighting.

Captain Duboc told his story at the 2007 National Press Club conference as well as on *UFO Hunters*. He said that, at first, both the steward and Duboc's copilot identified the object as a weather balloon. But he said that he when he observed it, he saw it as a UFO changing shape at an angle of forty-five degrees. He said, "It seemed to be a huge flying disc."

The object stabilized and stopped moving, "totally stationary in the sky." Then it seemed to disappear gradually. When they were looking at it, the object was a reddish-brown color with blurred edges and was about 1,000 feet wide. Duboc said that the object was partly obscured by a translucent field, which he took to be an electromagnetic envelope that gave it a "fuzzy" appearance. Then, he said, "The most incredible aspect is that it became transparent and disappeared in about ten to twenty seconds."

Captain Duboc said that he reported his sighting to all the appropriate authorities, especially because the airspace over Paris is restricted and there is a military base nearby. Whatever the intentions of the UFO, the mere fact that it was hovering near an air base made it a threat in military terms. Captain Duboc said that the report of his sighting made it to the official French COMETA report on UFOs, a report that made it clear that the experts, some from the military, investigating the incidents cited believed that UFOs were real and a potential threat to the national security of France. To this day, Captain Duboc's Paris UFO sighting remains unexplained.

UFOs over the English Channel

Captain Duboc told assembled press in Washington, D.C., that he fully supported the story told by Captain Ray Bowyers of Aurigny Airlines about his 2007 UFO encounter over the English Channel. Captain Bowyer was also a speaker at the National Press Club conference and a guest on *UFO Hunters*, during which he flew the route he took over the channel when he and his passengers spotted the UFO.

On April 23, 2007, Captain Bowyer and his passengers were en route over the channel heading south when about ten miles south of the Isle of Wight, Captain Bowyer spotted a large yellow light in the sky just below him. At first he believed that he was looking at a reflection from a cloud or from the water, explanations debunkers quickly set forth in commenting on the case. But when Bowyer grabbed his binoculars to get a better look at the object, he was able to see a clear circular shape. It was not an airplane, at least not an airplane that he had ever seen during his years as a pilot, especially flying the channel route for the previous ten years.

Realizing that this was a strange sight, Bowyer alerted his passengers, who, from their respective seats behind the cockpit, could also see the object. Had the object been a unique reflection off the surface of the water, or off a cloud, or even a reflection of the sun off the room of a greenhouse on one of the islands below (another explanation that skeptics proffered), then Bowyer's passengers, looking at the sight down from a different angle, might not have been able to see the same thing.

ALERT

When pilots, both commercial and military, report UFOs, and when those UFOs are also picked up as targets on radar, and when governments intervene to silence the story and hide the evidence away, you can bet that the UFOs are probably real.

Captain Bowyer notified the Jersey tower that he had picked up a large object visually, which should also have been visual to air traffic control. The tower notified Bowyer that the object was also being observed by the pilot of another plane nearby. It was at that point that Bowyer spotted another bright object in the sky near the first and reported that as well.

He continued on his route, landing and disembarking his passengers. However, he was not silent about what he saw, and just over six months after the sighting, he was in America talking about it with other pilots at the Press Club.

Bowyer's sighting made headlines in the United Kingdom because, by 2007, after the *Chicago Tribune*'s O'Hare Airport story, UFOs were making big news in the media. Skeptics argued that all Bowyer saw was a reflection that he was able to track because of unique weather conditions. However, even the skeptics admitted that the weather conditions they say were responsible for Bowyer's sighting that day had never occurred before and had not occurred afterward. They were totally unique. Ray Bowyer, for his part, stuck to his story because he and his passengers say that they were able to make out a structured shape in the sky and not a reflection that changed shape with the varying wind and water conditions.

CHAPTER 16

UFOs and Time Travel

Almost all UFO researchers understand that if Einstein's special theory of relativity is correct, space and time are related in an inverse proportion. The higher the acceleration toward the speed of light, the more time slows down. At the speed of light, time is zero, even though time onboard the craft traveling at the speed of light continues on course. At *Star Trek* hyperlight or "warp" speeds, time would run backward unless some other aspect of physics comes into play. Therefore, time travel, either as part of a grand government conspiracy, exotic science, or a factor in interstellar travel, is a part of UFO research. As anyone can imagine, just the thought that it might be real—and it is—could have catastrophic consequences, especially if a time-traveling entity could manipulate the past. What if time travel is something an extraterrestrial culture has been engaging in with respect to infiltrating our own society here on Earth? Worse, what if human beings are capable of time travel but don't know it? And what if that's one of the biggest secrets that the secret keepers are withholding? Wouldn't that be a conspiracy all by itself?

The Philadelphia Experiment: Fact or Fiction?

The story of the USS *Eldridge* has been a mainstay of UFO conspiracy theory for over forty years. The USS *Eldridge*, a World War II destroyer escort docked at the Philadelphia Navy Yard in October 1943, became the focus of a bizarre story once it was featured in the 1984 science fiction feature film, *The Philadelphia Experiment*. Although consistently debunked as a hoax, the story's place in UFO lore merits a look. What really took place in the Philadelphia Navy Yard, who investigated it, and how was it ultimately debunked?

FACT

Admiral Arleigh Burke was an important naval commander in World War II and the Korean War. Chief of naval operations during the Eisenhower administration, Burke was a friend of Lieutenant Colonel Philip Corso when Corso was a military staff officer of the National Security Council during Eisenhower's presidency. Corso had become a friend of most of the senior officers in the military in the 1950s because of his position in the White House and had many interesting stories about events during World War II.

The Planned Invasion of Japan

According to Philip Corso in *The Day After Roswell*, Admiral Arleigh Burke of the U.S. Navy told him that by the latter half of 1943, the United States was preparing for an invasion of the Japanese home islands. Every military planner believed that the invasion would be a blood bath for the military on both sides and for civilians. To accomplish such an invasion, the United States would have to firebomb Japanese cities into a complete wasteland, a naval bombardment more intense than what was already in the planning stages for the invasion of Europe across the English Channel. However, even to get close to the Japanese coast, the navy would have to cross a barrier of sea mines to put its forces in position not to mention contend with kamikaze pilots hurling themselves into the navy warships. However, the navy had developed a possible plan.

The Electronic Invisibility Cloak

Because sea mines were set off by the electromagnetic current running through a ship's hull, what if that hull were demagnetized? Perhaps by lowering the magnetic signature as well as by sweeping mines, navy ships could get close enough to the shore to support the landing. Demagnetizing the hull meant that the ships would be electronically cloaked, invisible to the mines. Their signatures would be erased by demagnetizing the hulls in a process similar to what is still used today on analog tape, called degaussing, named after Carl Gauss, who researched magnetic fields. The process to degauss ships' hulls so as to make them invisible to German underwater mines had already been developed by a Royal Canadian Navy officer named Charles Goodeve. Admiral Burke explained to Corso that the U.S. Navy wanted to try that same process on navy ships heading to Japan but needed to test it first. The candidate was the destroyer escort USS *Eldridge*.

The method used to degauss ships was called "wiping." It involved running a heavy-duty electric cable along the hull, which reduced the electromagnetic field to a level that would, in theory, not trigger the fuse on an underwater mine. This was the procedure used on the USS *Eldridge* in October 1943. It was a procedure done in complete secret because the navy did not want Japan to know its intentions. However, the current running through the cable was so high, over 2,000 amps, that it created a heat so intense that part of the deck melted, killing two crew members. Their bodies actually fused into the deck.

As a thick, heavy fog enveloped the navy yard on that October day, the *Eldridge*, still a part of a top-secret project, was sent down the Intracoastal Waterway to the navy base at Norfolk, Virginia, for repairs and to remove the bodies of the two crew members. Witnesses who knew little about what happened have said that the USS *Eldridge* simply vanished into the fog as if she had disappeared from view completely. In fact, it didn't vanish; it was only enveloped in fog as it sailed south, but, to some observers, it appeared that the *Eldridge* simply slipped through a seam in time, never to be seen in the Philadelphia Navy Yard again. For the next decade, the story was forgotten.

The Story Re-Emerges

The story of the USS *Eldridge* came to light again in 1955 when a man calling himself Carlos Allende, a.k.a. Carl Allen, wrote to UFO author Morris K. Jessup (*The Case for the UFO*) about the case. In their exchange of letters, Allen tried to convince Jessup that the USS *Eldridge* had traveled in time and that he was a witness to it. However, Jessup wanted more proof, and Allen could provide none of it. It turned out that the entire story of the *Eldridge's* time travel was concocted by Allen to be foisted onto Jessup. Allen also wrote to the navy, whose Office of Naval Intelligence (ONI) asked one of its officers, George Hoover, to investigate the case. Hoover found no evidence of time travel but was fascinated by it and heavily annotated Jessup's book. His notes later appeared in an authorized edition of the book printed by the Varo Publishing Company.

ESSENTIAL

George Hoover had a very interesting career. He advised Walt Disney on the *Man in Space* television series in the 1950s and later invented the heads-up cockpit display for fighter planes. Hoover was fascinated by UFOs and time travel and had an extensive library on the subject. Also, for conspiracy theory enthusiasts, Hoover said that when he was on patrol off Pearl Harbor in November 1941, he spotted a Japanese fleet of aircraft carriers. His ship reported the news but was told to maintain radio silence, to return to Pearl Harbor, and not to tell anyone of this sighting.

The Philadelphia Experiment and UFOs

Because *The Philadelphia Experiment* motion picture stirred up such interest in the original case and because witnesses subsequently came out of the woodwork to claim that the sailors onboard the USS *Eldridge* traveled into the future and exchanged identities with individuals living in the 1980s, the case has been connected to UFOs and time travel theory. But the Arleigh Burke explanation, according to Corso, makes the most sense, because the intent of the navy was to cloak the vessel by making it invisible to under-water mines. Hence, a story fell into the purview of UFOs by the power of motion pictures, UFO lore, and conspiracy theorists' fascination with time travel.

The First Human Time Travelers

In the late 1970s into the 1980s, the CIA and the U.S. Army experimented with psychic spying. Individuals, some more psychically endowed than others, were trained to focus in on a signal they were said to receive from somewhere in the universe that allowed them to use their minds to transcend their physical presence both in space and time. Popularized by the movie *The Men Who Stare at Goats*, these people were the first remote viewers.

QUESTION

How does remote viewing work?
According to former army remote viewers, most human beings, regardless of psychic ability, are able to receive signals or impressions from what Dr. Carl Jung called the collective unconscious. However, most people tune these signals out because the concept of receiving psychic or extradimensional impressions conflicts with their sense of logic. Remote viewers, however, are trained to listen to these signals and write down their impressions so as to describe what they are seeing in a nonanalytical and nonjudgmental manner.

Remote viewers, or psychic spies, as they were called, were part of a program already in use by the Soviets in which the viewers tried to pick up on a set of coordinates or an impression of a place in another person's mind, almost like the stage performer Kreskin. The place was supposedly where some secret was being housed.

Remote Viewer Paul Smith and Time Travel

One of the remote viewers was U.S. Army Major Paul Smith, who wrote about his experiences in *Reading the Enemy's Mind* and who has written for *UFO Magazine*. In his interviews about his experiences in the army remote viewing program, Paul Smith described a strange incident in May 1987. Paul was working with his trainer, Ed Dames, to see if Major Smith could remote view a UFO.

In his session with Dames, Paul Smith said that he viewed a desert landscape bordering on a narrow body of water. He was watching a vessel on the water making its way when suddenly he saw a cylindrical object streaking toward it. In an instant the cylindrical object struck the vessel, and Smith said that he could see the twisting and molten metal and hear the shouts of men as the vessel caught fire. He could smell the burned structure on the vessel. Then he saw a second cylindrical object hit the vessel and viewed men with black mustaches and beards on a jet plane nearby. They seemed to be in a panic, seemingly over what had happened to the ship. Then a second plane came into view. He recognized it, although he tried not to. It was a large aircraft with lots of radar scanning equipment. That craft, too, had a crew of men with dark facial hair, and Smith knew he was looking at Middle Eastern men. He wrote down his impressions and left the report for his supervisor.

A Trip into the Future

The following week his supervisor called him into his office to ask him about the report. Smith said that he drew no conclusions, except that he imagined after the session that he was looking at some territory near the Persian Gulf, probably the narrow Straits of Hormuz. He believed that he saw a naval vessel hit with an Exocet or some other type of antiship missile. Smith's boss told him that days after he had completed that session and filed the report, an Iraqi jet fired two Exocet missiles at the USS *Stark*. Major Smith had somehow managed to pick up a signal from the future that penetrated the present. Or, conversely, during his session, perhaps he had actually traveled into the future to witness an event that had yet to happen in his physical time but was happening in a future time. That experience intrigued Major Smith (who years later would earn his PhD in philosophy) about the implications of viewing a future event and what actions one could take in the present if one knew the future.

A Trip to Saturn

In a second 1980s session, ostensibly to look for flying saucers, Smith said he saw a cylinder-shaped object descending through the atmosphere of a distant moon. Then he saw that the moon was orbiting around a planet with rings. It must have been Saturn. Smith watched as the disk descended and disappeared from view. To himself he wondered if he had actually seen a UFO or a flying saucer, but, as remote viewers are trained to do, he withheld judgment so as not to interfere with the raw impressions of what he was viewing.

QUESTION

What are the philosophical implications of remote viewing time travel?
A question posed by remote viewers was, "What would happen if you remote viewed an event in the near future you knew you could change?" Would you intervene? If you did, what would happen? If Paul Smith knew what he was remote viewing when he received the impression of the USS *Stark*, should he have notified the crew of the impending attack? Was his seeing the future really seeing another version of an event that had already happened in the past of an even more distant future and, hence, unchangeable? These are the philosophical questions worth pondering.

It wouldn't be until January 2005 that what Major Smith viewed became a reality. He had seen a craft, but the craft was from NASA, and the moon was Saturn's moon Titan. The name of the craft was Huygens, a European/American space probe that accomplished the first landing of a spaceship on a body in the outer solar system. It was a triumph for NASA, and it was remote viewed by an army major looking for UFOs twenty-eight years before it happened. Did the army ever embrace the possibility that it could send spies traveling through time to see the future and what this might hold for looking for UFOs?

Government-Trained Time Travelers: Project Pegasus

The same wonderful folks who worked on what would become the Internet, the Defense Advanced Research Projects Agency (DARPA), also instituted a potentially chilling project in the 1960s called Project Pegasus, a time traveler training program. According to one of the self-described time travelers, author Andrew Basiago (*Celestial Secrets*), DARPA had been researching and then developing Nikola Tesla's teleportation theories. Ultimately, they were able to come up with a plan for a proof of the concept of time travel, but they needed time travelers, or chrononauts, as Basiago says they were called.

Personal Evidence of Time Travel

The training program lasted at least a decade, culminating in 1981, when the first missions were launched. Basiago says, and offers evidence in the form of a photo, that he was transported back in time to the Gettysburg battlefield during the American Civil War. He says that he was also teleported to the planet Mars twice, once alone and once with his trainer, CIA operative Courtney Hunt. Mars, Andy Basiago has said, is inhabited, and American intelligence and space agencies have dealt with its inhabitants.

ALERT

One theory among conspiracy theorists is that time travel has been going on for a while and that history is already being tampered with. As an example, some conspiracy theorists cite the 2000 presidential election in Florida where former CIA director and forty-first president George H. W. Bush had already ordered vote tampering in the past to ensure that his son George W. Bush would win the Florida electoral vote.

The What-Ifs of Time Travel

If Basiago is correct and his evidence holds up under scrutiny, his story of a timeline that could be changed by trips through time via a teleportation mechanism has the potential to change, if it hasn't already changed, every aspect of human experience. Imagine traveling to a distant time the way you might go on vacation to Williamsburg, Virginia. Or imagine that a military power in control of such a teleportation device would use the power to alter history in such a way that key moments would always break its way. For example, the Allied landing at Normandy is turned back by the Germans, or JFK is protected at the last minute in Dallas by a Secret Service agent throwing his body on top of the president. Or what if the Spanish fleet is warned in advance about a storm off the coast of France and turns back, only to return, avoid the British channel fleet, and make a landing in England? The Armada succeeds, Queen Elizabeth is removed from power with extreme prejudice, the pilgrims never land at Plymouth Rock, and the title of this book is *El Libro todo de los Ovnis*.

The Time Travel UFO Theory

More than one UFO researcher has suggested that what are referred to as extraterrestrial space travelers are really time travelers either from some other planet or from right here on Earth. There is lots of intriguing, though hardly any dispositive, evidence. For example, in Egyptian, Sumerian, and Mayan hieroglyphics, there are symbols of craft that look like a modern helicopter, a human being or humanoid in a space suit of today, and craft that look intriguingly like the space shuttle. In fact, *Legendary Times* magazine editor Giorgio Tsoukalis wears a piece of jewelry that is a model of a bird deity that was worshipped by the indigenous peoples of Central America. What was this bird creature that looks not at all like a bird? When Tsoukalis appeared as a guest on *UFO Hunters*, he explained his theory that what many paleoanthropologists called a bird was really an aircraft.

UFO Hunters tested this theory and created a scale model with balsa wood to see whether it might actually glide back to Earth if launched from a catapult device. Would the wings support it? Would the odd-looking tail assembly on the artifact act like a modern aircraft tail assembly? This was the challenge.

The Flight Test

UFO Hunters modeled the artifact, launched it from a catapult, and, to everyone's delight, the bird/space shuttle-like craft climbed into the air. Then, because it was unpowered, it settled back on its tail assembly that stabilized it. Its delta wings provided the lift for the nose to rise as the craft settled easily down to the ground in a perfect landing, just like the space shuttle. This doesn't prove the theory of UFO time travel, but it showed that if a time traveler visited the past in a shuttle-like lander and stayed, imparting a jump-start to Mayan or Inca technology, the bird artifact might have been the result of a cargo-cult memorialization.

FACT

In the South Pacific during World War II, islanders saw cargo planes for the first time. Believing that these craft were indeed gods, the islanders built artistically styled models of these craft and worshipped them. The religions that grew up around these models of cargo planes and warplanes were called "cargo cults."

Another intriguing part of the story came from Philip Corso, who claimed he saw a strange, otherworldly craft in the New Mexico desert at the Army Missile Proving Grounds in Red Canyon in the late 1950s. Corso said that when he was flying over the missile range in an army Piper Cub, he looked down into the scrub brush and chaparral landscape below him and saw a shiny metallic object on the ground. It wasn't huge, but it was, he said, clearly the size of something a human being could pilot. Corso told his pilot to head back to base, and when he landed he got his staff car and drove out to that spot in the desert.

The object was still there, almost shimmering in the desert heat. Corso got out of his car and approached the object, wary about touching it, but, after his experience with the Roswell cargo at Fort Riley ten years earlier, more curious than wary. He touched the surface of the object, feeling a little disoriented because the object seemed to be fuzzing around the edges as if it were winking in and out of reality. It was surprisingly cold to the touch. He noted its oval shape and stepped back as the thing began to hum, as if reacting to his presence. Then, right before his eyes, the object simply disappeared.

Corso was a man who kept his secrets close while he was in uniform and did not make a big report of what he saw. Instead, four years later when he was head of Foreign Technology at the Army Office of Research and Development in the Pentagon, he told former Nazi rocket scientist Hermann Oberth about what he saw in the desert that day. Hermann Oberth, once quoted as having said that the Germans were helped in their technological development by people from another world, suggested to Corso that it might be that the craft he saw was not an extraterrestrial spacecraft but actually a "timeship."

It was a statement that stayed with Corso for the rest of his life, and during his television appearance on NBC's *Dateline* in 1997, forty years after the incident, he told correspondent John Hockenberry the story of the craft in the desert. It was one of the most memorable moments of Corso's appearance.

Temporal Dislocation

There have been many other hints concerning the relationship between UFOs and temporal dislocation, as if time manipulation were part of their ability to navigate through space and, thus, time. Witnesses have reported short periods of missing time, moments when they could not account for the passage of time. Clocks mysteriously stop that should not because they're not electric and should not have been affected by an electromagnetic field. Engines that cut off when a UFO passes overhead mysteriously start up again as if they were never stopped but only hesitated in time and were running the entire time. Plants and trees touched by beams from UFOs seem to age years in an instant. And UFOs themselves simply don't accelerate as if they are gathering speed. They disappear in a direction in an instant as if they've passed into another time continuum.

Perhaps, if ever the secret of UFOs becomes public knowledge, the secret of temporal manipulation will be exposed. At that point, it is to be hoped that humankind will hopefully be ready for that astounding knowledge and won't, like the Krell people of the motion picture *Forbidden Planet*, destroy the population with that power.

CHAPTER 17

UFO Hunting

While it's true that UFOs, like gold, are rare, there are places where you'll be more likely to see and perhaps photograph UFOs than others. For starters, most UFO hunters begin by keeping an eye on Internet traffic reporting sightings of UFOs. You can visit historical hot spots, of course, to see for yourself what previous witnesses might have seen. You can also see what stories of UFO sightings have made it into the news and travel there. You should always bring some basic equipment with you, including a good set of binoculars, a camera, and a voice recorder, all of which should be separate from your smartphone. You should also bring along a lightweight computer or tablet for on-the-spot research if you are in a wireless hot spot or have radio connectivity.

The Best Places to Find UFOs

Tracking current UFO sightings and breaking news about UFOs is probably the surest way to keep up-to-date on the latest sightings. Begin by looking up all of the websites where individuals report having seen UFOs, such as the Mutual UFO Network websites. By going to the main MUFON website at *www.mufon.com*, you will not only get some of the latest sightings and the areas where they took place, you will also find some great tips on what equipment people used to capture the sightings on video or even cell phone cameras.

Another great reporting site for UFOs is George Filer's files at the National UFO Reporting Center, *www.nationalufocenter.com*. Here you'll find weekly updates of the latest sighting reports by private individuals, and you can also sign up for Filer's weekly e-mail updates. Chances are that between MUFON and Filer, you will be able to build your own current sightings map.

Another sighting report center is published in every issue of *UFO Magazine*. You can go to *www.ufomag.com*, where you can order digital copies of the magazine. By following the sighting reports in Rick Tropman's column, "Rick's Picks," you will be able to keep track of sightings around the country.

UFO Hot Spots

Many people like to travel to various UFO hot spots around the country to see what they can find. The most popular (but by no means the only ones) are described in the following sections.

Area 51 and the Nevada Desert

Perhaps the most intriguing UFO hot spot in the United States is the Nevada desert outside of the legendary Area 51. You can't enter the top-secret air force base. In fact, the air force doesn't even admit there is an Area 51, which actually opened up not in 1951 but in 1953. However, ever since Bob Lazar went public with KLAV newsman George Knapp about the reverse engineering of alien spacecraft at Area 51, the area has become a tourist mecca for UFO hunters.

Bob Lazar told George Knapp and test pilot and CIA pilot John Lear about scheduled tests of reverse-engineered alien craft at the base. He said he worked there as a propulsion systems expert. When Lazar took them out to the desert on nights the craft were being flight tested, sure enough, George Knapp and John Lear said they were able to see the craft that Lazar described. The television show *UFO Hunters* also visited Area 51 in 2008 and set up cameras around the perimeter of the base. To the displeasure of the powers that be who run the base, *UFO Hunters* captured a UFO on film, a craft that did not display the flight characteristics of a conventional aircraft.

To add to the lore of the area, years ago the son of one of the air force pilots who was a guest on *UFO Hunters* was driving across the Nevada desert in the very early hours of the morning. As he skirted the roads around Area 51 near Rachel, Nevada, he saw a giant triangle in the sky, lit at its three corners with bright lights. The triangle seemed to be shadowing his car, making him very nervous. Then it hovered over his car for a while, as he floored the gas pedal, and finally floated away across the desert back to the Area 51 airspace. If you're looking for an adventure like that, then plan a trip to drive across the Nevada desert at night, perhaps in an RV or camper filled with camera equipment. Make sure you stop in the area of Rachel—you could spot a UFO.

FACT

One of the great tourist stops in Rachel is the Little Ali'e Inn, a roadside convenience store and camping spot that has become home to UFO enthusiasts and campers looking to catch a UFO on camera.

Underwater UFOs and the Redondo Beach Channel

According to 911 calls to the Lost Hills sheriff's station in Malibu, California, witness reports from Catalina Island, twenty-six miles off the coast, and reports from boaters out in Santa Monica Bay, there might be a base of USOs (unidentified submerged objects) deep in the Redondo Beach Channel. USOs become UFOs when they leave the water. Late at night on the

Venice and Santa Monica piers, beachgoers have told stories of seeing lights entering and exiting the water. From Point Dume in Malibu and from nearby Paradise Cove, the location where Jim Rockford of television's *Rockford Files* was filmed, witnesses have told stories of seeing lights fly into the water late at night as they sat on the beach.

All these stories make the Southern California beachfront from Redondo to Malibu a prime UFO viewing area, if you have the patience to enjoy the beach in the day and the cool temperatures at night. With plenty of reasonably priced hotels along the Pacific Coast Highway, there are lots of places for you to stay and still have beach access to walk at night with a pair of binoculars or a telescope.

ESSENTIAL

Out in the Redondo Beach Channel is Santa Catalina Island, which you can reach by boat, ferry, or plane. There are plenty of camping spots on the island, and you will meet other sky watchers looking for UFOs. The light pollution is very low on the island, and it is easy to spot all kinds of phenomena in the sky, from shooting stars to satellites, as well as strange objects making hairpin turns high overhead.

Panama City, Florida, and Gulf Breeze

Gulf Breeze is known for the famous Ed Walters sightings. It has been home to underwater sightings as well. There have been sightings even after Ed Walters sold his house and moved away, probably because of the area's proximity to the Pensacola Naval Air Station and other military bases in the area. In nearby Panama City, where President Obama recently visited, pleasure boaters as well as night fishermen in the Gulf of Mexico also reported lights beneath the surface of the water that circled their vessels and then suddenly took off from below. A group of midnight shark fishermen told the crew of *UFO Hunters* that they recognize the lights of fish in the water. When they see a large light near their own small boats as they drag their lines for shark, they know they're not looking at the biochemical lights of small underwater schools of fish. They're looking at USOs.

For an exciting, if not downright exhilarating, UFO hunting experience, try joining the shark fishermen on the Gulf side of Panama City beaches to see if you can spot underwater lights that you can't identify.

Dugway, Utah, and the Army Proving Grounds

One of the closely guarded military facilities, Area 51 notwithstanding, is the United States Army Proving Grounds at Dugway, Utah. In a desolate area of hilly high desert, this most secretive base—an area where biological weapons and nerve gas were developed in World War II—hosts U.S. defense contractors developing some of our most advanced weapons. If you think that cloaking devices and invisibility shields are only for Klingon and Romulan birds of prey on *Star Trek*, think again.

If you can find a safe spot off the rear gates of Dugway and not get spotted by the constant security patrols, or photographed by the black helicopters patrolling overhead, you just might hear the sound of an F-16's jet engines roaring by at a low altitude. But when you look up to find the plane, there's nothing there, even though you can still hear the sound of the engines almost on top of you. What's going on? You've experienced an invisible warplane flying by.

The same holds true for the clouds of dust kicked up by vehicles driving on the other side of the fence line. You can see the dust in the distance and follow it along the dirt track as it drives out of view, but there's no vehicle to be seen. Like the jet you couldn't see, this vehicle is completely invisible, cloaked by the device that army defense contractors are testing for use in combat.

Then there's the bright blue beam of light that seems to shine from the ground to nowhere in the sky. If you're lucky enough to get out there at night with either an ATV or dirt bike and can pitch either a tent or a sleeping bag arrangement in a safe place, you might see a blue beam shoot up from the ground. As strange as that seems, the beam seems to attract whirring lights around it like insects, only much bigger. These lights are actually UFOs, whether alien or domestic is hard to tell, but for some reason they're either attracted to the blue beam or maybe are able to draw energy from it. "Alien" Dave Rosenfeld and his crew of Utah UFO hunters are constantly monitoring the base for signs of UFOs. They also log reports from Native American witnesses that have seen animal mutilation nearby.

Workers at the base also have sent out messages of strange craft flying overhead. One worker handed off photos to a member of the tribal police showing a large, hovering, soft triangular object with an air force insignia, flying at a low altitude over an army vehicle. The photograph, quietly secreted away lest it identify the person who gave it to an unauthorized individual, is either one of the best faked photos ever put together or proof positive that the United States military is testing its own flying saucer.

Dugway, according to two former law enforcement officers who are frequent travelers to the area, also is ringed by underground tunnels. On one trip, the officers saw a convoy of trucks, some of them military, approaching the base. Then, suddenly, the trucks seemed to go downhill and just disappeared. From their experience watching the movement of traffic at Dulce in New Mexico, these trucks simply entered into an underground tunnel. It is common for top-secret military bases to have underground tunnels, and there are rumors that underground tunnels and underwater channels run all the way from Santa Monica Bay to Area 51. This would allow for navy submarines to get to the base undetected by any enemy satellites. Perhaps these underwater tunnels are channels for USOs as well.

ALERT

Just like Area 51, the military takes its secret facilities very seriously. Crossing the baseline perimeter can get you in a lot of trouble with the military as well as with local law enforcement. Therefore, be careful where you camp out.

Gilliland Ranch at Mount Adams

One of this country's top UFO sighting locations is the Gilliland Ranch at Mount Adams in Washington State. Known for almost ten years as the best UFO hot spot in the northwest, the ranch has hosted thousands of visitors since 2003 when ranch owner James Gilliland began hosting UFO sighting events. Gilliland has hosted not only private individuals but, reportedly, members of the military services and various government agencies. Even representatives of the CIA have paid visits to the ranch to see not only UFOs but orbs that seem to respond to Gilliland's calling them with a powerful searchlight beam. According to some who've spoken to Gilliland, among his many visitors are people who claim they've worked on reverse-engineered UFOs or extraterrestrial craft now in the UFO reverse-engineering program. Some of the government visitors have said that the United States has nothing like these craft in its arsenal.

One witness reported that close to midnight, sky watchers at the ranch and at Mount Adams can see what look like satellites in the clear sky. Some of them will make ninety-degree hairpin turns without losing any speed. These, Gilliland tells his guests, are not conventional satellites at all because satellites orbit. To change a satellite's orbit is a gradual process for controllers to accomplish, and it's not done by jerking a craft into a ninety-degree turn. When you see a light in the sky perform those kinds of maneuvers, you're looking squarely at a UFO.

For some dazzling photos and videos of the kinds of phenomena people have seen and photographed at Mount Adams, you can visit the James Gilliland website at *www.eceti.org*.

ESSENTIAL

As exotic and bizarre as this sounds, more than one visitor to the Gilliland Ranch has said that you can telepathically communicate with the orbs floating around and actually bring them to you. For that reason alone, to experiment with another life form, it might be worth a visit to the ranch.

Mount Shasta, California

There are UFO hot spots, areas where you can see them fly overhead, and UFO sites where the craft actually disappear into a mountain. One of those reported spots, visited by *UFO Hunters* in 2009, is Mount Shasta, California, one of the most intriguing areas for dedicated UFO sky watchers. There, people report seeing UFOs actually flying out of the mountain. Long known as a historic site of great significance to Native Americans, the mountain in northern California has been inhabited for thousands of years and was a place where shamans held rituals and religious ceremonies. Native Americans considered the mountain to be the site of the creation of the world.

Perhaps one of the reasons that Mount Shasta is regarded as an important UFO area is not just because thousands of witnesses have seen UFOs, and in particular triangular craft, flying over the mountain. It's because the area was said to be home to a race of superbeings called the Lemurians. The question, of course, is whether the Lemurians are actual extraterrestrials who live on Earth and whose ships land on Mount Shasta, or whether they are original residents here, as the Native Americans believe.

Mount Shasta is a great site for UFO watching, and it can be reached from Interstate 5 traveling north from Southern California and San Francisco. It is about fifty miles from the border with Oregon and has a highway that runs up to about 8,000 feet, almost half the way up the mountain. Climbers can make it up to the top, but you don't have to be a mountain climber to camp at various places along the slope and take photographs of strange events in the sky. You have to be able to identify the lenticular clouds that are sometimes mistaken for UFOs, but if you watch for movement of lights, sometimes lights connected to a rigid triangular structure, you may be lucky enough to spot your own UFO.

Phoenix, Arizona

The most intense and celebrated sighting of UFOs took place in Phoenix, Arizona, in March 1997, when thousands of area residents saw not just strings of lights float across the state but also a rigid, structured craft hover above the rooftops (including Governor Symington's backyard). The Phoenix Lights were heavily covered by the media. Area residents say that the sightings continue, especially outside of the city in the areas of Native American rock inscriptions. Not only can visitors see strange lights in the sky, but different videographers have reported capturing images of oddly shaped craft during the daytime hours. At least one videographer, Jeff Woolwine, has told Pat Uskert, of *UFO Hunters*, during an episode of the program that he has seen UFOs in the area that had the same shapes as some of the drawings made on rocks by Native Americans. Woolwine believes that the rock art isn't just abstract paintings but attempts to memorialize the visitors and craft that the Native Americans saw thousands of years ago.

Requisite UFO Hunting Equipment

Although there is no official UFO hunting kit, there certainly are items that you should bring, depending upon whether you're looking to stay a weekend, camping out overnight, or wanting to record what you're looking for.

Outdoor Equipment

You will need some outdoor equipment, depending upon the season and particularly if you intend to spend extended time outdoors. A tent, sleeping bag, and a campfire cooking kit or camp stove are a must for outdoor camping, as are multilayered wilderness clothing and good, heavy boots. To give you an idea of the kinds of items you'll need, a visit to L. L. Bean or Cabelas online is a good place to start. Also, be sure to bring your IDs along, especially if you're planning to visit areas alongside restricted military areas.

ALERT

As with Dugway, the government takes its military security very seriously. Don't cross the perimeter of Area 51 under any circumstances, and be aware that you are being surveilled the moment you arrive close to the base's fence.

Area 51 Don'ts

Area 51, according to those in the military who say they know it well, is ringed by both audio and video sensors. Walking along the trails leading up to the gates, if you look in some of the shrubbery, you can see sensor devices. The area is heavily patrolled by helicopters and cameras that can spot interlopers before they get on the base.

The base is also guarded by snipers who have served in Delta Force, part of the military's Joint Special Operations Command. These snipers, as the warning signs say, are authorized by the federal government to use lethal force to protect the base from intruders.

Radios and Walkie-Talkies

If you are going out in groups, you should rely on short-distance inexpensive walkie-talkies rather than trying to communicate in remote areas using cell phones. Radio Shack and other electronics stores have battery-powered, hand-held walkie-talkies, which you can also recharge with your car's inverter port, that are far more efficient than cell phones. Just remember that depending upon the area you're in, there could be other people on the same frequency, so it might be best to look for hand-held devices that have multiple frequencies you can switch to in case the air traffic is high. And remember, when you get near restricted sites, radio traffic is constantly monitored by those guarding the sites. Everything you say will wind up in some agency's digital recording logs.

Camera and Video Equipment

Cell phone cameras and video cameras are great, but they're definitely not for getting high-resolution, close-up detailed photos of UFOs. Most will capture a blurry ribbon of light in the sky if you try to overfocus at long distance. And most will not have a night-vision shutter to let in more light. Worse, some cell phone cameras have auto flash, which, for stealth photography, is the last thing you want. Overriding an automatic flash might be too difficult for getting off quick shots of a fleeting UFO moment.

The trick in capturing good stills and video is to recognize that unless you're on surveillance for long periods of time, you're going to have to get what you can get when the moment comes. That means you have to have equipment that will allow you to snap off quick shots without too much setup. Therefore, a good digital consumer camera, one that you can turn off the flash and turn on the night shutter, is the best bet. There are inexpensive SLR combined still and video cameras that offer surprising broadcast quality video and allow for interchangeable lenses. You want an optical zoom feature, the kind where the lens actually moves, in addition to digital zoom. And you want the ability to snap off a series of shots without waiting for the camera to spend time recharging its battery.

There are plenty of cameras in a low to moderate price range that offer video (MPEG) as well as JPEG settings without having to spend time with hard-to-read menus on a screen. This is important because when the time comes that the light appears overhead, you will only have seconds to take your shot. And don't neglect the tripod. Probably one of the most frustrating things about watching UFO videos is the shaky camera. Sure, people will brace their camera hand against a pole or a tree to steady it, but at a telephoto setting even the slightest movement will bounce your object out of frame. Therefore, make sure you set up a tripod. It is the best way to make sure that the money you've spent on camera equipment pays off in good photos.

GPS

You should be able to account for your position at all times so you have an accurate reading of where you are when you spot a UFO. There are inexpensive hand-held GPS devices for campers that you should take along with you so that you can plot positions accurately. Also, if you get lost in the wilderness or desert, giving a 911 dispatch your GPS location will enable a sheriff or search team to get to you fast.

Star Maps and Reference Guides

Many people will stand aghast at a great UFO sight only to find out later they've been watching Venus or a very bright star. Experienced UFO watchers will tell you that if you're planning to go on a sky watch, you should have a good star map, either in book, print, or electronic form, that you've read before you head out. Here's the reason. When the magic moment comes that you see your UFO (and it surely will if you stay at it long enough), you want to make sure it's a real UFO. Most of the ones that people see are not huge triangles but lights in the sky that move in strange ways. Retinal drift—the appearance of movement when there is none—is a common optical illusion in UFO spotting. You should know what's already in the sky and be able to position it and yourself so you know where you are and where it is.

Some star guides and computer program star guides also have listings of satellites that pass over certain areas. These are invaluable as well because a moving light in the sky, if not a falling meteorite, may often be a satellite, and you want to be able to recognize that right away.

The fun part is not to be afraid to get out there with some camera equipment, a GPS, and outdoor clothing, even for a day trip or an overnight stay at a local hotel. If you're following UFO sighting reports and can pack up for a weekend, you just might wind up with your own million-hit YouTube video of a UFO.

Sighting a UFO

One of the most exciting moments in the hunt comes when you believe you've actually sighted a UFO. There's a flash of insight, an overwhelming feeling of wonder, and a sense of accomplishment. Of course, a lot of this depends upon whether you're seeing a dot of light in the sky perform strange maneuvers, such as hairpin turns, or an actual structured craft overhead. Whatever you see, flying triangle or balls of light, it is thrilling. However, you want to record the object and record the moment.

What Do You Do When You See a UFO?

You will want to be swallowed up in the moment at first because you know you have arrived at a point where your world has met another world. All of your reality will have changed because you will suddenly know, first-hand, that there is another reality out there and you have touched it. But you have to get right down to business. Pull out your notepad and jot down:

- Time
- Location: where it is and where you are
- Weather condition and condition of the sky, as well as visibility
- As complete a description of the object as you can give
- Description of what the object is doing: ascending, descending, landing, hovering, and the direction it is traveling
- Duration of the sighting and what the object did when it left the scene. Did it vanish, go behind a cloud, hover, then speed away?
- Were there any other events accompanying the sighting or other things that you saw? This will refer to specific things about the sight-

ing itself, such as whether you saw actual creatures inside the craft or whether you saw creatures exiting the craft after it landed. You should also describe events that accompanied the sighting, such as your car's electrical system encountering problems or shutting down, your watch stopping, or your walkie-talkies shutting down or becoming staticky.

Where to Report a UFO Sighting

Now that you've seen a UFO, what do you do about it? You should contact MUFON at *www.mufon.com/reportufo.html* and follow the instructions on the online reporting document.

You can also contact the National UFO Reporting Center at *www.nwlink .com/~ufocntr* and click on "Report a Sighting," where you will follow the reporting instructions online. In addition, you can contact *UFO Magazine* at *www.ufomag.com* and follow the "Report a Sighting" on that website as well.

Many people contact their local 911 dispatch to report a sighting even if the dispatcher on the other end seems less than enthusiastic about taking the report. If the sighting is near an airport, power plant, or other facility in restricted airspace, make sure you tell that to the dispatcher so that the facility itself can be alerted and the public safety agency handling the call can get confirmation as well as issue a warning.

Anomalous Sightings

These are events that sometimes accompany a UFO sighting and may include the way a UFO appears, either by simply materializing or emerging from water, or by seeming to come out of nowhere to hang in the air. Sometimes you may feel that you are being observed by the UFO or that the object is following your car. It's important to take note of these things as well.

Then there are other anomalous events, such as whether or not you encounter missing periods of time, whether you see the UFO do something such as fire a beam of light at an object, or deliberately seem to hover in a certain way over a particular spot. You may see the UFO land, ideally not next to you, in a field or a pasture. Some witnesses have said that they see humanoid creatures emerge from the UFO.

Finally, of course, there is your own experience if you have a close encounter with a UFO and actually have either a psychic or telepathic connection to the craft or its occupants or an actual physical contact. These seem frightening and you should not look to initiate it.

Are You in Danger?

This is the ultimate question. If you listen to the stories of involuntary abductees like the Hills, Travis Walton, Hickson and Parker at Pascagoula, or Ed Walters at Gulf Breeze, then you can see that there certainly can be danger in a UFO encounter. However, if you are simply observing a strange object in the sky that seems to show no interest in you, then you are likely not in any danger resulting from contact. Write your observation and enjoy the experience. For most UFO hunters, just having a sighting is a success. After all, you get to say, "I saw a UFO."

CHAPTER 18

UFOs and the Mainstream

Any reasonable person might ask, "If UFOs are observed by so many people and have appeared over military bases around the world, including restricted skies over Washington, D.C., and if they have been caught on camera, surely the media would have covered their appearances at least over the past sixty years." This is a good question that deserves a good answer. UFOs have been in plain sight for over sixty years, and, at least back in the 1940s, the media didn't look the other way. But since 1947, when the Roswell cover-up began, the government has consistently sought to marginalize the topic of UFOs as well as any UFO witness, especially members of the military or anyone in a position of credibility who might pose a threat to the secret. The media has willingly gone along with this strategy because no media organization wants to be marginalized by being referred to as the "UFO Network." This is how UFO stories have been kept out of the mainstream and continue to be relegated to the sideshow area of experience.

Area 51: The Rational (but False) Explanation

Area 51 author and *LA Times* editor Annie Jacobsen (*Area 51: An Uncensored History of America's Top Secret Military Base*) recently appeared on *The Daily Show*. She talked about how the Roswell crash story was really a story about a sinister plot cooked up by Josef Stalin and Dr. Joseph Mengele to frighten Americans with a World War II vintage Horten brothers' flying wing, piloted by creatures deformed by Mengele. She wrote that an unnamed source told her that the craft was a conventional jet aircraft, a flying wing, developed by German engineers and Nazi officers Walter and Reimar Horten as early as the 1930s and improved so that it could be fitted with jet engines by the 1940s.

FACT

The easiest way the media has for keeping UFOs out of the mainstream is the "snicker factor," a subtle, derisive way of ridiculing any UFO story, even one that seems credible, by laughing at it and the witnesses. Who wants to be laughed at? Better to shut up and stay out of the news rather than subject yourself and your family to public ridicule over seeing something that the government and the media says does not exist. Thus, the snicker factor successfully keeps real UFO stories out of the mainstream.

The Mengele Experiment

Jacobsen wrote that the "extraterrestrials" that witnesses at Roswell saw—she neglected to mention the witnesses who claimed to have seen and communicated with the living ETs—were actually children who had been biologically deformed by the Nazi concentration camp doctor Josef Mengele. Mengele was the doctor at the Auschwitz concentration camp in Poland who conducted horrific experiments on camp prisoners. He used subjects such as twins, people with deformities, and even some children for physical tests, including torture, to examine their reactions. Mengele was a war criminal whose name has become synonymous with cruelty and torture under the cloak of medicine.

In Jacobsen's book, she argues that the ETs retrieved from the Roswell craft were human beings who had been deformed by Dr. Mengele, upon the instructions of Soviet Communist Party chairman Josef Stalin, to frighten the United States. Her source suggested that the Horten flying wing design was so exotic that the American military would not have recognized it, or the jet propulsion engines, and also would not have realized that the recovered bodies were human beings. Thus, the U.S. military would have confused the wreckage with a UFO.

This story implied that the Roswell case could be put to bed. No aliens, thankfully. No spaceship. What a relief it was. And the real story, told by an informant whom the author can't reveal, makes sense. Only it doesn't.

The Horten Flying Wing: The Real Story

The Horten brothers' flying wing (similar in appearance to the U.S. Air Force's B-2 stealth bomber) was made out of wood, certainly not an exotic material. By 1945, it was powered by jet engines, assuming that Stalin was flying the latest model. The United States had jet engines by 1945, too—nothing exotic there. The United States also had its own Horten brothers' flying wing, captured after the war. The Luftwaffe, by the way, never actually put the flying wing into development and never deployed it. It was only a test aircraft. The flying wing was inherently unstable and really couldn't fly that well. Therefore, deformed children created by Dr. Mengele for Josef Stalin notwithstanding, there's nothing secret about that craft. The base intelligence officer, Major Jesse Marcel, certainly would have recognized it, as would his boss, Colonel William Blanchard.

Would Stalin have been in secret contact with Mengele? Remember, all the Allied powers were still looking for Mengele because they wanted to try him at Nuremburg. By 1947, according to every available record, Mengele was trying to find a safe haven in South America. This is the very same Mengele who killed Russian prisoners at Auschwitz and whom Stalin reportedly wanted to execute if he could his lay his hands on him.

The story, told by Jacobsen's informant, whose name we now know as well as the reasons for his having been told a false cover story, is far from the truth. It even goes so far as to indicate that Area 51 was named after the year of its founding, 1951, when in fact it was founded in 1954.

It's "Anything but Aliens" All over Again

A very real (and sometimes unfortunate) fact is that no one wants to deal with UFOs because of the ridicule factor. UFOs are completely ridiculed, as are the people who hunt for them. Mention a UFO in mixed company and suddenly you're in the tin hat crowd, that you believe in little green men and flying saucers from Mars. Assert to your dismissive audience that government documents, credible eyewitnesses, physical trace evidence, and stunning photos all indicate that UFOs are a reality and that the government knows about them, and the yawns will start. Yet, these are probably the very same people who would sit in rapt attention and listen to a ghost story about a cavalier soldier from Charles I's army trapped by a troop of Cromwell's roundheads during the Interregnum. Ghosts aren't ridiculed. UFOs are.

Even a Harvard medical doctor like John Mack, who began to take the stories of self-described alien abductees seriously enough to come up with commonalities in their stories and report them, was held up for ridicule by fellow faculty members. He was eventually given a tenure hearing because of his academic pursuits in the field of UFO studies. In a tenure hearing, a board of faculty peer reviews the tenure (lifetime employment) status of a faculty member for reasons of the faculty member's engaging in unprofessional contact unbefitting a scholar at the institution. In his defense he had to claim that academic freedom in the bastion of an Ivy League university should allow him to pursue noninvasive research into human anecdotal experiences. At the conclusion of the hearing, Dr. Mack was allowed to keep his tenure, although he was severely questioned for his research on self-described UFO abductees. Ultimately, John Mack was killed when he was run over by a truck when he looked the wrong way while crossing a street while attending a conference in the United Kingdom.

FACT

There is a theory that because John Mack wasn't removed from a position of power at Harvard Medical School, his research had to be stopped by other methods. One of those methods, according to conspiracy theorists, was to run him over while he was attending a conference in England.

Ask yourself why, after the Chicago O'Hare Airport UFO story broke in 2007, both the FAA and United Airlines were caught, in print, denying their own investigations into the strange circular object hovering over the United terminal. Ask why the ground safety crew stated that a CNN reporter would dismiss the whole story as the rants of just a bunch of kooks or nuts. Why would that be?

Denying UFOs

The larger issue is: Why are UFO stories so far out of the mainstream that just by associating with them it means a person also is no longer taken seriously? J. Allen Hynek marginalized himself when, after his years of service to Project Blue Book as a UFO debunker, he came out of the "UFO closet" to say that the evidence in the stories he was debunking was overwhelmingly persuasive and that UFOs were real. Carl Sagan publicly dismissed the possibility of UFOs while at the same time writing the novel *Contact*, a story about contact from an alien civilization that reaches the SETI radio telescope array at Arecibo. The UFO community asked: What did Sagan really know? As a scientist, he knew that of the billions of stars out there, some have to have planets, and some of those planets have to have life on them.

Among the deepest conspiracies in the UFO community, there is the story that even while J. Allen Hynek was calling cases like the Hillsdale, Michigan, sightings "swamp gas," not only was he aware he was dissembling, but he was already in the inner government loop. He worked with officials with special access who had come into contact with "the humanoid," one of the extraterrestrial life forms the government had captured and was studying. Even Carl Sagan, it was said, had to publicly debunk the concept of a UFO presence in order to keep his special access to the inner circle.

The Silencers: Harassing and Silencing UFO Researchers

What was keeping UFOs out of the mainstream to such an extent that even the CIA's own agents admitted that if anyone in the know about UFOs ever went public the official first step was to ridicule and marginalize the person? If ridicule and marginalization didn't work, or a job loss didn't work, then it was time to use more creative persuasive measures.

In the case of Professor James E. McDonald of the University of Arizona, it was time to get creative. He went so far as to testify before Congress about the best cases of UFO encounters and the science behind them. He also contacted the Soviet mission and the UN to find scientists to talk to about UFOs.

McDonald wound up attempting suicide twice because his wife, a self-described Socialist and member of the Socialist Party, became involved with a strange person at Socialist Party meetings. Over the course of their getting together at party meetings, Mrs. McDonald and the stranger developed a relationship that she said blossomed into love. The first time his wife told him she wanted a divorce, Professor McDonald shot himself in the head but didn't die, succeeding only in blinding himself by severing his optic nerve with the bullet. Now blind and dependent upon his wife, who already professed love for another man, McDonald was despondent. He attempted suicide again, and this time he was successful. He was no longer a threat to expose any UFO secrets.

Was McDonald's Death an Elaborate Form of Silencing?

What could Mrs. McDonald's affair with a stranger at a Socialist Party meeting have to do with UFOs? The answer, although circuitous, makes sense. McDonald was a threat because of his pursuit of UFO revelations. He had already brought his research to Congress. He had contacted the Soviet Consul at the UN about Soviet research into UFOs. He was an influential scientist in his field. His interest in UFOs and the kinds of data he was researching would have garnered interest among other scientists and academics. He could not be allowed to continue. But how to stop him?

In his private journals, McDonald had written of committing suicide. Therefore, anyone who knew about suicidal ideation could, by having broken into his home and reading his private diaries, predict that, given the right motivation, McDonald would attempt suicide. By setting up Mrs. McDonald with someone whose job it was to romance her, wooing her away from her husband, those plotting to silence McDonald found a way to interfere with McDonald's life. After McDonald committed suicide, the stranger broke off his relationship with Mrs. McDonald and eventually disappeared. Thus, there were no loose ends, and the threat from Professor McDonald was eliminated. This is how the government silencers work.

Suiciding

"Suiciding" is one method of choice government black operations agencies employ for silencing threatening people or to discipline them into silence. For example, author Morris K. Jessup, who went too far in his investigations into UFOs and time travel, wound up dying under very strange circumstances. In April 1959, his body was discovered in his station wagon in Dade County Park in Florida with a hose taped to the exhaust pipe of his vehicle and running through the driver's side window. The window had been closed as tightly as possible around the hose. The engine was running and Jessup had asphyxiated himself, which was the official cause of death. However, Jessup would have had to perform this operation in broad daylight in a public park. It was difficult to begin with, because of the taping of the hose to the exhaust pipe. UFO conspiracy theorists believe that Jessup was murdered and the scene staged to look like a suicide.

His death was all part of a process. Whatever group or groups control the UFO secrets needed to dismiss those who wanted that secret out in the open. Today, there really is a kind of gentlemen's agreement that UFO stories will be relegated to a certain part of the tabloid media, or to tabloid syndicated television shows, as bizarre stories not to be taken seriously. But they will never be allowed to penetrate into real news, even when media from around the world are broadcasting the videotape of a flyover, as they did in Phoenix in 1997.

Governor Fife Symington's Prank

Case in point was the then-Arizona governor Fife Symington, who had been indicted by a federal grand jury on charges of extortion, bank fraud, and making fraudulent financial statements and was then convicted in September 1997. Symington's conviction was overturned by an appellate court two years later. Governor Symington, after promising to get to the bottom of the Phoenix Lights phenomenon in March 1997, an event that he himself witnessed, held a press conference in which his chief of staff appeared in full alien regalia. Everyone had a laugh, including Symington. This was a joke, he later admitted, to lighten the tense situation caused by consternation over the nature of the Phoenix Lights.

Why did Symington play the joke?
Although former governor Symington has since apologized a number of times to the people of Phoenix for staging the press conference with his chief of staff dressed up as an alien, the question still remains as to his motives. Frances Barwood suggested that he staged the event as part of a deal to defuse the situation. Others suggested he wanted the entire event to go away and joking about it was the best way to get it out of the media. We only have Symington's own statement that he wanted to "lighten the mood."

Beam Me Up, Barwood

A Phoenix City Council member, Frances Barwood, who dared ask what was happening in the skies, was ridiculed and was given the nickname "Beam me up Barwood" and eventually retired from public office. The story of the Phoenix Lights languished for the next fifteen years, until Fife Symington publicly appeared on *UFO Hunters* to apologize and tell his real story of having seen a rigid-structured craft at 8:30 P.M. on the night of March 13, 1997, and being as much in awe of it as other witnesses were.

Who Will Make UFOs Mainstream?

If UFOs are real phenomena, you can go out and probably find one yourself. Government records, many of which are unclassified and can be found in a variety of sources, confirm the UFO reality. Pilot and military testimony about the appearances of UFOs can fill entire rooms of the National Archives. There is so much physical evidence, in the form of artifacts, soil samples, pieces of bones with alien DNA, and photographic evidence, that anyone taking the time to sift through it would agree that there's something there. If all this is true, why can't UFOs be mainstreamed, and if they can, who is the one to do it?

Many scientists have tried, just like James McDonald, only to find that the barriers to penetration of the mainstream were too great. UFO researcher Jacques Valle reportedly said to Peter Sturrock (*The UFO Enigma*), who chaired the Rockefeller panel on UFOs, that astronomers see UFOs all the time in their telescopes. However, no reputable astronomer whose institution receives federal funding will ever go public in a peer-reviewed journal for fear of losing that funding. It's just not worth the cost to cross whatever entity is keeping the UFO secret close.

FACT

You might remember the character Claude Lacombe, portrayed by Francois Truffaut in Steven Spielberg's *Close Encounters of the Third Kind* (1977). In real life the character Lacombe was based on Jacques Valle.

Finding the Truth

How, one might ask, does a college professor like Michio Kaku manage to talk about the possibility of UFOs without losing his faculty position and winding up as a marginalized figure? Easy. Kaku, who some ufologists criticize as being too timid in his statements, can get away with what he says by doing just that: being timid. By stating his opinions in hypothetical terms, playing "what if" and "as if" with elements he may believe to be true—but too dangerous to assert if they are true—Kaku can say what John Mack could not. He can say that there are some things about UFOs and the people whom they encounter that can't be explained away by conventional science, at least not at the moment.

UFO author Stanton Friedman has said that the overriding rule when dealing with the unconventionality or anomalous nature of a specific phenomenon is to explain it conventionally, no matter how implausible that explanation might be. Thus, Annie Jacobsen's source can say that Area 51 was established in 1951, and Jacobsen herself will repeat it verbatim as if she didn't simply go to any of the sources readily available to check the true date of the site's establishment. This is not investigative journalism. In so doing she would have immediately realized that her unnamed secret source was either lying or simply repeating a cover story without any knowledge of the facts. As implausible as this is, Friedman would say that the standing rule of "anything but alien," or ABA, governs any argument about UFOs. As the implausibility index gets higher and the logic stretched until UFOs are a more plausible explanation than the contorted conventional one, the arguments turn to derision and in that way end the debate. Case in point: debating with Seth Shostak of SETI about UFOs. When he asks, rhetorically, how the government can keep such a big secret as UFOs when it can't even run the post office, you have to answer that he is making a false analogy because the government doesn't manage the post office even though the post office is an agency of the U.S. government. Moreover, when it comes to keeping big secrets, the government kept the secret of the Japanese balloon bombs laced with biological agencies that landed in American cities during World War II. They have kept this secret since World War II, and very few people know about it.

From Derision to *Ad Hominem*

If derision doesn't work, the arguments become *ad hominem*. UFO researchers become "UFO promoters." The science behind physical trace evidence becomes "pseudoscience." UFO research organizations become "cults." There are cults, UFO promoters, and pseudoscience, but these aren't necessarily within the mainstream UFO community. And, yes, there is a mainstream UFO community.

What the CIA did in the early 1950s to marginalize UFOs and flying saucers worked absolutely well. They gathered the scientists they had to in order to research the nature of UFOs and outsourced real evidence to defense contractors. They went to motion picture producers and the tabloid newspapers with some of the best stories—retold for popular audiences—and encouraged them to produce and publish them. They went to science fiction authors like Isaac Asimov with some of the real stories and brought him into the loop. It worked.

Today, UFOs are more likely to be the product of fiction than of fact. Real cases like the flying saucer invasion of Washington, D.C., in 1952 are simply relegated to the past. When skeptics ask, "If UFOs are real, why don't they land at the White House?" and when the answer is, "They are and they did," there is only a denial of the very photos of UFOs over the nation's Capitol and the Washington Monument. Whom do you believe, your own eyes or what the government tells you you're not seeing? Unfortunately, most often the answer is: You believe what you're told.

All of this means that if after you go out and find a UFO and tell your story, don't be surprised that you're not fully believed. If the photos you've taken don't automatically stir up excitement, don't be disappointed. Privately, most people want to believe in UFOs. Publicly, most people wouldn't be caught on the same planet with one.

The happy fact, however, is that you could find one, maybe floating over a desert at 3 A.M., or over the ocean on a bright day, or even over your backyard. The extreme happiness, satisfaction, and thrill of knowing that there really is something out there that's not of this world is its own reward. You will be in the select group of those who know and for whom no contorted conventional explanation will ever work again. You know the truth, and you are free.

Online and Print UFO Resources

Print Resources

There are plenty of good UFO books on specific areas of UFO investigation and incidents, many of which go into great detail about the specifics of individual cases. However, for the beginner, the most informative books are encyclopedias or more general books about the phenomenon and the government cover-up of the phenomenon. Among these are:

Above Top Secret by Timothy Good, 1999

Crash: When UFOs Fall from the Sky: A History of Famous Incidents, Conspiracies and Cover-Ups by Kevin Randle, 2010

The Expanding Case for UFOs by Morris K. Jessup, 1957

Flying Saucers and Science: A Scientist Investigates the Mysteries of UFOs, Interstellar Travel, Crashes, and Government Cover-Ups by Stanton Friedman, 2008

Flying Saucers 101 by Harold Burt, 2003

The Flying Saucers Are Real by Donald E. Keyhoe, 1950 (reprint 2004)

Flying Saucers from Outer Space by Donald Edward Keyhoe, 1953

Little Giant Encyclopedia of UFOs by Jenny Randles, 2000

Open Skies, Closed Minds by Nick Pope, 1997

The Report on Unidentified Flying Objects by Edward J. Ruppelt, 1956 (with introductory material by Colin Bennett 2011)

Top Secret/Majic: Operation Majestic 12 and the United States Government's Cover-Up by Stanton Friedman, 2005

The UFO Book: Encyclopedia of Extraterrestrials by Jerome Clark, 1997

The UFO Cover-Up by Barry Greenwood and Larry Fawcett, 1992

UFO Encyclopedia, edited by Jerome Clark, 1996

The UFO Encyclopedia by Margaret Sachs, 1981

The UFO Enigma by Peter Sturrock, 1999

The UFO Magazine UFO Encyclopedia, edited by William J. Birnes, 2004

UFOs and the National Security State by Richard Dolan, 2002

UFOs: Generals, Pilots, and Government Officials Go on the Record by Leslie Kean, 2010

Unsolved UFO Mysteries by William J. Birnes and Harold Burt, 2000

Online Resources

Although a quick search on Google will return many good websites with UFO resources, perhaps one of the best sites is from Dimitris Hatzopoulos, who continually updates his research for visitors to his site at *www.hyper. net/ufo*. Like most good UFO reporters, Hatzopoulos focuses on the more intensive UFO incidents and not just the lights-in-the-sky reports. Other good general UFO resource websites are those tied to official investigative and research organizations. The sites below contain links to more specific sites to allow visitors to expand their search. These include:

Above Top Secret

This is one of the largest and most comprehensive UFO and paranormal sites on the Internet, containing news, updates, and discussion forums about the most popular controversies in the field.

www.abovetopsecret.com

BLT Research

BLT Research contains reports on a wide range of anomalies, but focuses on crop circles and the physical trace evidence of UFOs.

www.bltresearch.com

CUFOS

The official site of the Center for UFO Studies, one of the oldest and most reliable UFO research organizations. The material on CUFOS is comprehensive and science-based with links to some of the most important official and semiofficial studies of the UFO phenomena.

www.cufos.org

MUFON

This is the official website for the Mutual UFO Network, containing sighting reports, an opportunity for visitors to file their own sighting reports, and the latest UFO news.

www.mufon.com

UFO Casebook

UFO Casebook is a comprehensive site that covers historic UFO cases as well as modern sightings. Casebook is one of the best archival resources for beginning as well as experienced UFO researchers.

www.ufocasebook.com

UFO Magazine

This site contains an index to all past issues and forums for visitors to post their own information.

www.ufomag.com

APPENDIX B

The Best UFO Videos

There are some very compelling UFO videos available on the Internet. However, given the quality of screen resolution, some of these videos are hard to evaluate. Here is a short list of some of the most intriguing ones from YouTube, all of which also link to other videos. For the researcher looking for visual evidence, these represent a very good start. Also, some of the best UFO videos are part of UFO documentaries, some of which made it to theatrical or television release and some of which were released on the Internet. These include:

Best Evidence: Top Ten UFO Sightings
Paul Kimball features coverage of some of the most important cases in UFO history.

Out of the Blue and I Know What I Saw
These two documentaries by James Fox, both of which were broadcast on television, cover many sightings, including the March 1997 Phoenix Lights incident, and feature not only fascinating interviews with eyewitnesses, but footage of strings of lights and other apparently anomalous aerial phenomena.

The Phoenix Lights Documentary and the updated The Phoenix Lights—Beyond Top Secret
This is an award-winning documentary by Dr. Lynne Kitei about the March 1997 Phoenix Lights incident that contains the filmmaker's own photos and stills, as well as videos from other sources that make the case for an anomalous or otherworldly presence over the Phoenix area.

Pilot UFO Sightings
A documentary that covers major cases in which some of the nation's most credible witnesses describe their UFO encounters.

Secret NASA Transmissions: Smoking Gun
By Martin Stubbs, who as a station manager in Vancouver, British Columbia, Canada, linked directly to NASA transmission feeds to record UFO encounters that NASA never intended the public to see.

UFO

From 1956, one of the early documentaries featuring a historic interview with Pentagon press officer Al Chopp on the 1952 UFO invasion over Washington. It also contains footage of UFO images from other incidents in the 1950s. A piece of UFO history.

UFO: The Greatest Story Ever Denied

This video by Jose Escamilla contains some great archival footage of statements and interviews from important experts in the field. Covers stories about presidents Eisenhower and Carter and their alleged UFO encounters.

UFO Hunters and UFO Files

From the History Channel, these are probably the best professional UFO documentaries ever made, covering not only historic UFO sightings but current incidents including Stephenville, Texas, and Needles, California.

UFOs: 50 Years of Denial

This video by James Fox contains some very good footage of UFOs along with interviews with eyewitnesses and well-known witnesses such as Edgar Mitchell, Jesse Marcel Jr., and Lt. Col. Philip Corso.

UFOs Past Present and Future

Presented by Rod Serling, this is perhaps one of the greatest professional documentaries on the history of UFO cases, including the purported UFO landing at Holloman Air Force Base.

Index

We Have

EVERYTHING

on Anything!

The Everything® list spans a wide range of subjects, with more than 500 titles covering 25 different categories:

Business	History	Reference
Careers	Home Improvement	Religion
Children's Storybooks	Everything Kids	Self-Help
Computers	Languages	Sports & Fitness
Cooking	Music	Travel
Crafts and Hobbies	New Age	Wedding
Education/Schools	Parenting	Writing
Games and Puzzles	Personal Finance	
Health	Pets	